THE NEW INTEGRATED DIRECT MARKETING

THE NEW INTEGRATED DIRECT MARKETING

Mike Berry

Gower

Published by
Gower Publishing Limited
Gower House
Croft Road
Aldershot
Hampshire
GU11 3HR
England

Gower
Old Post Road
Brookfield
Vermont 05036
USA

British Library Cataloguing in Publication Data
Berry, Mike
   The new integrated direct marketing
   1. Direct marketing
   I. Title
   658.8'4

ISBN 0 566 07960 7

Library of Congress Cataloguing-in-Publication Data
Berry, Mike, 1958–
     The new integrated direct marketing/Mike Berry.
       p. cm.
     Includes bibliographical references and index.
     ISBN 0–566–07960–7
     1. Direct marketing. I. Title
HF5415.126.B47   1998   97–31504
658.8'4--dc21   CIP

Typeset in 10 point Plantin Light by Photoprint, Torquay, Devon, and printed in Great Britain by MPG Books Limited, Bodmin.

CONTENTS

LIST OF FIGURES AND PLATES

Figures

Plates

PREFACE

One day, every marketer will be a
DIRECT marketer at heart.
The Institute of Direct Marketing

This book is intended for marketing professionals. It may be useful to students, academics, journalists and others who observe, comment on and analyse marketing from the wings of the profession, but these groups do not constitute the primary audience.

The book is about direct marketing:

**The establishment and maintenance of
a one-to-one relationship between an
organization and its customers and
prospects.**

It is about how direct marketing fits into what could be called the 'integrated communications mix'; this comprises the set of all marketing communications disciplines (including advertising on TV, in the press, on radio, posters, the Internet and in other media: sales promotion, public relations (PR), design, event marketing, exhibitions and other activities).

The book sets out to define and understand all these disciplines, then to focus specifically on direct marketing, exploring its strengths and weaknesses as a basis for demonstrating how it can be employed most effectively by the marketer, and how it will become increasingly important as a discipline within marketing. The main purpose of the book is to make the case for direct marketing as a discipline which will progressively come to dominate all marketing communications, not in terms of execution, but in terms of attitude of mind and overall strategic viewpoint. This idea is controversial but I believe the case is unassailable.

This book is intended for those who find themselves working in direct marketing (whether as client-side marketers, in agencies or supplier companies) but who do not (yet) consider themselves to be direct marketing *experts*; perhaps they have embarked on a direct marketing career after a more general marketing role, or perhaps they have joined a direct marketing agency or direct marketing department as a first job, or following a background in sales promotion or advertising. It will also serve as a 'crash course' in the basics of direct marketing, including its role within total marketing, for senior managers (with little or no personal experience of direct marketing) whose overall responsibilities include direct marketing activities.

Early in the book, we establish that the marketing world is changing fundamentally and that direct marketing, sales promotion and advertising can never again be viewed as discrete, non-overlapping disciplines. Gone are the days when the majority of marketing managers and directors chose (almost without thinking) to spend their entire promotional budget on TV or in 'image' press. Neither do direct marketing agencies, on the whole, walk into a prospective client's office these days and demand that the entire TV expenditure be switched to direct mail. On the contrary, more and more companies, in the UK and overseas, are using direct marketing as one *part* of their overall marketing mix; it is therefore vital that its strengths and weaknesses are fully understood so that it can harmonize cost-effectively with sales promotion and 'above-the-line' advertising. Only this *integrated* view of marketing, based on understanding rather than hearsay and/or prejudice, is appropriate for the 1990s direct marketer who plans to be successful as we move into the twenty-first century.

Much has been written in the marketing press about the 'overlap' between direct marketing and sales promotion and about the blurring of 'the line' that separates them from general 'image' advertising. This book sets out to evaluate comprehensively the strengths and weaknesses of each discipline both separately and in combination, with a view to structuring multidiscipline marketing programmes in such a way as to maximize the overall cost-effectiveness of the activity. Many of the observations contained in the book come directly from personal experience of marketing communications (integrated and otherwise), gained across a range of sales and marketing roles: on the client side, and within direct marketing, sales promotion and integrated agencies.

In the course of the book, various 'myths' are debunked, including:

- 'Sales promotion is all starbursts and plastic daffodils'
- 'Below-the-line agencies are full of failed admen'
- 'Ad agencies are only concerned with winning creative awards and funding their extravagant lifestyles – doing a selling job for the client is sometimes a by-product'

- 'Direct marketing and sales promotion are basically the same'
- 'Direct marketing is more cost-effective than advertising'
- 'The best marketing brains are to be found in advertising agencies'
- 'The Internet will soon replace all current forms of marketing communication'

The book's (admittedly controversial) central theme is that direct marketing, as an approach to marketing centred on the creation and profitable exploitation of customer relationships, is the marketing of the future, and that regardless of the specific media employed, marketers must increasingly think as the best direct marketers currently do. This theme emerges chapter by chapter.

Chapter 1: Direct marketing introduces the discipline, from its roots in mail order, through its adoption by charities and insurance companies, until it emerged in the 1980s as a fully fledged marketing tool, capturing an increasing share of the budgets of automotive, financial services and finally even fast-moving consumer goods (FMCG) companies.

Chapter 2: Sales promotion starts by defining the discipline and its associated terms and describes in necessary detail the various mechanisms employed by sales promotion specialists, both client companies and consultants. The historical development of sales promotion agencies, from 'refuges for spivs and failed admen' into strategic marketers is traced, and the role of sales promotion within an integrated marketing mix is examined.

Chapter 3: Advertising seeks to analyse, from a professional's viewpoint, a discipline with which we are all familiar as consumers. We look at what is meant by branding, chart the deployment by successful established companies of sustained 'above-the-line' image-building communications campaigns, and establish the unique role of such communications in creating and nourishing brands. This is important in the context of the main theme of the book, as it is made clear that advertising *cannot* be superseded by 'pure', traditional direct marketing as a brand-building tool.

Having provided a reasonably detailed introduction for the reader into the above core communications disciplines, the book now develops the main theme further as we return to direct marketing and examine how customer relationships are becoming the main driver of successful marketing communications campaigns, cutting across some of the traditional categorizations of such activity.

Chapter 4: The changing scene – integration. In this chapter we consider the effect of 'the winds of change' which are sweeping through marketing communications in the closing years of the twentieth century and into the twenty-first; the old 'pure' disciplines we examined in Chapters 1–3 are pure no longer. We are experiencing 'convergence' and overlapping of marketing communications activities, as clients increasingly seek 'integrated communications'. There is also a highly topical section dealing with the Internet, the World Wide Web, and CD-ROM technology – what they offer to the (direct) marketer and their importance in turning the tables on the old 'one-way' broadcast communications as advertisers rush to embrace these new 'interactive' media. A note of caution is also sounded: the interactive bandwagon is seductive but, realistically, online communications should be viewed as additional arrows in the marketer's quiver rather than as a whole new replacement weapon.

Chapter 5: Direct marketing and sales promotion: one discipline or two? We now focus on a topic of much debate in the industry, which the professional direct marketer (and the promotions executive) is likely already to have encountered in his/her career: are direct marketing and sales promotion really distinct, or just different parts of the same branch of marketing communications? The conclusion is that there are many areas of overlap, but that the two aspects are nevertheless fundamentally different, so that there is a valid role for both as complementary specialist disciplines in an integrated communications future.

Chapter 6: The creative process. We now switch our attention to the core discipline in any communications agency (and arguably the one clients get most excited about) – the process of creating and executing the communications *ideas*. We analyse some of the great advertising ideas of history, and consider what sort of minds come up with these famous campaigns (and how to get the most out of them). We examine how ideas can be extended from, say, a TV commercial or press ad into other media and other disciplines, and look at how direct marketing can successfully draw on communications ideas which first find their expression in pure image-*advertising* executions.

Chapter 7: The marketing database. This key chapter explains what a marketing database can achieve if properly constructed and exploited. We discover that the database can become far more than a mailing list; rather, it can be a highly effective tool for media planning, research and targeted communications. It will lie at the heart of the new, powerful integrated direct marketing of the twenty-first century, in which the intelligent acquisition and manipulation of data will be critical.

Chapter 8: The integrated communications agency. Having established that integrated direct marketing is the way of the future, we move on to the practical (and thorny) issue of how marketers in client companies can *achieve* it. If they choose to engage the services of an outside agency, what should be their selection criteria? From the point of view of such consultancies, how can they best structure themselves to meet the emerging needs of the clients who seek the new integrated direct marketing? We examine strategies for agencies to re-engineer themselves, and depict a model integrated agency.

Chapter 9: Making it happen – integration in action. We look at the process by which integrated direct marketing can be most effectively planned and executed, with reference to the respective roles of both client and agency personnel at various levels. Some pointers for the kind of agency–client relationships and methods of working most appropriate for the new integrated direct marketing future are provided.

Chapter 10: An integrated future? The premise of this book is that integrated direct marketing is rapidly arriving and that its emergence as the dominant system of marketing, in terms of understanding and strategic approach, rather than media choice, is now inevitable. Against this contention, we view various alternative future scenarios, recognizing that the new interactive media are currently rewriting the media rule book and forcing all those who intend to be part of the emerging marketing scene to 'take a step back' and to reassess their views of the total media universe. The conclusion is that we must both learn from the past and also free ourselves from historical prejudices if we are to plan and implement the new integrated direct marketing with maximum success as we enter the twenty-first century.

Along the way, the book tackles 'hot' issues including:

- the integration of marketing communications – client- or agency-driven?
- planning and implementing customer loyalty programmes; and
- the impact of the Internet and World Wide Web on direct marketing; are these new disciplines a subset of direct marketing? a threat to it? or neither of these?

Above all, this book establishes and explains the uniquely influential role direct marketing will occupy at the centre of marketing communications in the twenty-first century.

I hope you find it challenges some of your preconceptions and provides you with some insights.

Mike Berry, January 1998

ACKNOWLEDGEMENTS

Many people have contributed, directly or indirectly, to the writing of this book. To an extent everyone I have ever worked with (colleague, mentor, protégé, friend, client, agency or supplier) has had some influence on the thoughts and opinions which appear in the pages that follow.

I have learned much about how to do things (and on occasion how *not* to do things) from the many characters I have had the pleasure of working with, of working for, and of managing during my career to date. This isn't the book I would have written when I started at Procter and Gamble as a graduate trainee in 1981; nor is it the book I might write 20 years into the future. Like all books, it represents a snapshot in time and, like most books, it reflects one person's opinions and areas of interest which are inevitably biased and to an extent personal – so be it.

I thank everyone who has taken the trouble, over the years, to stop and teach me things, who has put up with my impatience and tolerated my often over-zealous desire to get things done, and to everyone who has given 100 per cent, and at times seemingly more, in the various teams I have managed over the years.

Specifically I would like to thank the following for their assistance in compiling the various case histories which I believe put real 'flesh' on the more theoretical bones of the text:

- Simon Jacobson and Andy Lee from Intel Corporation (UK)
- Beverly Le Cuirot and Steve Cartwright from Standard Chartered (Offshore)
- Jonathan Gibson from Creative IQ for IDV (Smirnoff)
- Nick Houghton from Playtex
- David Horncastle and Neil Williamson from Nissan Motors (GB)
- Joanna Thurrock from Virgin Atlantic
- Peter Humphrey from Option One for Shell UK
- Andrew Pickup from Microsoft UK
- Nick Stephens from Marketing Principles for Alfred Dunhill
- Richard Downes from BMW (GB)
- Susan Goldsworthy from Digital

• Miles Templeman and Stuart McFarlane from Whitbread (Boddingtons)

These are all great case histories, from great companies, featuring great brands. There is something to be learned from each one of them. I am grateful to the above marketers, and their agencies, for permission to feature their successful campaigns. I must also thank Julia Scott, Solveig Gardner Servian and everyone at Gower for their patience and encouragement.

Lastly, I would like to thank Jane, my wife, and Lorna and Julia, my daughters, for sharing my belief in this book over the time it has taken to put it together and for accommodating my reclusive behaviour (impacting on evenings, weekends and even holidays) during the many hours spent labouring towards the end result.

I've enjoyed writing this book; I hope you enjoy reading it – if not, please don't blame any of the above.

MB

INTRODUCTION

Direct marketing, in the UK and internationally, as a discipline and as a profession, finds itself at a crossroads. These are uncertain times. Changes are taking place that seem irreversible – things may never be the same again.

What has been happening over the last decade, but with a noticeable acceleration over the last two to three years, is that barriers have been broken down – barriers between direct marketing and sales promotion, and between these disciplines and so-called 'above-the-line' image advertising.

One illustration of the extent of these changes is that some client marketing departments are structuring themselves along product group lines, so that one manager is responsible for all communications activity to support a particular brand or range of brands, with specialist input from others in the organization and from outside suppliers. In these companies, job titles such as 'Advertising Manager', 'Direct Marketing Manager' and 'Sales Promotion Manager' are being replaced by 'Marketing Communications Manager' and 'Advertising and Promotions Manager'. Other companies, especially in fast-moving consumer goods (FMCG), are grouping the roles of several brand managers together under the new job title of 'Category Manager'. Job functions are being redefined and client company marketers need to change to fit them.

Agencies, too, are changing. In the 1970s and 1980s, a large number of specialist direct marketing agencies sprang up in the UK, mainly due to a massive explosion of interest from clients – in financial services, business-to-business and, latterly, FMCG, to name just three sectors of rapid growth. At the same time, separate consultancies specializing in sales promotion were proliferating, devising and implementing a range of on-pack and in-store promotions for petrol companies, retailers, and food and drink manufacturers, among others. These 'below-the-line' agencies tended to be set up and staffed by, respectively: (i) in direct marketing: ex-mail-order entrepreneurs and executives; and (ii) in sales promotion: ex-advertising-agency account handlers or ex-clients.

Sales promotion agencies, in particular, were often accused of employing 'failed admen' who had dropped (or been pushed) out of 'proper' advertising agencies and found themselves obliged to peddle the 'free plastic daffodil', the 'free fluffy duck', the 'grand prize draw' and other classic promotions. There was certainly a view that 'below-the-line' agencies were in some way the 'poor relations' in terms of calibre of people, strategic marketing understanding, quality of service and, above all, creativity. In some cases, this was deserved – certainly the rapid growth in direct marketing and sales promotion encouraged some less than reputable operators with their eye on a 'fast buck' to enter the business, with consequent damage to its image and professional reputation.

Those days are, generally speaking, behind us. The 1990s have seen the emergence of new, highly professional, multidiscipline agencies both in the UK and across the world. The best of these 'communications agencies' offer an entire orchestra of disciplines, embracing on-pack and in-store promotions, direct mail, telephone marketing, database management, direct response advertising (in all media) and a host of other services, even, in some cases, pure 'image' advertising. They are staffed by intelligent and creative professionals, combining the business understanding and planning skills of above-the-line advertising agencies with the numeracy and executional thoroughness of the more accountable discipline of direct marketing and the 'quick-fix', added-value, 'whizzy' ideas of sales promotion. The below-the-line people in such agencies are, generally, equally accomplished marketers, equally intelligent and equally creative as their advertising bedfellows and, importantly, are acknowledged as such by their colleagues and by client companies. However, these integrated agencies are still comparatively few in number and, as the twentieth century draws to a close, 'specialist' agencies (in advertising, sales promotion or direct marketing) are still the norm. We shall examine the current environment and future prospects for agencies in Chapters 8–10, as they attempt to 're-engineer' themselves in order better to meet the needs of their clients and, indeed, to ensure their very survival.

This book aims to equip the emergent twenty-first-century marketer with the direct marketing skills, knowledge and understanding needed to play an active role in this new marketing world. Although the emphasis is on strategy, rather than execution, there is a discussion of integrated direct marketing creativity, that is, copy and design issues, in Chapter 6. This book is written by a direct marketing practitioner who has worked on the client side and in both sales promotion and 'integrated' agencies as well as in pure direct marketing agencies. It is based on extensive personal experience of integrated campaigns – some highly successful, some less successful – for a range of clients, from multinational corporations to small family concerns.

This is not a textbook on sales promotion or advertising. It does, however, pay more than passing attention to these disciplines, which are increasingly closely related to direct marketing, illustrating the many areas of significant overlap by means of several case histories of integrated campaigns which cause us to question our definitions and ask whether we really can any longer talk about direct marketing, sales promotion and advertising as distinct disciplines. (Indeed, the reader might ask, if the activity meets its objectives – whether to generate immediate sales, increase brand awareness or build long-term customer relationships – why categorize the techniques used at all?) For completeness, we also discuss public relations (PR), design, conferences, exhibitions and sponsorship in Chapter 6; after all, the new generation of integrated direct marketers will require a broad grasp of how direct marketing can dovetail with *all* the other communications disciplines, including the rapidly developing field of online communications (see Chapter 4 for a discussion of the Internet and its potential for marketing).

This book is intended to be read straight through (although pausing between chapters is permitted!). It is aimed primarily at those who are new to direct marketing but who do not expect to spend the rest of their career in 'pure' direct marketing. It will also be of value to 'classically trained' direct marketing people who now find themselves working alongside sales promotion and possibly advertising professionals and are expected to integrate 'seamlessly' with these possibly somewhat alien disciplines.

David Ogilvy (the advertising guru who founded the Ogilvy and Mather agency group) once predicted:

'One day, all agencies will be direct marketing agencies.'

I would dare to disagree with the great man and rephrase this aphorism:

'One day, all communications agencies will embrace direct marketing.'

Arguably, that day is already here. There will always be *specialists* in TV advertising, design, PR, on-pack offers, exhibition stands (design and build) and sponsorship. However, there are fewer and fewer careers in marketing communications, particularly on the client side and in the account management departments of agencies, to which direct marketing skills are not relevant. Indeed, in more and more cases, they are essential.

This book aims to provide a thorough, primarily *strategic* grounding in direct marketing as part of the range of communications disciplines in the armoury of the 1990s marketer which will carry marketing successfully into the next century. I hope you enjoy reading it. I hope you find it helps you to do your job better. Finally, I hope it helps you to become a more effective, more successful and more *integrated* direct marketer.

1 DIRECT MARKETING

Today, direct marketing is an idea so timely
that it almost has a life of its own, so
popular that it has spread through every
kind of business and every country of the
world, so effective that . . . it chalks up so
many victories and successes . . . One
measure of its success is that it is now the
basis for a half-dozen sub-disciplines.
'Database Marketing' is now a basic tool of
some of the largest packaged goods
companies. 'Relationship marketing', 'one-
on-one marketing', 'MaxiMarketing',
'integrated marketing' and others all offer
interesting extensions and variations of its
basic techniques.

Ed Nash, 1994

Definitions

Marketing has been defined as follows:

Marketing is the business task of

(1) selecting attractive target markets
(2) designing customer–oriented products
and services

and

(3) developing effective distribution and
communication programmes with the
aim of producing high consumer
purchase and satisfaction and high
company attainment of its objectives.

Philip Kotler, 1974

Direct marketing can be defined as:

An interactive system of marketing using one or more advertising media to generate a measurable response/ transaction at any location.

The American Direct Marketing Association

This is hardly the snappiest or most compact of definitions, but at least it has the merit of including the key ingredients. Specifically and first, direct marketing is interactive. It is not 'one-way traffic'. This is critical; in general, direct marketing asks for a response, a reply of some sort. It therefore seeks to initiate and maintain a *dialogue* between the advertiser – anything from (say) a major multinational corporation selling a wide range of products in food, toiletries and pharmaceutical markets to a one-man band selling seeds to gardeners by mail order – and the (prospective) customer. It is not a *monologue* – an expression conjuring up images of a 'John the Baptist' figure crying out as a lone voice in the wilderness, proclaiming to the world that 'Guinness Is Good For You', that 'Persil Washes Whiter', or 'Beanz Meanz Heinz' or even 'Coke is it!' with no attempt to accommodate the various subgroups within the target audience or any particular interest in receiving a response as a result of the communication (other than an improvement in the all-important Nielsen market share figures).

Direct marketing employs one or more *advertising* media. Is this not a contradiction in terms? – you may be asking yourself at this point. We haven't yet defined advertising but the question is a fair one; we need a set of definitions to work with or confusion rapidly ensues. A *medium* is a channel through which information is distributed. The important factor here is that direct marketing is not itself an advertising *medium* (as are TV, radio, press, direct mail and so on), but a *system* of marketing, a subset of total marketing. The various media upon which both direct marketing and image advertising rely to convey messages to the target audience (of prospects and/or customers) are simply means to an end – they are conduits or channels of communication. Once this has been agreed, it is obvious that direct marketing is a broader term than direct mail, which is merely one of the media that direct marketing employs.

Direct marketing generates a 'measurable response/transaction at any location'. One of the reasons behind the phenomenal rise in direct marketing expenditure by companies of all kinds, in all sectors of industry and commerce over the last 20 years, has been its accountability. If you can measure results, you can evaluate cost-effectiveness. This has become something of a 'Holy Grail' to marketers in the USA and Western Europe since the late 1980s. In the 1990s, times have become comparatively tougher, with advertising and promotional budgets being squeezed and marketing managers under increased pressure from their senior management to demonstrate 'value for money'. The measurability of direct marketing, coupled with the plunging costs of storing and manipulating data on computers, has earned it an increased share of the advertising and promotional 'cake', even in years when the cake itself was either not growing or was actually shrinking.

Other definitions of direct marketing, such as 'accountable advertising' or 'action advertising', have their appeal, but are inadequate as complete descriptions of the direct marketing discipline – let us stick with the definition above.

Direct mail is defined as follows:

**Personally addressed advertising,
delivered through the post.**

The key factor here is the personal address – in general, we are talking about a named individual, at a specific postal address. This may be either someone's home (consumer direct mail), or work (business-to-business direct mail). In other words, direct mail involves a letter of some description, sent by an 'advertiser' (that is, a company selling a product or service) to an identified individual potential purchaser. An acceptable alternative definition might be 'one-to-one advertising in an envelope'.

'The post', which in the UK effectively means the Royal Mail, conjures up rich historical images of quill pens and parchment, of Penny Black stamps, sealing wax, coaches and horses and, later, steam trains and mailbags; these days, however, we are more likely to be talking about optical character recognition (OCR) of addresses, mechanized sorting procedures and sophisticated distribution networks (road, rail and air).

Direct mail is unusual among advertising media for its reliance on few (and, in some countries of the world, monopoly) suppliers, that is, the Postal, Telegraph and Telephone Administrations (the PTTs), the postal services of the country of dispatch and delivery. Mailings of quantities in excess of one million are regularly posted and delivered along with thousands of other items including personal letters, cards, magazines and a host of other correspondence, by these 'media owners' who publish their 'rate card' (thus setting their prices) and are not, generally speaking, prepared to negotiate. Such discounts as are available (for example, Mailsort in the UK and Third Class (Bulk) rates in the USA) generally result from doing part of the sorting task yourself, with (part of) the consequent saving, quite reasonably, being passed on to the mailer. Attempting to negotiate with a monopoly supplier which knows (or believes) you can afford its rates does not, in general, offer much scope for cost saving.

'Direct mail' is an advertising medium – the major medium of direct marketing. It is not 'mail order', which is historically the origin of direct marketing – selling direct to the consumer without the involvement of a retailer. Mail order (whether driven by 'off-the-page' direct response advertisements, or 'cold' letters backed by a weighty catalogue featuring photographs of hundreds or even thousands of items for sale) is best viewed as a method of doing business. It is not an advertising medium; rather it employs direct marketing (and at times image advertising) as part of its armoury of communications weapons. In this case, the channel of distribution happens to be the post. There are of course many, many applications of direct marketing which are quite distinct from mail order, as we shall see throughout this book.

Direct mail is not 'door-to-door' (and doesn't even include it). 'Door-to-door' is defined as:

**The distribution of unaddressed
advertising material directly into
consumers' homes via the letter box.**

Clearly this is another advertising medium – it differs significantly from direct mail in that it doesn't require the consumer's name and address. Although a certain degree of targeting is possible, distribution is, to a greater or lesser extent, 'random' or 'blanket', and consequently the communication is correspondingly impersonal and could thus be less effective. On the plus side, however, cost per thousand consumers reached is in general significantly lower than with direct mail.

'Direct response' advertising refers to any advertisement in any medium (although mainly press or TV) which seeks an immediate response. This might require the consumer to complete and cut out or 'clip' a coupon, or perhaps to telephone their enquiry using an 0800 (toll-free) or other telephone number, or respond via e-mail or the Internet, say. Thus defined, direct response advertising is integral to direct marketing.

I hope these working definitions will serve to help us distinguish between the various terms *direct marketing, direct mail* and *mail order*. We shall use them throughout this book.

The history and development of direct marketing

We have established a set of basic definitions of what direct marketing is and what direct marketers do. It is possible to take issue with some of the technicalities, but they will serve as a framework for the arguments and descriptions that follow. In order to understand where direct marketing is today, and, most importantly, where it is going, we can profit from reviewing its history.

As mentioned previously, direct marketing has its roots in mail order selling, which is probably as old as commerce itself, or at least as old as the postal service in each country. In the USA, the sparsity of the white population in the latter part of the nineteenth century meant that for people in remote locations, placing their orders with retail stores remotely (either by letter or telegraph), with delivery by stage-coach, was the only practical way to buy certain goods. To this day, the USA has a booming magazine subscription mail order service, since retail newsagents are simply inaccessible to many people. In the early 1900s, a railroad employee by the name of Richard Sears found he was able to clear an unwanted consignment of gold watches by mailing a list of his colleagues – a very early example both of niche marketing and of direct marketing! Famous mail order companies such as Montgomery Ward, L L Bean and Franklin Mint became successful because they gained their customers' trust by delivering high-quality merchandise reliably and conveniently ('to your door'). Sears, Roebuck was a pioneer of 'the store in your living room' with its catalogue containing hundreds of items, which was a revelation to its customers many miles away from the emporia of 5th Avenue. In the 1950s, the charge cards launched by Diner's Club and American Express gave the mail order entrepreneurs the facility to offer 'cashless telephone shopping'. In 1965, the first newspaper inserts appeared (another godsend for direct sell operators). This was followed by the arrival of toll-free telephone numbers in 1966 and the making of zip codes compulsory in 1967; direct marketing as we know it is indeed a young business.

In the UK, the major catalogue operations (Great Universal, Littlewoods, Kays, Grattan, Marshall Ward, Freemans and so on) grew up in the 1950s and 1960s. This growth owed much to the success of the 'agent' concept. These 'agents', mainly housewives, would agree to act as representatives of the manufacturer, selling merchandise (aided by the attractive, full-colour illustrations in the bulky catalogue) mainly to friends and family. They took the orders and collected the money, forwarding both to the catalogue firm. The items were then delivered to the home of the agent, who distributed them to the purchasers, receiving a commission for their efforts. This was a very successful method of trading in the years when there were sufficient willing agents (keen to earn extra income by part-time work) and sufficient eager buyers who appreciated the convenience of the whole operation (including the option of extended credit) and enjoyed buying from friends. With the increase in the number of working women, agent catalogues suffered during the 1980s and 1990s at the expense of their 'home shopping' equivalents, through which busy people of both sexes could buy *what* they wanted *when* they wanted, regardless of retail opening hours, and completely avoiding the crowds which for many people constitute the worst aspect of shopping in stores.

In the 1960s, there was a tremendous boom in the UK 'Sunday supplement off-the-page' market. In rapid succession, most Sunday newspapers launched free 'colour magazines', taking advantage of improvements in printing technology. Suddenly, colour press advertisements, offering the chance to 'order now', reached a large section of the adult population, and mail order without the agent took off in a big way. Companies like Scotcade and later Kaleidoscope and Innovations were highly successful at selling a range of electronic products (for example, alarm clock radios) straight off the page and via loose inserts (with direct mail catalogues employed against the database thus created).

The proliferation of credit and charge cards in the late 1960s and over the following two decades provided a further tool for the specialist mail order companies, making telephone ordering (by quoting one's credit card number) a practical reality. A further step forward followed in the 1980s when the UK's British Telecom (BT) launched the 0800 toll-free service ('straight through for free'). It is perhaps difficult today to recall that 'Freefone' via an operator was, before this, the only free telephone response service.

A glance at today's colour consumer magazines throws up a list of successful modern-day mail order practitioners including, besides the mail order catalogue operators listed above, Franklin Mint, The Bradford Exchange, Danbury Mint, John Harvey, Langley House, Lawleys by Post and Compton and Woodhouse. To these we can add those companies using loose (and bound-in) press inserts and mini-catalogues, including Innovations, Time Life Books, Book Club Associates (World Books, The Literary Guild, Reader's Choice, Executive World, Children's Book of the Month Club, The History Guild and so on), and of course The Reader's Digest. These companies are all mail order specialists, with little or no reliance on retailers, agents or other intermediaries. They build an ongoing trading relationship directly with their customers on a one-to-one basis. The normal technique is to generate first orders off-the-page, or via inserts, door-to-door or even in certain cases direct response TV (DRTV), with subsequent customer selling messages conveyed via direct mail; as such these companies could be described as 'pure' direct marketers. Pure awareness advertising and brand building, as distinct from hard-nosed 'selling' communications, have, in general, no place in their marketing plans. If asked to explain their business philosophy, they might say, in the words of David Ogilvy, 'we sell – or else'.

As we have noted, however, direct marketing is a much wider discipline than mail order. As the definition in the previous section suggests, it includes any communications activity which *builds and maintains a direct relationship between buyer and seller*, so that the following are all examples of direct marketing activity:

- a mailing to generate appointments for a photocopier sales force
- a mailing to sell insurance policies 'direct' with an 0800 'help line' service if required
- an 'outbound' telephone marketing campaign to invite purchasing managers to a seminar
- a TV commercial inviting viewers to call an 0800 number for details of local suppliers
- a targeted door-to-door leaflet including a 50p voucher redeemable at a local supermarket.

Having come of age in the 1970s and 1980s, and then established itself as a key part of the marketing mix during the dark days of the early 1990s recession, direct marketing is now entering a new phase of its development. The media scene is fragmenting, with cable and satellite home shopping channels increasing their penetration of households, along with such developments as 'power dialling' outbound telephone marketing and laser printing in several colours. Personal and business communications and home entertainment technology are converging at a bewildering rate. Just as CD players replaced turntables, so VHS has become the dominant video cassette format and now personal computers appear on almost every desk, in every classroom and in an increasing proportion of homes. Video on demand (via telephone lines) on a pay-per-view basis is being trialled. New interactive media (notably CD-ROM, the Internet and specifically the World Wide Web) have emerged, offering even greater opportunities for relationships between seller and many individual buyers. There is more about these new media in Chapter 4, where we tackle the changing media landscape in greater detail.

With the increasing demand among consumers for convenience, choice and service, direct marketers are facing new opportunities and new threats. The early 1990s recession hastened the incorporation of 0800 and Freepost reply devices into even the most 'image-oriented' TV 'awareness' commercials and press ads. Increasing volumes of direct mail (both business and consumer) and ever more restrictive data protection legislation (particularly in France, Germany and the UK) are also factors which will shape the future of direct marketing into the twenty-first century.

Undoubtedly the main issue which will impact on the development of direct marketing over the next ten years and beyond, however, is that of *integration* – between direct marketing and sales promotion, between direct marketing and advertising, and between direct marketing and each of the other weapons in the marketer's arsenal. Trends are emerging which suggest a progressive convergence of all these disciplines; some practitioners are even arguing that such 'purist' labels as direct marketing, sales promotion and so on are now inappropriate and will rapidly become obsolete. This traffic is not all one-way, however. Others claim that 'integration' and such new buzz phrases as 'direct promotions' and 'action marketing' are nothing more than the latest fad and that this issue will rapidly be forgotten when the next marketing communications 'craze' arrives. I disagree and I shall make the case that integrated marketing and, specifically, integrated *direct* marketing is the marketing of the future which all marketers need to get to grips with now to meet the opportunities which are currently developing.

These issues are all pertinent to the central theme of this book, that is, *the central role of direct marketing in the integrated communications mix*, and we shall return to them repeatedly in what follows.

Direct marketing today

Today, direct marketing is both a respectable discipline within the overall marketing mix and a substantial industry in its own right; it is estimated that in 1997, around 20 000 people (source: UK DMA) were employed in client companies, suppliers (printers, lettershops, data bureaux and so on) and consultancies/agencies in the UK direct marketing industry. Let us examine the overall process of direct marketing by reference to the process chart (Figure 1.1).

At the risk of demystifying the whole process to the extent that direct marketing 'experts' fear for their continued job security, I would argue that

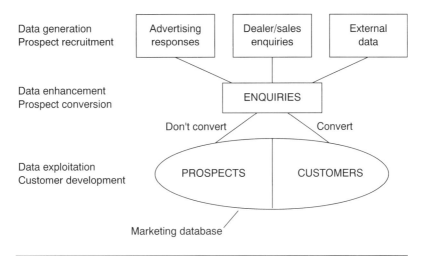

Figure 1.1 The process of direct marketing

it is clear from the chart that the whole of direct marketing may be conveniently broken down into two fundamental activities:

1. Customer acquisition
2. Customer retention/development.

Terminology naturally varies from one company to another, with activity 1 often dubbed 'prospecting' (or 'conquest' in automotive companies) and activity 2 the subject of a thousand conferences on 'Customer Loyalty' or 'Targeted Relationship Management' or some variant on the above, but basically, this is what direct marketing covers.

First we must find our prospective customer, effectively getting them to 'hand-raise', that is, to identify themself as a suitable target for more communications and specifically some information about a particular product or service (as 'teased' in an ad, mailing or outbound telephone call, say). Then we must convert them to a customer (either with a fulfilment mail pack, or an outbound telephone call, or alternatively via a third party, for example, sales executive, dealer or retailer). From then on, the task is to 'maximize their lifetime value' to us (that is, the present value of the aggregated future stream of earnings generated by that one individual, in other words, to keep them coming back for more product, more often, that is, locking them in and achieving maximum *customer loyalty*. This process can be summarized as that of locating a prospect, and progressively forging and deepening a relationship with them via *customer* and *client* to *advocate* (effectively an unpaid salesperson for your company/ product/service – see Figure 1.2).

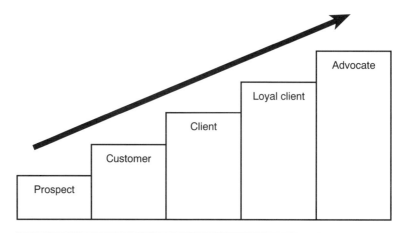

Figure 1.2 The loyalty ladder

This is what today's direct marketing involves: it is a complex and fascinating discipline, representing the fusion of the *creativity* of copy and design with the *scientific* disciplines of testing and database management. Far more than advertising, direct marketing is a *dialogue* rather than a *monologue*; in inviting a response, we are acquiring data which can and should be employed to target future communications; we are building a *relationship* with the prospect or customer which we must subsequently manage in order to extract the maximum profit from each customer over their lifetime with us. Clearly intelligent collection and exploitation of data is crucial to successful direct marketing; so also is an understanding of marketing strategy, of branding, and of the respective roles of the other communications disciplines (including advertising) alongside which direct marketing operates. Let us next examine in turn the key media by which direct marketing achieves the dual objectives of acquisition and retention.

THE MEDIA OF DIRECT MARKETING

Direct mail
Direct mail offers certain unique advantages as a marketing communications medium. It is:

- *personal* – you can address your target individually and personally in a personalized, one-to-one communication;
- *selective* – you can zero in on exactly those customers or prospects you wish to target, with a message which is tailored to them, recognizing their relationship with you (if any) and using relevant selling messages. You can minimize wastage by avoiding other individuals;

- *flexible* – you can send your targets anything from a massive mail order catalogue to a teaser postcard, include audio, video cassettes, CDs, floppy discs, CD-ROMs, tell your story in as much or as little detail as you wish. Your message is comparatively unrestricted by space or time limits which constrain other advertising communications (especially TV, press and radio);
- *discreet* – direct mail is not a broadscale medium: the communication is not the same for everyone, and, to an extent, you can control who receives it. This makes it more difficult for your competitors to monitor exactly what you're doing. If you sell by mail order, you can even test offering the same product at two different prices (often the higher price, because it makes the product more 'credible', proves to be more cost-effective overall) without customers comparing notes. The relatively 'low profile' of direct mail (compared with, say, TV, posters or press) makes it easier to keep the competition guessing;
- *measurable and cost-accountable* – because it is normally possible to count how many responses you obtain to a mailing, and because you generally know how many you sent out, and how much they cost you, it is easy to get some kind of a measure of the overall cost-effectiveness of your direct mail. Indeed, pure mail order (where the product is dispatched directly from the customer's mail or telephone order with no inter-mediary) is arguably *the* most scientific form of marketing; all variables (except the legendary fickleness of the consumer) are under the marketer's control. However, measurement is less easy in cases where you are selling via a distribution chain, for example, car dealers, insurance salespeople, wholesalers and retailers and so on. In these cases, it is often not straightforward to track the exact source of a given sale, so that to match mailing responses to incremental revenue can be extremely difficult. In such cases, self-styled direct marketing 'gurus' are overclaiming when they proclaim that direct mail is a 'completely accountable medium'.

Direct response press

Press advertising has several key advantages as a medium. It is flexible in terms of format and, if properly planned, it can deliver good coverage of the target audience. With sufficient insertions over a period of time, it is possible to build awareness highly cost-effectively. When response is the objective, certain techniques come into play. Creatively, prominent coupons which are easy to cut out, visible 0800 free telephone numbers and e-mail addresses for immediate enquiry are important. Tip-on reply cards are also accepted by certain magazines. In media terms, it is important to analyse historical response by publication, by day of the week, by position, by size of ad, and by creative treatment/offer. With this information, future media planning (for optimum quality/quantity of response) becomes more scientific and less based on judgement/guesswork than much conventional media planning.

Direct response TV

Much of the above also applies to direct response TV (DRTV). TV has the great advantage of being able to communicate moving colour pictures and sound together – which is pretty much the closest that advertising media can get to a real salesman at your front door. When this is combined with a device to allow response (via telephone, Internet/ electronic mail/keypad in your hand), we have an extremely powerful medium. DRTV requires specialist skills in media planning and buying, in creative execution (strong call to action, prominent 0800 numbers on-screen and in the voice-over and so on) and in organizing appropriate response handling and fulfilment, all of which distinguish it from the equally specialist discipline of pure image TV advertising. In some cases, the commercial is required to do a 'double-duty' job, that is, to combine awareness/attitude change with generating a pool of enquirers. It is essential in these cases to set clear objectives and to take a realistic view of what is achievable from a single communication.

Loose inserts

An alternative to taking 'space' in a newspaper or magazine is to place a loose insert inside the publication. This medium has received much bad PR (most people claim never to read them), but results show they can be highly cost-effective in certain cases. The cost per thousand is relatively low, and the advertiser has complete control over the quality of the finished print (which must be supplied to the publication). Loose inserts are also a convenient medium for true split-run *testing*: you can arrange a pure 'A/B test' where two different creative treatments are interleaved so that you can conduct a scientific test and draw confident conclusions about the offer/creative treatment from the resulting responses. Perforated reply cards also allow easier response than do space ads.

Telephone marketing

Also known as telemarketing, this is arguably a branch of marketing all of its own, although more often regarded as a subset of direct marketing. It can be most conveniently and logically subdivided into: (i) outbound and (ii) inbound. We shall look at each in turn.

(i) Outbound, at its simplest, involves phoning people up (at work or home) as part of a marketing or sales campaign. Outbound telephone marketing can have the following objectives:

1. *Telesales* – trying to get people to agree to buy something (or donate to a charity, say) purely as a result of receiving a telephone call. With the increasing penetration of credit and charge cards, this technique has come of age in recent years. However, it is illegal in some countries and arguably inadvisable in most, as the success rate is likely to be low and the negative reactions likely to be numerous.

   The method requires considerable operator skill, and has at various times attracted significant adverse comment from those opposed to the techniques of 'pressure' selling employed by some of the less scrupulous practitioners in this area of telephone marketing.

2. *Appointment setting*. Outbound telephone marketing can be highly cost-effective as a tool for fixing appointments for salespeople/ representatives. The less savoury side of this would be calling consumers on behalf of a double glazing or timeshare company, but much legitimate activity in this category is business-to-business, and could be on behalf of an office equipment supplier, a firm of headhunters, or an advertising agency.

3. *Customer care*. This is an increasingly important use for outbound telephone marketing; it is a key part of customer loyalty programmes, both consumer ('Good evening Mr Berry, I'm calling on behalf of XYZ motors to make sure you're still happy with your Z . . .') and business-to-business ('Good morning Mike, I was just giving you a call to make sure everything was OK with Karen; I know she's very happy and feels joining you was a really good move for her . . .').

4. *Market research*. Certain categories of market research depend heavily on the telephone. Some audiences are difficult or even impossible to get along to focus groups (especially senior executives, who are much more likely to agree to talk on the phone for five or ten minutes), whereas for a quick 'dipstick', when there is not time to use interviewers or recruit group members, the telephone (used to call, say, a subset of the company's sales/marketing department) can be indispensable.

These examples show the telephone at its best: immediate, personal, difficult to ignore and not difficult to use. It should be borne in mind, however, that the telephone is not a *cheap* medium. Like direct mail, it is not suited to mass awareness tasks or the transmission of information to a large audience – the numbers just do not make sense in these contexts.

It is important to bear in mind that each marketing communication medium has its own strengths and weaknesses. Successful direct marketers, in particular, know how to use direct mail, direct response press and TV and telephone marketing individually and in combination, employing the individual strengths of each for maximum overall cost-effectiveness.

(ii)   Some would dispute that inbound telemarketing represents a marketing discipline at all, rather describing it as a technique employed for handling responses, which could just as easily have arrived via the mail (as coupons/reply cards) or via electronic mail or on the Internet, among other delivery channels.

With the growth of DRTV, the planning of inbound telephone marketing has become of crucial importance to a number of large companies. Considering the vast sums of money spent on creating the correct impression and motivating a call in response to the communication, it is sheer folly to fail to handle the response properly, that is, promptly, professionally, and in a manner consistent with the original communication and with your company's overall image.

Despite this, it is still perfectly possible to call the 0800 number on an ad or mailing, only to get:

● engaged (busy);
● a message telling you you're being held in a queue (better, but still frustrating);
● an answering machine inviting you to leave a message;
● a live operator who is poorly briefed, unhelpful or downright rude.

The importance of planning to handle inbound telephone calls cannot be overstated. The logistics involved are basically the same, whether your arrangements are for an in-house call centre or an external bureau. Although the investment required for the former is much greater, many large users of inbound telephone marketing are now setting up such operations, since they offer increased control of the customer relationship rather than entrusting such communications to non-employees.

There are of course many highly professional telephone marketing agencies which would disagree with this extreme attitude, but most are realistic enough to acknowledge that many clients do feel this way about something as fundamental to their relationship with their customers and potential customers as the telephone interface, and as a consequence many have built a valuable business out of acting as consultants to organizations looking to set up their own 'call centres' both in the UK and internationally.

THE DIRECT MARKETING INDUSTRY

We shall look at the industry under three headings:

1. Clients
2. Agencies
3. Suppliers.

Although there is some overlap of people between the various categories (particularly supplier → agency and agency → client), the culture in each of these categories of company is fundamentally different and, on the whole, so are the individuals who work in them.

Clients

There is a tremendous difference between working in direct marketing in, say, a packaged goods company, and in a major mail order catalogue vendor; in the latter, the chairman is likely to be a former direct marketing specialist, whereas in the latter, direct marketing may still be regarded with at least suspicion and in some cases contempt. Direct marketing exists as a separate department in some organizations, whereas in others the direct marketing function may be managed by, say, product managers or marketing executives as part of their job responsibility. In some financial services companies there is a very sophisticated direct marketing function – often effectively an in-house agency, with 'creatives' and even a studio in-house. In other organizations, one of the key roles of the direct marketing executives, at all levels, is to manage the company's relationships with agencies and other suppliers to achieve the most cost-effective overall solution.

The main users of direct marketing are the following:

- Mail order firms
- Charities
- Financial services (banks, building societies, insurance/investment companies)
- Automotive companies and their dealers
- Retailers
- Airlines
- Other travel/leisure organizations
- Political parties
- Packaged goods (FMCG) companies.

This last is perhaps the last 'unconquered' (by direct marketing agencies) sector of major advertising spenders who have not yet fully committed to direct marketing as a discipline. Agencies have, for at least 20 years, been trying to make the case to FMCG companies for including direct marketing within their amply funded marketing mixes. Only in the 1990s, with the increasing power of retailers, the decreasing cost of data processing and the new recognition of the cost of finding customers compared with the lower cost of retaining them effectively, have companies like Procter and Gamble, Unilever, Nestlé, Heinz and Mars begun to invest significantly in building and exploiting consumer marketing databases. Clearly making a single sale via mail order of, say, a jar of coffee, a tube of toothpaste or a can of baked beans will never pay back. However, if you can identify 'heavy user households', and keep them loyal to your company's range of products over the long term, then the mathematics begins to make more sense, especially if you account for the advertising effect of, say, direct mail or telephone marketing communications.

Agencies

Although we should include telephone marketing agencies in this category, we are primarily talking about full-service direct marketing agencies. Typically they will have the following departments.

Account management   This department comprises the 'suits', who fulfil a role directly comparable to account management in advertising agencies: they represent the client within the agency, and the agency to the client. They meet the client, take a brief, brief the agency's creative department, sell the creative work to the client (tricky one, that) and send out the invoice. Of course this can be a demanding and stressful process, requiring the tact and patience of a saint, the effortless good humour and persuasiveness of the natural salesperson and ample supplies of determination, energy, and eagle-eyed attention to detail. It is also tremendously fulfilling and rewarding when it works! It is the central role in the agency in so far as people in account management are the coordinators; no one is in a better position to see the totality of the agency's efforts and their results – both favourable and otherwise.

Creative   As with advertising, this is the 'ideas' department. As with advertising also, it is the part of the agency clients least understand, and are most fascinated by. As with advertising, its occupants may be unruly, eccentric and difficult to live with. However, they are the generators of the agency's product, the finished output and, as such, need to be nurtured, cajoled and (to an extent) cushioned from some of the realities of life (including, on occasion, contact with the clients). Some direct marketing creatives may be suffering from an inferiority complex (and some may indeed be failed advertising creatives), but increasingly below-the-line creativity is being recognized as a respectable skill in its own right and both art school alumni and English graduates are actually seeking to work in the creative departments of direct marketing agencies; this represents progress indeed since the late 1970s when direct marketing agencies first began to emerge. Thus direct marketing creative people can, these days, be just as 'difficult' and even 'precious' as their advertising counterparts and, in some cases, just as well paid!

Production   The production department may include print buyers, art buyers, press production executives and traffic/progress chasers. These people are primarily technicians; they are less thinkers than doers, and none the worse for that. Indeed they turn the strategic musings of Account Management (and Planning, where it exists as a separate department) and the wild ideas of Creative into a reality which can actually be sold to clients (an important consideration if the rest of the agency wishes to continue its thinking in relative security). The best production people are cheerful, practical and capable; they gently (?) restrain the creatives' worst excesses, while the traffic executives chase up Account Management to fix meetings with the client and to push the client to approve the work so that deadlines can be met. A good production department can make all the difference to client perceptions of the agency as 'getting the job done', which surveys have shown is a key determinant of client loyalty to agencies. The art-buying role of this department is crucial to the *execution* of the creative ideas (as opposed to the original *conception*) and the cost control role can have a crucial impact on the profitability of the entire agency. It is essential to buy from suppliers of appropriate quality at an appropriate price; this is a job for specialists.

An effective direct marketing agency production department has to have a detailed knowledge of the various types of direct mail suppliers (see below) and must be able to 'make the trains run on time'. This demanding task is, of course, critical to the agency's profitability and, ultimately, to its survival.

Suppliers

These come in a variety of shapes and sizes:

- Lettershops (= mailing houses)
- List brokers
- Database bureaux
- Printers
- Envelope manufacturers

Each has a crucial role to play in the production of cost-effective and successful direct marketing campaigns. They may work directly with clients (as telephone marketing agencies generally prefer to do) or alternatively via agencies (acting in the role of consultants to their clients which may extend to sourcing and managing the best suppliers on their clients' behalf). See Figure 1.3 for an illustration of the relationships.

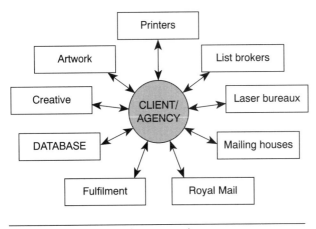

Figure 1.3   Direct marketing supplier management

Although this is perhaps a less glamorous sector of the direct marketing industry than the agency world, it can be both satisfying and profitable, as successful entrepreneurs who have founded list brokers, lettershops (mailing houses) and specialist direct mail printers will (privately, at least) testify. These suppliers are, however, particularly exposed to the vicissitudes of the economic cycle: during the early 1990s recession, several large and apparently soundly financed organizations went out of business. The quality of the job done by these companies also has a direct impact on the effectiveness of direct mail (in particular); thus whether the client ends up with good or bad address quality and a print job which conveys prestige and professionalism as opposed to shoddy 'junk mail' is largely down to the relevant supplier. Telephone marketing agencies are often in the position of representing their client to the client's customers (often incognito) – a heavy responsibility indeed. Thus suppliers have a very real impact on the *quality* and therefore the *results* of direct marketing activity.

There is a famous quote by Jerry della Femina about advertising being the most fun one can have with one's clothes on (see the start of Chapter 3). Various pundits have taken issue with this; I personally feel it betrays a disappointing lack of familiarity with the best Saint Emilions, the chess games of Bobby Fischer, the middle period of the Lennon–McCartney songwriting collaboration and Beethoven's late string quartets (the enjoyment of none of which is in any way enhanced by nakedness, to the best of my knowledge), but let's not split hairs. Advertising, and direct marketing and sales promotion, are *fun* – if you like that sort of thing. Certainly enough people seem to like it (or what they've heard of it) to ensure that agencies in London and other advertising centres are inundated with applications from would-be employees at all levels. People want to be in communications and, increasingly, bright, able young people are positively choosing to enter direct marketing, which is evidence of its growing respectability as a profession in its own right. Indeed, direct marketing appears to offer the greatest prospects for growth of all the marketing communications disciplines, as data become increasingly cheap to store and manipulate, consumers become increasingly differentiated and individualistic, and communications media fragment and offer seemingly limitless choice for the consumer. Thus old-style mass marketing becomes more and more inappropriate, and the importance of retaining customers is recognized even by those who previously threw all their marketing budget into mass advertising on TV and in the press. It is my belief that the future belongs to direct marketing – a theme we shall develop throughout the remainder of this book.

To illustrate companies' successful use of direct marketing, the following case histories are offered.

Case history

Company	**Intel Corporation (UK) Ltd**
Background	Intel, founded in 1968 in California, is the company that invented the integrated circuit – the microprocessor chip. To this extent, one of the founders, Dr Bob Noyce, has been called the father of the computer revolution. Today around 80 per cent of the world's PCs use Intel microprocessors.
	The Overdrive® processor is aimed at existing PC owners wishing to upgrade their computer without the cost of replacing it altogether. It could enhance the computing power of a machine with an i486 processor up to almost the power of a Pentium processsor.
Marketing objectives	Communicate the benefits of the Overdrive® processor to an elusive audience of:

  - MIS directors
  - IT directors
  - CEOs throughout Europe

and generate qualified sales leads.

Solution The direct mail campaign employed identical designs in three languages (English, French and German). The targets were mainly drawn from Intel's extensive in-house corporate database, concentrating on named senior IT decision makers in companies with a large number of Intel 486-based PCs on site.

The offer (communicated to this carefully selected audience by a personalized direct mail letter) was to 'test drive the Overdrive processor for yourself' in return for which the respondent would be allowed to keep it.

Plate 1.1 Intel – 'Test drive the Overdrive processor for yourself'
Source: Intel Corporation (UK)

The fulfilment pack to the initial mailing was one of the most valuable ever mailed – it included a fully functional Overdrive® processor (worth £300–£400) with an evaluation form. Results were excellent, with sales exceeding target by a ratio of nearly 2:1.

Case History

Company	**Standard Chartered Bank (CI) Ltd, Jersey, Channel Isles**

Background Standard Chartered Bank (CI) Ltd offers a comprehensive range of offshore banking facilities, from interest-paying cheque accounts in sterling or US dollars to specialist mortgage services that offer structured lending for the tax-efficient purchase of UK property.

There are a number of advantages to banking offshore in Jersey:

- Offshore banking services can be provided to non-resident investors on advantageous terms.
- The Jersey Government has a stated policy of maintaining the existing arrangements, which allow for bank interest to be paid to offshore investors free of island taxes.
- Jersey has a well-established, sound and prosperous economy and is recognized worldwide as an important financial centre.
- Although closely associated with the UK, Jersey is financially and politically independent.
- The island is politically stable and enjoys a special relationship with the European Community that ensures its continuing status as an independent centre of finance and taxation.
- No exchange controls mean capital may be moved in and out of the island without restriction.
- Jersey banks are not required to make automatic returns to fiscal authorities regarding individual customer accounts.

Marketing objectives
- To increase awareness of Standard Chartered Bank (CI) Ltd and its services
- To position Standard Chartered Bank (CI) Ltd as the offshore bank which truly understands its customers' practical and emotional needs in relation to finances
- To establish a distinctive brand identity for the bank
- To reassure existing customers that they have made the right choice
- To attract new customers and generate new accounts.

Solution The bank and its agency came up with a distinctive campaign showing prospective (and current) customers that Standard Chartered Bank (CI) Ltd understands the dilemmas customers face when making decisions about their finances. The advertising targeted specific customer types by showing their own dilemma literally 'writ large' as the advertisement's headline. Every ad in the campaign shared the verbal structure: 'I do . . . I don't . . . do I? . . . don't I?'. This was turned into a compelling visual device

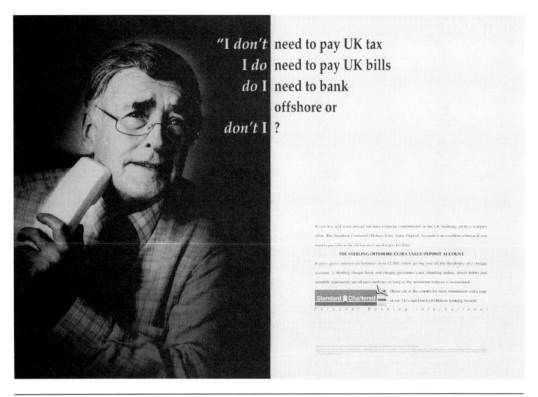

Plate 1.2 Standard Chartered Bank – the 'Do's and Don'ts' campaign
Source: Standard Chartered (Offshore) Ltd

by isolating the key phrases in white-out type within a photograph of a typical member of the target audience.

The 'Do's and Don'ts' campaign led to a significant increase in awareness of the bank and its range of services. At the same time, it positioned Standard Chartered Bank (CI) Ltd as a bank that made considerable efforts to understand its customers' needs – a bank that asked questions before it offered answers.

The underlying tactic of the campaign was to generate reassurance among the target market, by establishing the bank as a highly experienced authority in the world of offshore banking, through advertising that appeared to *advise*, rather than to *sell*. This tactic was supported by the offer of a complimentary booklet, 'The Do's and Don'ts of Offshore Banking', commissioned by Standard Chartered Bank (CI) Ltd as an independent guide, offering objective advice on such matters as how to choose an offshore centre from the 50 or so around the world. The creative theme was extended right through to the 'I do/ I don't' boxes on the advertisement's coupons.

The 'Do's and Don'ts' campaign was truly international, covering such titles as *Middle East Expat, USA Today, Resident Abroad, High Life, The European, International Herald Tribune, The Economist, The Guardian Weekly* and *BBC Worldwide*.

For a relatively modest media expenditure of £250 000 per annum, the results were outstanding and well over target: there was a 57 per cent increase in enquiries over previous levels, and a similar increase in the rate of conversions. Cost per response was also substantially lower than the levels initially projected.

Media used: international and expatriate press, in-branch posters, literature and fulfilment packs.

2 SALES PROMOTION

Trying to define what is and isn't sales promotion can be as difficult as trying to draw a map of the lava erupting down the side of a volcano. But it's precisely this lack of clearly defined boundaries that represents sales promotion's constant potential for original solutions to marketing problems – cost effective solutions. The very lack of well-established traditions in sales promotion encourages radical answers to fresh challenges as they arise. In no other part of the whole spectrum of marketing activities is there more call for imagination and inventiveness; for lateral as well as logical thinking; for understanding of what will not just gain attention but will maintain an audience's interest. In no other marketing activity is there greater scope for creativity, and in no other can creativity produce commercial dividends so cheaply.

Quoted by Alan Toop in '*Crackingjack*' 1994.

Sales Promotion tends to be more tangible, more three dimensional, more solid, more tactile . . . [and is associated with] premiums and samples you can touch and hold, with cash in hand – not merely with promises and claims, with images in the mind.

Petersen and Toop, 1994

Definitions

In this chapter we examine a discipline many consider to be exclusively tactical and short-term and some would even dismiss as 'brand-threatening'. Others, however, swear by it, as a sure-fire way of 'shifting volume' and getting some 'pull-through' (that is, helping the retailer to sell 'off the shelf'). I shall seek to show that the truth lies somewhere in between.

Sales promotion can be defined as:

> Any activity which adds value to a product
> or service for a limited time period by
> offering an incentive to purchase.
> UK Institute of Sales Promotion

Sales promotion is about making 'extra benefit' offers. It is perhaps most easily explained by looking at a typical consumer offer. Imagine Mr/s Smith in the supermarket at the soap powder fixture, and suppose s/he feels fairly neutral about soap powder; this is for Mr/s Smith a low-interest category, and s/he has no strong allegiance to any particular brand. Depending on how s/he feels at the moment of the purchase decision in any particular week, s/he may plump for either 'brand X' (the most expensive), or 'brand Y' (a little cheaper but still TV-advertised and a product s/he feels 'good' about buying) or, if it's getting near the end of the month (salary giro time) and things are tight, s/he will settle for the store's own-label 'Sainsbo basiclean' which s/he feels doesn't really quite deliver on whiteness but does a reasonable cleaning job for 85 per cent of the price of brand Y. This week however, the game has changed. Brand X has a special offer – 'Buy One, Get One Free' – that is, buy one packet of brand X, cut out the special token on the top, mail it to the address given and within 28 days receive a voucher for a free packet of brand X – no strings attached. Mr/s Smith doesn't have to think long about this one – it's brand X this week. Here, then, is an example of a sales promotion mechanism ('BOGOF' – Buy One Get One Free) working superbly. However, this isn't the end of the story. Brand X's manufacturers are not stupid (it is safe to assume). On the face of it, they have just given away one packet of brand X for nothing (although they have admittedly made one sale). But they run promotions of this sort because they *work*. By this I mean that such offers pay for themselves (and then some). Although this sort of thing is notoriously difficult to measure, the thinking might go as follows:

Mr/s Smith tries brand X to take advantage
of the promotion, that is, s/he buys X
instead of the normal Y. Two weeks later,
having used up the packet of X, s/he
returns to the store and uses the voucher to
'buy' another packet of X. Having now
used X for four weeks, s/he realizes what a
good product it is – it's getting the clothes
really clean and they smell fresh too – just
like the man on the TV says. Yes, it does
cost a few pence more, but it performs a
whole lot better and surely using an inferior
product is a false economy – who wants to
walk around in dirty clothes (or worse –
smelling stale)? No – it's going to be brand
X every time for Mr/s Smith from now on
– s/he'll just have to trade down on (say)
washing-up liquid to make up.

If sufficient non- (or occasional) users of brand X participate in the
promotion with these results, the 'lifetime value' of these new users who
have been 'brought into the brand' as brand X purchasers into the future
will comfortably exceed the cost of giving away the free product (and
administration and any other costs associated with the promotion).

However, consider the following: what might be the long-term effect of
this promotion? Suppose another shopper, Mr/s Jones, is passing the same
soap powder fixture. S/he buys X from time to time and knows that it
does an excellent job but has a suspicion that it is rather overpriced
compared with brand Y; X is a 'Rolls Royce' product whereas a good old
'Ford Escort' (brand Y) generally does the job and doesn't break the bank.
What does the 'Buy One Get One Free' offer on X suggest to him/her?
Perhaps brand X is 100 per cent overpriced – after all, they can afford to
give one packet away for each one they sell (Mr/s Jones will certainly feel
less happy about paying a premium price for brand X in the future). In
this case, we may conclude that the promotion has actually damaged or
eroded the 'brand values' which have been carefully, and expensively, built
up over years of TV press and poster advertising (brand building). For
this reason, many 'premium priced' products which sell on quality have a
policy of avoiding discounting as a promotional tool (although of course
such principles are easier to stand by when business is good, and more
likely to come under pressure during recessions).

Clearly, then, the planning and implementation of successful sales promotion (like successful direct marketing) campaigns requires judgement and skill. There are no easy answers and much 'real-world' decision making relating to promotional activity owes more to knowledge gained from previous experience and pure 'gut feel' than to 'scientific logic'. Considerable skill and expertise also come into play when one seeks to forecast response and to limit exposure; there is a thriving sector of the insurance industry which will, for an agreed premium, underwrite one's risk of running a promotion which 'over-redeems', the only thing which uninsured promoters fear more than failure being a raging success. (The Hoover 'free flights' promotion provides evidence of the damage an unexpectedly high level of redemptions can cause – see page 34.)

Let us next consider some of the mechanisms employed by sales promotion managers in client companies (such as the manufacturers of brand X in the previous example) and their sales promotion agencies; when one gets down to basics, there are only so many different types of 'offer'.

PRICE PROMOTIONS

These are arguably the least 'creative' sort of promotion in that they are simply variations on the theme of 'giving your product away'. The main types are:

- Cut price (discount), for example, 10p off (instant saving)
- Extra fill, for example, 12.5 per cent extra free
- Buy One Get One Free (instantly), for example, 'banded' pack
- Money-off coupons offering a saving, normally a straight discount on a single future purchase.

These promotions have the advantage of being easy to understand and, by offering an 'instant reward' at the point of sale, they encourage brand switching by users of competitive products. However, giving product away has a cost attached (albeit far less than the 'saving' the consumer makes on the promotion, that is, the 'perceived value') and there is also the potential damage to the 'brand image' inherent in any discounting of your product, especially if it is premium priced, as noted above. Promotions of this type are, of course, the easiest for client companies to plan and execute without any outside help (from their sales promotion agency); however, it is very difficult to measure the total annual expenditure on such promotional activity.

PRIZE PROMOTIONS

Free prize draws (and lotteries)

These are contests where all entrants' names go 'into a hat', and winners are decided by chance. In the UK it is illegal, under the 1976 Lotteries and Amusements Act, to make entry into a prize draw contingent upon a purchase of a product or service; the same applies in France, Germany and an increasing number of other markets around the world. Thus the UK National Lottery required an Act of Parliament to make it legal. In other words, you can't use a prize draw directly to incentivize a sale. Why then are free prize draws so popular? (You'll see them on-pack, especially on grocery products, in-store and in the press, not to mention as an incentive to respond to direct mail.) Very simply, they are popular because they add excitement, interest and even drama to the most mundane, low-interest product, because many people (mistakenly) buy the product in order to enter the draw, and because people notice the draw, note that it's free but buy the product anyway. If the prizes are selected and purchased with care, such promotions can have a powerful effect on sales, for a reasonable cost.

Another important reason why free prize draws are among the most widely used of all sales promotion mechanisms is that they are popular with the retail trade, that is, with supermarkets, independent grocers, off-licences, pharmacies and so on. The way promotions interact with the trade can be complex. For instance, if the retailer believes, after a presentation from a manufacturer's national account manager, that a particular prize draw (for example, on a can of Beanzo baked beans to win a holiday in Florida) is a very strong offer which will attract a large number of extra buyers, that retailer may order double their normal weekly volume of Beanzo to avoid running out of stock and consequent disappointment of customers, resulting in loss of sales (and anarchy in the aisles!). When the massive delivery arrives (from the depot or direct from the manufacturer), it takes up so much space in the stockroom that the retailer displays it prominently near the entrance to the store. Since this is a good position to display a product, Beanzo sells extremely well, even if the prize draw wasn't particularly motivating, and the retailer hasn't overordered after all – in other words, the promotion has worked (for one reason or another), and we are dealing with a self-fulfilling prophecy. (Cynical perhaps, but not entirely unrealistic.)

In recent years there has been an increase in UK promotions which test the law on linking prize draw entry to purchase. The 'plain paper' entry is the classic way around the restrictions of the 1976 UK Act. Suppose we consider an on-pack free prize draw. The pack is flashed with a message like 'Win a car a day with Heinz' or 'Thousands of Michael Jackson prizes to be won with Pepsi'. The on-pack copy focuses on the prizes. Only when one gets home with one's purchases and sits at the kitchen table to work out how to claim one's winnings does it become clear from the small print ('Prize Draw Rules') that 'no purchase is necessary', that is, if the consumer sends in their name and address on a piece of paper, the promoter will enter them into the draw without the on-pack entry form. The Institute of Sales Promotion Code of Practice and the Committee of Advertising Practice (CAP) Guidelines recommend that this phrase is clearly displayed on the outside of the pack, but there is no doubt that many recent UK promotions have sailed very close to the wind in this respect – it has to be admitted that it is likely that some consumers have been misled into purchasing the product in order to have a chance of winning the prize; thus the spirit, if not the letter, of the 1976 Act and the various industry codes has been broken. Another example is the promotion of the type 'Is there a car in this can?' (used by petfoods and soft drinks among others). Again the small print includes the 'no purchase necessary' clause.

Legal grey areas of this sort are only likely to be clarified if test cases are brought. The picture is still somewhat uncertain in the UK at the time of writing, although there was a test case ('Telemillion') where a company was successfully prosecuted for running a prize draw where one effectively had to pay to enter. One implication of the current somewhat confused situation is that it is possible for certain highly reputable organizations to make a good living out of offering a professional legal advice service to sales promotion practitioners. Their fees are a small price to pay compared with the possible costs of getting it wrong, as Hoover found to their cost with their massively over-redeemed 'free flights' promotion, which damaged the company immeasurably and curtailed the careers of several of its senior executives. Hoover Europe's loss from the promotion, which offered free trans-Atlantic flights with purchases of its white goods products, was estimated at $60 million. It must be admitted that UK legislation in the area of free prize draws is something of a minefield. First-time and even relatively experienced promoters would be well advised to avail themselves of professional advice. The trap that promoters risk falling into with free prize draws where the need to purchase is implied is effectively that of operating an illegal lottery, that is, a contest in which prizes are awarded by chance and where entry is contingent on purchasing a ticket (or buying a product, which purchase is deemed to be one's entry fee). Examples of (perfectly legal) lotteries we are all familiar with include charitable raffles (for example, at charity balls or those conducted by youth organizations or churches on a localized basis). In other words, a lottery is defined as a prize draw where one must pay to enter. To all intents and purposes, lotteries for commercial organizations are illegal in the UK. It is possible to run such contests legally (for example, certain national 'scratchcard' promotions at £1 per ticket) but only if a proportion of the takings is donated to charity – 'avoidance' schemes become very complex.

So why is running a lottery where one has to pay to enter illegal in the UK and yet a competition requiring proof of purchase to enter perfectly legal? The only difference is that lottery prizes are awarded at random whereas competition prizes depend on skill (see page 36). So where is the sense in this situation? The reasons are historical: the law was originally intended to protect weak-willed consumers from ruining themselves, although given the plentiful opportunities to gamble perfectly legally on horses, greyhounds, football pools, various scratchcard 'instant wins' and, since 1994, the National Lottery, the UK law today could be viewed as making little sense. Nevertheless, the law exists and promoters (including 'innocent' direct marketers) ignore it at their peril.

Sweepstakes/games

This category of promotions is closely related to free prize draws; as the above terms may mean different things to different people, we shall, as usual, define our terms.

> **A sweepstake is a contest where the distribution of prizes is dependent on the random distribution of predetermined winning tickets.**

The most familiar example is probably the petrol station forecourt 'scratchcard' promotion, for example, 'Scratch off three symbols to reveal three similar playing cards – three Aces, Kings etc., and win a prize.' If you think about this sort of promotion, we are indeed dealing with a prize draw; it is just that, in a sense, the draw has already been made. Thus somewhere on the scratchcard one picks up with one's petrol or hamburger and fries (and on the point-of-sale material which advertises the promotion), it should say 'No purchase necessary'. If the promoters (and their agency) are wise, they will also limit the number of game cards available to 'one promotional piece per visit'. Arguably, even more than free prize draws, the 'game' mechanism *implies* a linkage between purchase and winning a prize – the legal implications of this need to be considered carefully.

Another variant of the 'sweepstake' idea is the 'rare' package (can, box, bottle) offering an 'instant win', for example, 'Is there a car in this can?',

'Have you won £500 000? – see inside', 'Thousands of prizes to be won with lucky ring-pulls' and so on. This mechanism has been successfully employed by manufacturers of canned soup, cat food, canned soft drinks and beer/lager, among others. All offer, in the small print, the option of 'plain paper' entry, that is, 'Write to this address enclosing a piece of paper on which you have written your name and address, and our representatives will open a can at random on your behalf and advise you if you are a winner.' Inevitably, the number of people who actually submit plain paper entries is small and it seems likely that the incidence of people being persuaded, by the prospect of winning the prizes, to purchase the product is significant. One feels a single major test case would be enough to put a stop to promotions of this sort. At the time of writing, they are widespread.

Competitions

A competition is a contest where the winner(s) are determined by the exercise of skill. (Promotional lawyers can argue over *how much* and indeed what 'skill' is.) In this situation, it is perfectly legal (though not obligatory) to ask for proofs of purchase (or even money, as in some 'spot-the-ball' competitions) as a condition of entry. But what if a number of entrants get all the answers to the questions right and there is only one first prize? You can't put all the names into a hat and draw out a winner (this would turn the competition into an illegal prize draw, that is, a lottery); hence the need for a *tie-breaker*, with the judges' opinion on appropriateness to be final. In this way, skill (and judgement) is deemed to be the sole determinant of success.

Competitions tend to generate lower levels of response/participation than free prize draws. The reason for this is probably in some way connected with the aphorism 'Nobody ever went broke by underestimating the public' – in other words, one man's mildly diverting test of skill and judgement is likely to be a lot of other people's nuclear physics degree final exam. The element of skill can imply an element of difficulty, that is, a deterrent to participation, whereas 'any fool' can enter a free prize draw with an equal chance of success. (And, after all, 'someone's got to win it'.) Even worse, competitions are more fiddly, involving, as they generally do, the collection of proofs of purchase which takes time and costs money. Indeed, some competitions have been known to generate depressingly low levels of participation, except from the small group of 'professional entrants' (with no interest in the product other than the competition itself) who are the bane of many a sales promotion manager's life!

So why do promoters run competitions? The main reasons are that a competition:

- *dramatizes the brand*. Particularly if the promotion is featured on-pack, the prospect of attractive prizes can attract the shopper's eye and attain that 'Holy Grail' of FMCG pack designers – 'on-shelf stand-out';
- *attracts trade support*. Any on-pack activity gives the manufacturer's national account managers some ammunition in their negotiations with the supermarket chain head offices. If a competition can secure (i) 'keen' (competitive) in-store pricing, (ii) in-store display or (iii) a place in the retailer's own advertising, or all of these, it will almost certainly more than repay the cost of running the competition itself and the retailer will see a corresponding increase in sales of the product (which the national account manager might even claim 'proves that competitions work, by building consumer interest'). In most of such cases, only the sales promotion manager (and the handling house) knows how many (or few) redemptions were actually obtained, however.
- *can be used to educate the consumer* (about product benefits). If the manufacturer is asking users of the product or service to answer a number of multiple-choice questions or rank some statements in order of appropriateness, it is a perfect opportunity to get them thinking about the brand, the situations in which they can use it, and the benefits it can offer them, that is, the various ways in which it can improve their personal or professional lives. The prizes, too, can be selected for their relevance to the brand. The idea is that all those who even contemplate entering the competition will ingest and retain some of the key messages that the manufacturer wishes to impart in all advertising and promotional activity. This benefit of running competitions should be reflected in medium- to long-term sales, if not in immediate promotional responses (and hopefully both).
- *forces purchase*. Unlike free prize draws, competitions can require one or more purchases, perhaps enough to build a habit (especially if the product delivers).

So much for prize promotions – but before we leave this branch of promotional activity, let us consider which sorts of prizes are most desirable. In descending order of attractiveness: cash, holidays and cars. In terms of cost-effectiveness, however, holidays and cars are the favourites, cash costing exactly its face value (if anyone knows how to obtain it for less, please contact me via the publisher: I'm certain we can come to an understanding). On the other hand, 'deals' can be done on holidays and cars provided that the promoter is prepared to share some of the exposure with the car or holiday provider.

SELF-LIQUIDATING OFFERS (SLOs)

These are promotions where the consumer is offered a 'gift' or other premium item in exchange for sending in a cash contribution and one or more proofs of purchase. The offer is 'self-liquidating', from the manufacturer's point of view, if the promotion covers its own costs, that is, the consumer's 'cash contribution' = cost price (to the promoter) + handling and distribution costs.

As such, SLOs could be described as the 'mean promoter's free mail-in' (see next section). SLOs (or SLPs – self-liquidating promotions) have been called the 'poisoned chalice', presumably because their drawbacks for the promoter are many – notably the risk of large-scale under-redemption (no joke when you have a warehouse full of cuddly Father Christmases – 'which kids will love' – in mid-January). The main advantage of the SLO for the promoter is that it is a comparatively cheap promotion to run (indeed, by definition, it should be 'no-cost'). However, the appeal to consumers may be limited – after all, we're asking them to find hard cash (and proofs of purchase) in exchange for a reward they can't (yet) see or touch, which they weren't shopping for when they purchased our product, and for which we proceed to ask them to wait 28 days (in many cases).

Naturally, the best, and consequently the most successful, SLOs offer high perceived value (a saving on retail price of a comparable product) and an item which is a natural fit with the product itself, for example, baby bath towel with baby wipes, cake tin with cake mix, make-up bag with shampoo and so on. However, the best advice about SLOs is – beware!

FREE MAIL-INS (FMIs)

This is the category of promotions where the consumer is offered a 'free gift' in return for one or more proofs of purchase (POPs). These POPs may be packet tops, labels, ring-pulls, bottle tops and so on; in effect, an SLO with no cost to the consumer. These promotions are a very popular way of adding value to a product by offering the consumer an item of relatively high perceived value without asking for money. They are ideal for building and retaining consumer loyalty by motivating a series of purchases (repeat purchases). They can also motivate trial 'across the range', for example, Lea & Perrins Spicy Sauces offered a free international recipe book with five proofs of purchase from their range (no more than two to be from the most popular Worcestershire Sauce variant). This type of activity is also known as *cross-selling*.

One key benefit of FMIs to the promoter is the phenomenon known as 'slippage', that is, consumers collect POPs with the intention of sending for the free item and, either through inertia or because they forget all about the offer, fail to do so before the closing date. Meanwhile, the manufacturer has obtained the desired incremental sales without troubling their fulfilment house or giving anything away – a promoter's dream.

Forecasting redemption levels is a key skill required in planning a free mail-in promotion. It is vital to build up a series of historical results based on similar promotions in order to reduce the risks and costs of over- or under-redemption. Factors to be considered, all of which will impact upon the attractiveness of the offer, include:

- Number of packs carrying the offer (known as the 'pack-out')
- Number of POPs requested
- Seasonal factors
- Duration of offer (closing date)
- Competitive activity.

As mentioned above, some companies specialize in offering insurance against over-redemption of FMIs; although it might be viewed as a nice problem to have, a flood of applications for free gifts can mean substantial costs (and dramatically exceed allocated budgets), so that insurance is a wise precaution.

Examples of FMIs are widespread, including Corn Flakes (and other breakfast cereals), Nescafé (label collection schemes for free mugs and the like), and 'cashbacks' (where the free item is actually a cash refund).

After 'price promotions', FMIs are probably the most common example of FMCG sales promotion today. Properly planned and executed, they can be very cost-effective.

PARTNER PROMOTIONS

This category of promotions includes all offers which involve two parties, that is, the promoter (the manufacturer of brand X, say) has got together with another organization (normally another manufacturer, say of brand Y, but possibly a retailer) to offer the consumer an added-value benefit (for a limited time period) and provide a reason to choose brand X, and frequently brand Y too, rather than competitive products. For a successful partner promotion, key requirements are:

- brand X and brand Y are non-competitive but have closely matching target markets; and

- both manufacturers participate financially and gain commercially from the success of the promotion.

Benefits include access to each other's customers (possibly in a 'privileged' medium with the endorsement of the partner organization) and, of course, cost saving.

Some examples will illustrate how such promotions should work:

- **Persil train tickets**. BR and Lever brothers combined to offer free travel to children (accompanied by a full-fare-paying adult) with proofs of purchase (since repeated by BR and Boots).
- **Nat West/Kall-Kwik**. Nat West Bank and Kall-Kwik (the High Street instant print franchise) got together to offer an incentive to new small businesses to open their bank account at Nat West by providing free business stationery from Kall-Kwik.
- **British Airways/Safeway**. Safeway, the UK supermarket chain, offered free BA flights as a reward for repeat purchases.

Partner promotions (like price promotions) grew dramatically in popularity during the early 1990s UK recession. When such promotions are properly planned and executed, having two parties sharing the costs (and funding the rewards) means that promotional budgets go further and the 'perceived value' on offer to the consumer is maximized.

Consider a partner (or joint) promotion between, say, a shampoo (X) and a moisturizer (Y). Ideally the promotion should be featured on both X and Y (on-pack). In-store, point-of-sale material could attract attention to X and Y on their respective fixtures. Press and radio advertising, covermounts, door-to-door coupon leaflets and even TV commercials could also be jointly funded for a heavyweight media campaign that would almost certainly impress the retail grocery and pharmacy trade (multiples and independents) and receive keen in-store pricing and possibly featuring and display. Thus, a well-constructed partner promotion can work extremely hard and generate substantial incremental sales for both manufacturers at relatively low cost.

As with any 'marriage', the companies and products should be well matched and fit naturally together, for example, a new car and free AA cover, a holiday company/tour operator and sunglasses, a soft drink and a snack brand, or either of these with a cinema chain. Partner deals also create interesting database-sharing opportunities.

CHARITY PROMOTIONS

These are promotions which appeal to the consumer's better nature – the 'hook' or 'reward' depends on our sense of altruism or the kick that we all get (to a greater or lesser extent) from giving to a worthy cause. A charity promotion for an FMCG product is typically structured as follows:

- The offer: consumers mail in wrappers/tokens (POPs). Each earns a certain amount for the charity, for example, 50p donated by the promoter/manufacturer.
- Logistics: at the end of the promotional period, the promoter counts the proofs received and pays the charity the equivalent sum (or pre-agreed guaranteed minimum).

These promotions need to be carefully planned. I would advise any promoter contemplating a charity link as follows. The first decision should be whether to run such a promotion at all – is it a good fit with your brand values? (A charity promotion may not be appropriate for a luxury fragrance, a diamond ring or a single malt whisky, for instance.)

Next, the choice of charity is crucial. Think about your customers: what sort of people are they; what are their concerns? What is/will be fashionable and/or in the news? (Children, animals, handicapped, inner-city, overseas and so on.)

Then find out what the *charity* wants. Understand the sort of promotion that fits *their* image and requirements. Tap into their historical results/track record. Above all, remember you are dealing with committed people who are more likely to be morally sincere supporters than cynical 'hired hands' – respect their integrity. Having done this, don't feel guilty about using the charity to gain incremental sales and profit for your organization – the charity is also benefiting; people feel good about giving; it's a win–win–win scenario.

TAILOR-MADE PROMOTIONS

Any of the foregoing consumer promotional mechanisms may be either *national* (that is, available to every consumer via every retail outlet where the product is sold) or *tailor-made* (that is, available only via the outlets of one retail organization). An example of the latter would be '£1.50 cashback with three purchases of Woodpigeon Cider from Albert Wine Stores only.' Retailers love these but they can be less effective for manufacturers than national promotions.

These, then, are the principal mechanisms employed in sales promotion. They have been covered in some depth, since a reasonable grasp of each of the various techniques is essential for a direct marketer who wishes to dovetail effectively with sales promotion specialists in an 'integrated' environment. We will discuss the linkages between direct marketing and sales promotion in Chapter 5, and how direct marketing and sales promotion professionals can work together in an integrated environment (as indeed many already are) in Chapters 8–10.

We have established that sales promotion is about making 'extra benefit' offers; that is, we are giving the end user or customer (business or consumer) a reason to select our product or service in preference to a competitive product or service and to make that purchase decision NOW. Moreover, we shall not be (entirely) satisfied if that is as far as it goes; rather, we hope to achieve a longer-term change of consumer behaviour (in the most extreme cases, we may be asking our target audience to 'break the habit of a lifetime'). In short, we wish to gain new, loyal customers who will come back to choose our product again and again and, in effect, deliver a future stream of revenue to us over years to come which represents incremental profit far in excess of what the promotion cost us to run. (Realistically, these 'good' consumers are required to subsidize the 'bad' opportunist customers who desert the brand as soon as the promotion ends.)

However, in my experience, few promotions are evaluated this scientifically; rather, judgement, experience and 'gut feeling' replace hard measurement. However, a promotion that only produces a temporary 'blip' on the Nielsen (a research service measuring retail sales of FMCG products) curve (plotting the brand's market share), after which the monthly sales revert to the level they were at before, would be agreed by most sales promotion professionals (and indeed most 'right-thinking people', which, generally speaking, includes the former group) to have been a waste of time and money (unless, of course, it could somehow be proven that without the promotion, the long-term position would have been inferior).

The history and development of sales promotion

Sales promotion is one of the core communications disciplines. As with direct marketing, we can best understand its current practice and future direction by pausing for a while to examine its history; let's go back to sales promotion basics.

Like direct marketing, sales promotion is almost certainly as old as commerce itself. As soon as primitive societies began to trade, the offering of something 'extra' became an option for clinching a deal (especially in a competitive situation). Indeed, it has been claimed that 'the first incentive was the apple that Eve gave to Adam' (quoted by Christian Petersen), although arguably the extra benefits of that particular special offer were more apparent than real (making this promotion a candidate for the title of 'earliest instance of a pig-in-a-poke'). A better-documented case of an early sales promotion is that of the 'Baker's Dozen'. With various bakers competing for the customer's penny, offering thirteen loaves for the price of twelve was either a good method of recruiting new customers (trial gaining) and/or an unexpected and welcome 'thank-you' to regular customers (loyalty building). This deal was effectively 'buy twelve, get one free' and was sufficiently widespread (in 'Olde England') for the phrase to enter the language (even if the original motives were more defensive than promotional!).

> Baker's Dozen.
> 13 for 12. In earlier times when a heavy
> penalty was inflicted for short weight,
> bakers used to give a surplus number of
> loaves . . . to avoid all risk of incurring a
> fine.
>
> Brewer's *Dictionary of Phrase and Fable*,
> Cassell

The history of sales promotion in the UK and USA is not one of logical, systematic development; rather it is a story of piecemeal and seemingly at times random growth, various techniques being used rather haphazardly, found to be successful and so repeated, refined and extended.

Christian Petersen, in his excellent book *Sales Promotion In Action* (ABP 1979), locates the origin of modern-day sales promotion as 1844 with the founding of the first cooperative society. Although the Co-op's 'dividend' was motivated by an ethical distaste for profit, rather than a more capitalist desire to build business and deliver profits to shareholders, it certainly had a powerful promotional effect in attracting customers to buy their groceries from the local 'Co-op'. Another milestone was the earliest recorded launch of trading stamps (Red Stamps, in Yorkshire in 1851).

In the second half of the nineteenth century, the multiple grocers began to establish branch networks and companies such as J. Sainsbury, Lipton's and Boots the Chemists expanded rapidly, often using powerful advertising and cut-price promotions to attract custom. F.W. Woolworth was meanwhile expanding the 'Nickel and Dime store' across the USA, reaching Britain (Liverpool) in 1909 with a shop offering 'nothing over 6d'.

At an international exhibition in Chicago, Mr H.J. Heinz offered 'free Heinz badges' to visitors to his stand. Pears Soap offered 'Bubbles' jigsaws while Bird's Custard were giving away Bird's Recipe Books before the turn of the century. A visit to antiques fairs and bric-à-brac stalls produces ample evidence of early sales promotion activity, for example:

- Illustrated biscuit and chocolate tin containers (to be retained for storage, free gift with purchase)
- Cigarette cards (an early in-pack free gift)
- Tea cards.

Other historical highlights include:

- Quaker's packing of china bowls inside their cereal packets
- *News Chronicle*'s 'Lobby Lud' giving away cash prizes at seaside resorts between the wars (cf. Kolly Kibber in Graham Greene's *Brighton Rock*).
- Radio Luxembourg's League of Ovaltineys, which, according to Petersen, proffered 'a special comic, a badge, and a cook book, and was designed to inculcate reassuring habits of obedience, helpfulness *and Ovaltine drinking* amongst the young'.

In the depression of the 1930s, prices collapsed, the new multiple retailers' power grew and the manufacturers sought to differentiate their products by means of 'gift catalogue' schemes, increasingly sold to retailers by a new breed of motor-car-travelling manufacturers' sales forces; long before the Ford Cortina/Sierra/Mondeo and Vauxhall Cavalier, the 'sales rep' had already been born.

There followed a hiatus from 1939–45 (when most people, at least in the UK if not in the USA, had things on their minds other than sales promotion). However, as rationing ended in July 1954, branded goods re-emerged, supported from 1956 by TV advertising in the UK and often reinforced by large-scale popular promotions which caught the imagination of a public which was, compared with the situation today, promotionally unsophisticated (as in the case of 'The White Tide Man', and later 'The Fairy Snow Man'). The new brands were increasingly distributed by a small number of large self-service retail chains – Sainsbury, Safeway, Fine Fare, Tesco and of course the Co-op.

When 'resale price maintenance' ended in 1962, price cutting again became the main promotional tool. However, as retailers' and manufacturers' margins tumbled, a new wave of US-inspired sales promotion consultancies sprang up. These agencies were structured along somewhat similar lines to the already well-established advertising agencies and their entrepreneur leaders were bursting with creative ideas for new and exciting promotions to influence consumer decisions by adding value (as opposed to discounting). Not all got past English law – one consultancy was ruined by an illegal promotion for Kit-e-Kat petfood. The 1950s and 1960s, however, spawned some now classic promotions, including the Glendinning agency's Shell 'Make Money' (matching half banknotes, based on an earlier US promotion for Getty Oil and later successfully revived by Shell) and Esso's Tiger Tails (self-liquidating premia) based on their advertising slogan 'Put a Tiger in your Tank' and the Tiger as featured in their TV commercials. Cigarette cards were replaced by coupons and Embassy cigarettes were launched in 1962 supported by lavish gift collection catalogues. Petrol station promotions were revolutionized by the arrival of Green Shield Stamps (also distributed by Tesco and various other retailers) which escalated to the extent that 'Quad', 'Quin' and 'Dec' (*sic*) stamps were offered by screaming forecourt posters to increasingly bemused motorists before the 1973 oil crisis, when petrol prices soared and the actual availability of petrol became more important to the consumer than any promotion.

In the late 1970s and 1980s, petrol promotions involving free drinking glasses enjoyed a vogue, while during the early 1990s recession points collection schemes proliferated (for example, the Esso Tiger Tokens Collection, Mobil/Argos Premier Points, and Total/Marks and Spencer/Boots gift voucher scheme). With tough economic times, the 1990s again saw widespread price cutting (following the boom 1980s emphasis on style, choice and customer service). However, one major change is the environmental issue – new products like Ecover have emerged, packaging has become increasingly (and visibly) recyclable and 'ozone-layer friendly' and 'green' or environmentally aware charity promotions have become widespread. Loyalty cards have been embraced by many marketers, pioneered by the airlines' frequent flier programmes (including the BA Executive Club, American Airlines AAdvantage, Virgin Freeway and Lufthansa Miles and More, all of which provide successful case histories), and subsequently followed enthusiastically by UK grocery retailers (Tesco, Sainsbury, Asda, Safeway and the like). It is interesting to speculate whether these programmes should be classified as sales promotion or direct marketing: are they a short-term method of influencing consumer choice by offering a reward, or are they a long-term route to building a relationship by encouraging fundamental behaviour change? In my view, the best of these loyalty programmes are *both* direct marketing *and* sales promotion. As with most marketing initiatives, however, the effect diminishes as the novelty of the pioneering programmes wears off, until every competitor offers something similar, and the consumer is unable to distinguish between the offerings of the competing brands.

Although economic and cultural factors will inevitably change with time and across national boundaries, the basic human motivations remain consistent. Thus, most consumers will always jump at 'something for nothing' and everybody feels good to have 'got a deal', especially when making a 'necessary purchase'. In a situation needing a decision to purchase one product or another (similar) one, from one retailer or another (similar) one, with all other factors roughly equal, the choice will invariably be the one offering 'extra added value'. It would appear that promotions will always be with us.

In the remainder of this book, we shall examine how promotions interact with other marketing communications, especially direct marketing.

Let us close this chapter by studying two highly successful sales promotions.

Case history

Company	British Airways
Background	Research during 1994 had indicated that BA's rapid growth and commercial success had left some of its leisure customers and potential customers feeling it was rather large and 'aloof'.
Marketing objectives	To demonstrate that BA was a warm, caring, fun company. For customers/prospective customers, the positioning 'nothing too big, nothing too small' needed to be reinforced. There was a secondary objective of involving and motivating the BA staff. Timing was Christmas 1994.
Solution	The 'Paint a plane' competition was chosen from several promotional campaign concepts as the best route to achieve the above objectives. Children under the age of 14 were invited to

'Paint a plane for Christmas'; judging was in two age groups, ten and under and 11–14. One winner and ten runners-up were selected from 19 356 entrants. All taking part received a certificate; all 50 finalists received a model plane, and the two winners were invited to London to approve their designs before BA Engineering transferred them to a real Boeing 737–200 aircraft!

A 'Winter Wonderland' launch event was held, featuring a Dickensian street market, performers, carousel rides and a 20 ft Christmas tree, as well as the formal unveiling of the completed painted plane.

BA and its agency achieved extensive UK and international press coverage and the whole promotion was judged to be a complete success in terms of demonstrating the relaxed, family-oriented and fun-loving side to British Airways.

Case history   Smirnoff Virtual Reality

Company	The Pierre Smirnoff Company
Background	Smirnoff developed its 'Pure Thrill' global positioning in the early 1990s. Its innovative 'through the bottle' advertising carries a consistent message to consumers all over the world and has helped increase awareness and sales for the brand.
Marketing objectives	The Smirnoff international marketing team, and their consultancy Creative IQ Group Ltd, wanted to repeat this success in the more difficult area of promotions. They wanted to develop a concept that could successfully communicate 'Pure Thrill', and also achieve global and local objectives in any country in the world.
	The key objectives that the promotion had to achieve were increasing trial and rate of sale amongst consumers between legal drinking age and 24, encouraging them to ask for Smirnoff by name and to obtain 'first pour' status in all participating outlets (i.e. Smirnoff is poured when consumers ask for vodka).
Solution	The competitive nightclub sector in Europe was targeted as the right testing ground for a new concept – Smirnoff Virtual Reality.
	Smirnoff national marketing companies pre-selected large participating night clubs on the basis that they gave the brand 'first pour' status.

Plate 2.1   Smirnoff – Virtual Reality
Source: Creative IQ Ltd

The Smirnoff Virtual Reality roadshow toured six countries in
Europe for three months and was 'live' in each club for three
nights. The events were heavily pre-publicized by flyers, local
radio and DJ trails in the clubs.

Consumers received an entry card when they bought a Smirnoff
(free on request in countries where this is not legal). The word
'*EXPERIENCE*' printed on the back of the card magically
transformed from black to red or green when moistened. Winners
with green cards tested their skills in the Smirnoff 'Zone Hunter'
challenge – a two-player virtual reality game. Each player's
progress could be watched by their friends on large TV monitors.

The road show was a huge success. Rate of sale increased by an
average of 2.9 times in participating night clubs. Playing a virtual
reality game is a thrilling experience, and the clubs were
consistently busier on the second and third nights as many people
returned with their friends to play another game.

Virtual reality succeeds in communicating the idea of 'Pure Thrill'
and links well into the theme transformation in the 'through the

bottle' advertising. It also has the advantage of being a strong incentive for young people all over the world.

Smirnoff monitored rate of sale and trial at each venue before, during and after the promotion, and were able to create a strong sales story for countries considering using the promotion in the future.

Smirnoff Virtual Reality subsequently rolled out internationally with countries typically taking the promotion for two to three months.

3 ADVERTISING

One of the intriguing things about the advertising business is the number of characters it throws up; most seem to have at least one famous quote attributed to them. A collection of a few of these will serve as an introduction to this colourful subject area:

> I know that half of my advertising budget is wasted, but I'm not sure which half.
>
> Lord Leverhulme (attributed)

> The consumer is not a moron. She is your wife. And she is grown up.
>
> David Ogilvy, 1956

(Much less sexist then than it sounds today.)

> Don't tell my mother I work in advertising, she thinks I play piano in a whore house.
>
> Jacques Seguela, Vice-President of Euro RSCG, 1979

> Advertising is the most fun you can have while keeping your clothes on.
>
> Jerry della Femina, 1970

> Remind me not to go out for a good time with Jerry.
>
> Tamara Ingram (attributed)

> I can look at a Benson and Hedges campaign and admire the technical skill and ingenuity. I can feel nothing but admiration for the craftsmanship, but regret the fact that it is there.
>
> David Abbott (attributed)

> Advertising isn't a science. It's persuasion. And persuasion is an art.
>
> Bill Bernbach (attributed)

> Advertising is simply a way of selling something, anything, in the most effective

way possible. No great mystery to it and
not really that much science – despite the
efforts of various people to turn it into one,
largely to justify their salaries, expense
accounts and very existence . . . The
bluffing point is that in many countries, but
not the USA, selling is seen as something
that is not quite nice. Thus advertising
often goes to extraordinary lengths to
distance itself from all those nasty used-car
and double-glazing salespeople . . . Since
advertising is essentially to do with human
behaviour, it can only be an inexact science
at best, and usually something of a gamble.

Nigel Foster, 1988

Definitions

Not an easy place to start, unfortunately. One option is to resort to yet
more quotes.

Advertising is the origination and/or
communication of ideas about products in
order to motivate consumers towards
purchase.

David Bernstein (attributed)

Advertising presents the most persuasive
possible selling message to the right
prospects for the product or service at the
lowest possible cost.

Institute Of Practitioners In Advertising

Advertising creates famous brands (as we shall establish, a brand is more
than a product). Anyone who doubts whether advertising works might like
to consider the following words and their 'meanings':

● McDonald's
● Kellogg's
● Coca-Cola
● Kodak
● Marlboro
● IBM

- American Express
- Sony
- Mercedes-Benz
- Nescafé
- Disney
- Toyota
- BMW

Each of these brands has been created (in most cases over many years) by careful management of the image, along with judicious improvement of the product itself, as well as updating of graphics, logos and packaging to ensure contemporariness without compromising heritage. Extensive and consistent advertising support has been a common factor in the creation and development of all these brands, as well as a host of others including Levi's, Bacardi, Seiko, Chanel, Colgate, Dunhill, Guinness, Heineken, Heinz, Hertz, Mars, Pepsi-Cola, Nike and Pampers.

Advertising is something everyone thinks they understand but which most (myself included) would be hard pressed to define adequately. The reader in search of a definition might like to select from the following (all offered by one 'expert' or another at one time or another):

- 'Advertising exists in order to sell things'
- 'Advertising is any means by which the seller communicates with the buyer, excepting face to face contact'
- 'Advertising is the sum of all remote communications intended to sell a product or service'
- 'Advertising is what Admen do' (?!)

(There are analogous definitions of direct marketing, sales promotion and PR.)

Anyway, we all know what advertising is – or do we? It may be easier to say where advertising starts than where it finishes: a TV commercial for Pedigree Chum petfood is 'advertising'; so is a black and white press ad for Tesco highlighting 'this week's bargain prices'. So too is a radio commercial singing the praises of the latest mobile 'phone from Motorola. The poster on the roadside urging us to 'visit Israel for the holiday of a lifetime' would also be described as advertising by most people, in or out of the business; but what about the following?:

- a TV commercial reminding viewers to visit McDonald's for a 99p breakfast (available only until X/X/XX);

- a press ad for the Literary Guild offering new members 'your first three books for £1';
- a radio commercial for a soap powder consisting mainly of a hard sell and a strong call to action, urging listeners to phone 0800 123 456 and give their names and addresses for a free sample. (Refer back to our definitions of direct marketing and sales promotion.)

We are coming up against questions of definitions; one of the unfortunate aspects of the marketing world is that different terms mean different things to different people. As elsewhere in this chapter, we shall now define our terms (I hope clearly) and subsequently adhere closely to these definitions so that although some may take issue with our usage of certain words, at least what follows will be understood as I intend.

For the purposes of this book, then, 'advertising is the collection of activities intended to increase sales of a product or service by:

- creating or increasing awareness;
- communicating the benefits (to the end user);
- creating (and building upon) positive attitudes towards and perceptions of the product or service.'

Advertising is generally a long- to medium-term process and involves the creation and development of a brand image (that is, a bundle of benefits which are properties associated with the brand) which is ideally based on a USP (unique selling proposition, a term coined by Rosser Reeves at the pioneering US agency, Ted Bates), giving the brand a substantial competitive advantage. When we use the term 'advertising' in what follows, we shall mean 'image'-based, brand-awareness communications using the following media:

- TV
- Press (magazines and newspapers)
- Posters
- Radio
- Cinema

and so on.

If a response is requested by these communications, it is incidental. The primary objective is brand building, that is, transmitting a consistent series of positive messages over a period of time to create favourable perceptions in the minds of the (poor hapless) target audience (whether consumer or business buyers).

Our definition of advertising is intended to exclude activities designed to communicate promotions and also communications intended primarily to build or enhance a database, that is, name gathering via a direct response device. In case the reader feels we still haven't got enough definitions: if PR is defined as

> 'the management of all relationships between an organization and its key stakeholders' (customers, distributors, suppliers, employees and shareholders),

then PR activity (including media relations, crisis management and parliamentary lobbying) is all marketing communications *except* advertising, direct marketing and promotions.

Obviously no set of definitions of the various terms employed to describe communications activity can be entirely satisfactory and no doubt the reader will be consciously or subconsciously framing questions intended to expose an inadequacy or area of overlap in the foregoing sections.

However, I believe that these definitions will suffice for what is to follow, and in any case, the central thesis of this book is that the disciplines of direct marketing, sales promotion and advertising, although distinct, are converging rapidly and overlapping increasingly. The definitions are important to an understanding of the three disciplines in isolation (as they used to be) in order fully to appreciate their power when two or more are used in combination (as they increasingly will be).

The history and development of advertising

As with direct marketing (Chapter 1) and sales promotion (Chapter 2), we can gain considerable insight into the current state of advertising and where it might be heading by taking a brief backward glance at the rich tradition of advertising campaigns as they have developed over the years.

The history of advertising is the history of brand building. Advertising is therefore as old as the need felt by manufacturers to differentiate their products and services from the competition. For many multinational companies, including McDonald's, Coca-Cola, IBM, Kodak, General Motors and Exxon, brands have been the main 'engines of growth' and are indisputably major corporate assets.

The word 'brand' comes originally from the Norse *brandr*, meaning 'to burn'. Brands were originally marks by which farmers identified their cattle – later 'hallmarks' (on silver items) and 'trademarks' (for example, by a potter on his pots) and eventually an identifier on any item to reassure the consumer of consistent quality and authenticity (and at the same time to distinguish this 'branded' product from the competition). Brands, once established, generate a stream of sales and profit for the manufacturer, a continuing supply of customers for the retailer and a level of 'peace of mind' for the consumer who knows what s/he is getting. Brands have been a major ingredient of capitalist economies since the 1850s. For their creation and development they have relied heavily on advertising.

Advertising is necessary to tell your potential customers what a great product you have, and, specifically, what it can do for them. In other words, branded goods' manufacturers have (especially over the last century and a half) employed advertising to inform and persuade, that is, to sell benefits to consumers. These years have seen many commercial milestones including:

- the development of mass production and packaging techniques (for example, in motor cars, food, household products);
- the rise of supermarket distribution;
- improvements in transport and distribution (shipping, railways, roads, personal transportation);
- commercial television (in the UK during the late 1950s and 1960s) and development of satellite and cable (1980s and 1990s).

Brands have recently been valued as a part of various companies' assets and in the late 1980s and early 1990s certain corporate acquisitions and mergers have been heavily influenced by valuations of the brands involved (for example, Guinness's controversial purchase of Distillers, RJR Nabisco's sale to its own management in 1988 and subsequent sale of the European businesses to the French BSN for some $2.5 billion, and the sale of Rowntree's Confectionery, makers of Kit Kat, Aero and Polo, to Swiss giant Nestlé for $2.5 billion).

Brands and their advertising have been inextricably intertwined. This may be why just about everyone you might stop in the street has an opinion about advertising – love it or hate it, you can't avoid it. In any shopping centre (mall) or public house (bar) the following slogans would produce recognition and a reaction (depending on the individual's attitudes to the appropriate brand):

_____ is good for you

A _____ a day helps you work, rest and play

_____ is it

Happiness is a cigar called _____

_____ refreshes the parts other beers cannot reach

Beanz Meanz _____

Drink a pinta _____ a day

Readers could doubtless supply their own additions.

TV

> Broadly, I think we in the agency business
> had better caution ourselves against being
> the retarding factor in our clients 'getting
> into' this new medium . . . many of us in
> this business, I feel, have more imagination
> than guts.
>
> Leo Burnett, 1949

> the foulest, ghastliest, loathsomest
> nightmare ever inflicted by science on a
> suffering human race
>
> P.G. Wodehouse, on the introduction of
> commercial TV, 1955

> That tuppenny Punch and Judy show
> Winston Churchill, of commercial TV

The arrival of commercial TV had a major effect on advertising. The first rudimentary TV commercials ran in the USA in 1940. At that time, only some 5000 receivers were in operation in the New York area, with an estimated five people watching per set. The first serious TV commercial is generally reckoned to be for Bulova watches during a baseball game between the Brooklyn Dodgers and Philadelphia Phillies on 1 July 1941: 'the Bulova Time Check', aired on WNBT in New York. The commercial cost Bulova $4 for the airtime and a further $5 for 'station charges' (*Advertising Age* special issue – '50 years of TV advertising', Spring 1995). The war slowed down the spread of TV. In September 1944 the 'Gillette cavalcade of sports' was launched. In 1945 Sears, Roebuck started selling TV sets and later that year TV commercials were aired from Pan Am, Firestone, RCA and Esso. Colour TV arrived in the USA when CBS broadcast the first colour programme in 1951 (received by only 25 viewers – real early adopters! – while 12 million mono viewers saw only a blank screen). The first colour commercial was shown in 1954. The first TV commercials in the UK were broadcast by Associated-Rediffusion at 8.12 p.m. on Thursday 22 September 1955: they were a 60-second effort by Young and Rubicam for Gibbs SR toothpaste and Colman Prentis and Varley's commercial for Cadbury's Drinking Chocolate. Other brands on TV that evening included Batchelors, Kraft, Esso, Ford, Crosse and Blackwell and Oxo. These ads played to some 165 000 viewers at a cost of £975 per minute. The UK's first colour commercials arrived in 1969.

UK advertising agencies, accustomed to promoting their clients' wares via press and posters, were naturally uncomfortable with the new medium when it arrived in the late 1950s. Similarly, their US colleagues, a decade earlier, had been reluctant to believe that TV advertising could offer much that radio and print ads did not, and had doubted that the new medium would catch on sufficiently to make it viable. Early commercials tended to resemble moving press ads rather than the feature films they later emulated. (Contrast the launch of the Apple Macintosh during the third quarter of the US Super Bowl with the famous 60-second 1984 Orwellian epic commercial by Chiat/Day which cost $400 000 to produce and £500 000 to broadcast in its single national paid airing.) However, the TV medium took off faster than most had predicted and, by the mid-1960s, blockbuster TV campaigns were the accepted way to promote FMCGs on both sides of the Atlantic. Classic US campaigns of that and the next decades were the 'Magnificent Seven' themed work by Leo Burnett for Marlboro, 'Hertz puts you in the driver's seat' by Norman, Craig and Kummel in 1961 and the original 'good to the last drop' work for Maxwell House, followed by the classic Doyle Dane Bernbach work for Volkswagen, McCann Erickson's 'I'd like to buy the world a Coke' and American Express's 'Don't leave home without it'. UK viewers were treated to such efforts as 'Persil washes whiter and it shows', 'A Mars a day helps you work, rest and play', the Oxo mum and the Brylcreem bounce. These campaigns remind us how successful advertising and especially TV advertising campaigns can enter the culture and language, win creative awards for the agency and, more importantly, create lasting brand properties that give manufacturers the sustained competitive advantage that they all crave. From time to time TV has been judged to be too powerful by governments keen to protect its citizens from its effects; in 1969 TV ads for cigarettes (a third of all spend at the time) were banned in the UK; the USA followed suit in 1971. Today there are also tight restrictions on TV advertising of a range of other products including toys, alcoholic drinks and sanitary protection products.

It is interesting to compare current attitudes to the new interactive media (the Internet and World Wide Web) with reactions to the arrival of commercial TV. Certainly broadcast TV is now seriously threatened by a range of newcomers, including satellite (Sky TV launched in 1989, BSB in 1990. Cable is showing signs of finally taking off in the UK in the late 1990s; the Americans have been heavy cable subscribers for decades). There is no doubt, however, that the combination of sound and moving colour pictures gives TV an ability to grab the viewer's attention and demonstrate product benefits second only to sending out door-to-door salespeople. Certainly TV can be used to generate response (DRTV is now an established and specialist craft requiring expert planning, buying and creative resources). However, the great strength of TV is to build brands, and if the need is to achieve rapid awareness for a new product or to add authority and credibility to existing brands, it is still an essential part of marketing communications plans.

To conclude this chapter, let us spotlight three famous brands which have been consistent and heavy advertisers for many years. Their manufacturers understand the importance of investment in brands and the returns that strong, healthy brands can deliver year after year.

Nescafé

Nescafé pioneered the instant coffee sector when it was launched just before the First World War. Consistent investment in advertising and product improvements and careful nurturing of the brand (the essence of successful brand management) have kept Nescafé as the number 1 in the world instant coffee market ever since. Advertising has been thoroughly researched and tightly controlled from Nestlé's head office in Vevey, Switzerland and brand extensions (for example, Gold Blend and Gold Blend Decaffeinated in the UK) have become star brands in their own right. To most Western consumers, Nescafé means instant coffee, the ultimate tribute to successful branding created by advertising.

Marlboro

Marlboro is the world's number 1 cigarette brand. Whatever you believe about the morality of promoting the practice of cigarette smoking, there can be no doubt about the success of the branding job done by Philip Morris, who launched Marlboro with the famous 'Cowboy' imagery in 1955. The associations with the outdoor life, with masculinity, strength and independence of character have been carefully created by heavy investment in skilfully crafted advertising around the world.

As restrictions on the advertising of tobacco products increase, Philip Morris will no doubt employ increasingly subtle techniques to maintain Marlboro's profile (for example, posters consisting entirely of a red strip).

In such circumstances, sustaining a strong brand built by significant and consistent advertising is a feasible marketing objective; defending an ailing brand which received little advertising support even when it was permitted is likely to mean fighting a losing battle; launching a new 'Marlboro' without the assistance of advertising would appear to be impossible. Such is the power of advertising.

American Express

'Amex' is a massively successful international brand and unusual in that it is not an FMCG product – the company's products are comparatively intangible.

Although American Express is a relatively broadly based financial services group, offering travellers' cheques, insurance and personal financial planning, to most people the company means the American Express card – a charge card which, through consistent and carefully managed international advertising (particularly in the USA, the UK and major European markets), has dominated its market despite intense competition from other heavily advertised brands including Visa and MasterCard.

In the UK, advertising slogans such as 'That'll do nicely' and 'Don't leave home without it' have burned or 'branded' themselves into the consciousness of the Amex target market (broadly: males 25–50 years old with high disposable incomes).

American Express is a powerful brand, like Nescafé, Marlboro and a host of others, and a monument to the power of advertising to build awareness and create positive attitudes in the minds of the target audience.

David Ogilvy once summed up the *raison d'être* of his worldwide network of advertising agencies and simultaneously encapsulated his philosophy of why advertising exists, in the motto 'We sell – or else'.

Good advertising identifies the key benefits of a product or service (ideally isolating a unique selling proposition (USP) as preached in the 1950s by Rosser Reeves, the co-founder of the Ted Bates Agency, and by many of his disciples subsequently) and communicates this message to the targeted consumers persuasively and memorably.

It is no coincidence that other disciplines, notably direct marketing and sales promotion, have broadly similar bases for their existence. As we shall discover in the remainder of this book, successful integrated marketing communications strategies are founded on the same principles as successful advertising campaigns. To illustrate companies' successful use of advertising, consider the following case histories.

Case history

Company	Playtex (*Wonderbra*)
Background	*Wonderbra* (the original push-up plunge bra) had been marketed in the UK under licence by Gossard since 1968 and had come to be regarded as a 'classic' style. It was something of an engineering achievement, requiring 44 components compared with only 25 in a standard bra.
	In 1994 it was decided by parent Sara Lee to switch the licence to Playtex and relaunch. Playtex had a traditional image and a 30-year-old product, compared with Gossard's fashionable image and their new push-up product (The 'Ultrabra'). The trade had doubts about what Playtex would do with *Wonderbra*. 'Bra Wars' had begun . . .
Marketing objectives	Relaunch the *Wonderbra* brand in the UK and introduce three new styles.
Solution	The launch budget was relatively limited (just over £300k for the first crucial six months). The controversial creative approach adopted by Playtex and their agency (TBWA) featured Czech supermodel Eva Herzigova and the end-line 'The One and Only *Wonderbra*'.

The creative execution had to be carefully judged. Extensive research indicated that *Wonderbra* woman was 'powerful, image conscious and in control, with a mind and body of her own. She was interested in how the product helped her to make the most of herself:

- PHYSICALLY by boosting her cleavage
- EMOTIONALLY by boosting her confidence

and
- ULTIMATELY by boosting her sex appeal.'

Product demonstration was considered to be necessary, in a way that was humorous and sexy, but not sexist or offensive. To avoid sending out the wrong signals, no men featured in the pictures, which were taken by a female photographer (black and white shots only). Eva Herzigova was selected as the model, as being beautiful, charming and sexy, with a smaller than average bust.

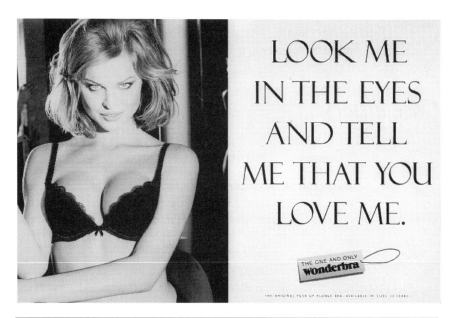

Plate 3.1 Playtex – the *Wonderbra* campaign
Source: Playtex

Playtex is traditionally a committed TV and press advertiser. On this campaign, £200 000 was spent in the predictable (and of course appropriate) core medium of women's magazines. But the secret weapon was a media choice – selecting the poster medium. Posters are generally viewed by lingerie marketers as too wasteful and too public. But for only £130 000 over two weeks, Playtex gained significant impact, visibility and interest.

The executions were described by Playtex's agency as being 'very bold, up-front and in-ya-face'. Substantial positive (and a certain amount of negative) PR was generated. (Playtex authorized an affectionate parody by Kaliber low-alcohol lager featuring comedian Billy Connolly on facing poster sites; they turned down numerous other 'less tasteful' proposed product linkages.) The estimated value of the PR coverage was £50 million.

The campaign was featured on-pack and in point-of-sale material. Playtex's distribution base doubled, getting the brand into a substantial number of new sales outlets. The advertising campaign took the UK by storm, and helped to boost sales by 41 per cent on the previous year. *Wonderbra* played a major part in the doubling of Playtex UK business in two years and it became a truly worldwide brand within 12 months of the relaunch.

Perhaps the most telling proof of the success of the campaign was that Playtex followed up with more activity, also featuring Eva Herzigova and including posters in full colour in contrast to the original mono executions.

Case history

Company	Virgin Atlantic (Upper Class)

Background During 1993/4, in an intensely competitive market, Virgin Atlantic had an 8.6 per cent share of voice (that is, proportion of advertising spend) in the region in which it operated, being outspent by 5:1 by British Airways. Fifty airlines spent a total of £40 million during the 12-month campaign period. As a business travel airline, Virgin had various problems to overcome: they were primarily viewed as 'young', trendy and 'bearded' (after the high-profile founder of the group, Richard Branson). Virgin Atlantic was perceived by many business travellers as something of 'a rock 'n' roll airline'. In the 'business class' market, the complication was that the Virgin fare structure was different from the rest of the market; its 'Upper Class' product offered '1st class service at a business class fare'. According to Virgin, this innovation had led to some misperceptions among the travel industry and customers; the superiority of the Virgin product over British Airways Club Class was not appreciated, and there was a mistaken impression that Virgin's Economy service ('Mid Class') was in fact a cheap business class product, which led to unfulfilled customer expectations.

Marketing objectives Virgin Atlantic wished to position itself as a carrier *for the business traveller* against the more traditional British Airways, which appealed to the more conservative members of the target audience. Specific objectives were therefore:

- TRIAL – to get new business customers to try Virgin
- REPOSITIONING – to establish Virgin as a serious business carrier in the minds of the target audience.

Solution The strategy adopted was a strong communication of Virgin Atlantic as a 'serious business carrier' to the target audience. It was decided to clarify the status of Upper Class and communicate it as 'A 1st class service at a business class fare'. The media were targeted at regular flyers of competitive carriers.

The creative solution was centred around the premise: 'It's a simple business decision.' The campaign presented, in a calm, rational manner, 'nuggets' of information about the Virgin Upper Class product in such a way that the business traveller could make up their own mind to choose Virgin! The TV commercials featured Terence Stamp as a spokesman for the frequent business flyer (research indicated high credibility). The tone of the campaign was intelligent, understated, stylish and adult to adult. Media employed were TV, press and direct mail.

The results were excellent. In the month after the campaign broke, first-time Virgin Upper Class bookings were up 31 per cent year on year. A similar increase was experienced after the second burst. Independent research indicated increased awareness and strongly positive attitudes to Virgin and the Upper Class product, linked with high prompted and unprompted recall of the campaign. (This must be viewed against the fact that BA outspent Virgin by 5:1 over this period.)

Case history

Company	Nissan Motors (GB)
Background	In the midst of the early 1990s recession, Nissan launched the new Micra, a premium-priced replacement for a car which had sold, on average, at a price 20 per cent lower than its competitors. Although Nissan Motors (GB) believed the car was of a quality which justified the higher price, they also recognized that this would mean attracting customers who were less price-sensitive than traditional Nissan buyers. All this was against the background of a highly competitive market, with dealer margins under pressure (and Nissan in the process of setting up a new UK distributor). Moreover, the budget available to launch the new Micra was limited.

Much rested, therefore, on the integrated launch communications campaign.

Marketing objectives
- To launch the new Micra successfully into the UK car market
- To establish Micra at a premium price and to build loyalty to the Nissan marque overall.

Solution   The central campaign idea was a striking visual device. The redesigned Micra had a very rounded appearance, which was believed to lend itself to a positioning incorporating 'friendliness', but was difficult to capture in photography. For this reason, in researching possible creative executions with consumer 'focus' groups, a 'cartoon-like' graphic of the car was employed. This was found to work as 'an extraordinarily powerful and attractive icon', providing an accurate expectation of the key attributes of the car itself. Moreover, Nissan found that the Micra 'cartoon' worked extremely well in print. Thus it was adopted as the central creative property of the entire integrated launch campaign. Some 270 small-space 'teaser' ads, in 40 different executions, were used in the national press in the week before the official launch. Direct mail, posters and TV also incorporated the 'friendly' Micra image.

Nissan comfortably beat its sales targets for the car, despite increasing prices by 20 per cent against an overall market of falling prices. Research showed that buyers of the new Micra were much more influenced by successful road tests and by advertising than by pure price considerations.

The integrated campaign comprised TV, press, posters, direct mail and dealer POS material. All work featured the Micra 'cartoon' and communicated a powerful and entirely consistent brand personality, despite a relatively restricted overall spend for a launch of this type.

4 THE CHANGING SCENE – INTEGRATION

> Is it necessary or desirable to do one
> campaign for brand reinforcement and
> another campaign to promote a premium
> or distribute a coupon? By careful planning
> of the use of space in print advertising, one
> ad can often accomplish both jobs, to the
> benefit of both.
>
> Stan Rapp and Tom Collins, 1987

> The 1:1 future holds immense implications
> for individual privacy, social cohesiveness
> and . . . alienation and fractionalization . . .
> from the breakdown of mass media.
>
> Don Peppers and Martha Rogers, 1993

> If you see a bandwagon, it's too late.
>
> Sir James Goldsmith (attributed)

The winds of change

We have, in the previous chapters, examined the definitions, history and development of the three disciplines on which this book focuses:

- *Direct marketing* – the building and exploitation of a 1:1 relationship between one seller and many buyers using a marketing database.
- *Sales promotion* – the temporary addition of value to a product or service by making a special offer.
- *Advertising* – the process of communicating positive messages about a product or service over time, thus building a brand.

These 'pure' disciplines are still employed, in isolation, by many clients. For example, *direct marketing* is used by a charity, mailing its regular donor file to solicit extra donations at Christmas; *sales promotion* by a beer brand offering its target market (BCC/C2 males 18–25) a booklet previewing the new football season, in exchange for five ringpulls/proofs of purchase; and *advertising* is used by a new female fragrance launching with a pan-European heavyweight TV 'image' campaign, with glossy production values and few words ('short copy'). These are three classic examples of 'pure' disciplines, as practised by traditional specialists employing their own unique craft skills.

However, such 'pure' activity is becoming the exception rather than the rule. Neat compartmentalization of activity into 'watertight' pigeon-holes marked 'direct marketing', 'sales promotion' and 'image advertising' respectively is becoming increasingly difficult and, indeed, irrelevant.

Since much marketing communications activity now incorporates elements of all three of these above disciplines (and others), client marketing departments are, in many cases, restructuring to reflect this change: specialist direct marketing, sales promotion and advertising managers are being replaced by marketing communications managers; their role includes what could be described as 'conducting the marketing communications orchestra', or finding someone to do this for them.

Inevitably, agencies are also having to change. Advertising agencies have traditionally structured themselves to mirror their clients' hierarchies, with a group account director 'facing off' against a marketing director, an account director against a marketing manager, account manager against brand manager and so on.

Below-the-line agencies have often been prepared (or compelled) to deal with client organizations at a relatively *junior* level (with, for example, MDs of direct marketing and sales promotion agencies routinely working closely with direct marketing managers and sales promotion managers who report to marketing managers). What then happens when the 'client' becomes a generalist, with responsibility for organizing his/her company's marketing communications across a *range* of media and disciplines? The specialist client has suddenly disappeared!

The nature of an agency's response will largely depend on what resources it has to offer. It would seem likely at this point that small specialist single-discipline organizations will continue to sell their services (in, say, direct marketing) to the new generalist client, provided of course that the client is happy to continue buying different marketing solutions from different suppliers. Indeed it could be argued that the generalist client has an even greater need for specialist *outside* expertise than his/her more narrowly focused predecessor.

However, depending on the client's marketing headcount (another casualty of the early 1990s recession which looks likely to become a permanent feature), the organization structure may not allow time for the luxury of briefing several separate specialist agencies on the same project. The message for the agency is, in this case, 'integrate or die', or at least lose the account, which, if the account is sufficiently important, is near enough to death for most agencies. In this situation, larger agency groups, with the resources to offer a wide range of communications services, are better placed. They can (at least in theory) reorganize themselves into an 'integrated agency', fronting 'super account directors' (generalists) who will 'handle' the (generalist) client and who will be backed up by the relevant specialist skills (in direct marketing, sales promotion and advertising) which they call on as necessary. As so often in the past, the agency is adapting (chameleon-like) to the changed marketing environment in which it finds itself. And, as Darwin might have predicted, those dinosaur organizations which are unwilling or unable to evolve will soon be extinct, or at best, left to decay in 'Jurassic Park'.

More of this in Chapters 9 and 10. Suffice it to say at this point that the winds of change are undoubtedly blowing, and when leading multinational agency groups embark on programmes of major structural change, we can be sure that this is, at least in part, a result of a fundamental shift in how their clients organize their marketing activities. This is something more than a recessionary 'blip' and merits further examination.

Some 'real-world' examples

So far in this book, our case histories have primarily been examples of 'pure' activity. As we have noted, however, things are changing. Consider the following (fictitious, but drawn from real examples) as examples of 1990s-style marketing communications campaigns.

CASE 1

A well-known petfoods manufacturer (company X) launched a new 'super premium' cat food, 'Kitticare', in the UK. The high quality and premium price meant that Kitticare would appeal strongly to the top niche of the market – those to whom their cat was a valued member of the family and therefore deserved the best 'prepared ' food money could buy. TV advertising was considered essential to launch Kitticare, powerfully communicating the desired brand values of luxury and cosseting, and convincing the retail grocery and pet shop trade that X was serious about the brand). However, marketing management at X calculated that TV advertising would involve a substantial wastage factor, however carefully airtime was planned. As a result, they also examined methods of targeting their communication more tightly, which would work alongside the 'umbrella' of the TV support.

It was decided to build a Kitticare marketing database, to contain, as far as possible, all actual and potential purchasers of the product. The key data required were:

• Name and address of owner, name, date of birth and breed of cat.

The following media were employed to build this database:

• TV (an 0800 free telephone number was appended to the commercial which included an offer for a free sample pack of Kitticare).
• Press (all newspaper and magazine ads carried a coupon as well as the 0800 number).
• On-pack and in-store. Various promotions communicated on the label of the can and via leaflets in a dispenser on the shelf.

This activity generated the data detailed above, which were captured and held as part of the customer record on the database.

A carefully planned and accurately targeted direct mail campaign, using names and addresses selected from the database, was then carried out. In addition, certain external 'cold lists', especially 'lifestyle databases' compiled from questionnaire responses were tested. X's agency reached an agreement with the list owners to mail a certain number of the names and addresses held on their database(s). Although X had use of the list once only (under the list rental agreement), all the respondents became X's property and could be added to the database.

Over the period of time since launch, company X has built itself a valuable marketing tool – its prospect/customer database. TV, press (and even radio) advertisements create awareness and change attitudes but also, crucially, feed the database, generating a constant influx of suitably qualified new owners who are prospective Kitticare buyers.

Promotions offer the customer added value over the competition and also generate data, often from identified Kitticare purchasers. Direct mail is the main medium by which X builds a profitable relationship with these individuals: it is used both strategically and tactically. Promotional offers are mailed to known competitive users (for example, 'Send us a wrapper from brand Z and we'll mail you 2 × £1 vouchers redeemable against Kitticare'). Kitticare buyers are rewarded for supplying details of friends and relatives 'who care as much about their cats as you do'.

The increasing investment in this programme by company X is testament to its proven and constant success in transmitting the right messages about Kitticare to the right audience cost-effectively.

Should we label this programme 'advertising'? 'direct marketing'? or 'sales promotion'? Clearly it incorporates elements of all these (and the picture could be broadened if we included X's involvement in exhibitions, conferences, video, incentives, training and retailer incentive programmes and the like). While individual elements of the activity could be pigeon-holed as direct marketing or sales promotion (say), we must conclude that Case 1 describes an integrated campaign with several (if not all) of the marketing communications disciplines working together in a coherent, synergistic manner.

CASE 2

A well-known UK company, operating in the hot drinks market, conducted a door-to-door campaign, distributing an unaddressed leaflet to gain trial of a new product (Y). The promotional mechanism was disarmingly simple: '50p off your next purchase' plus 'free recipe' (a chocolate cake recipe was printed on the leaflet). The targeting of the (approximately one million) leaflets was, however, far from simple: respondents to a number of on-pack offers were profiled (using a geodemographic market analysis system to identify potential purchasers) according to the type of residential area in which they lived. Next, certain external research surveys were 'overlaid' on this profile, with particular reference to heavy users of competitive brands (and supermarket own-label). Consideration was also given to regional variations in distribution of Y (areas where Y was difficult to find in the shops, that is, where distribution was poor, were down-weighted) while areas of known strength were up-weighted.

Finally, a UK postal sector ranking report was obtained. This listed every postcode sector (for example, OX3 1––) in order, according to the 'degree of representation of suitable geodemographic categories', that is, the extent to which they contain the 'right sort' of people to target for product Y. The activity was judged to be highly successful, in that response (percentage of coupons redeemed) was significantly higher than for previous (more crudely targeted but otherwise similar) campaigns, and massively greater than that to a (randomly distributed) 'control cell' (that is, a test area included in the same distribution). A selective telephone follow-up (as a 'toe-in-the-water' piece of research) confirmed that those people redeeming the coupons were, generally speaking, of high quality, that is, they were serious triallists of brand Y, and many of them were persuaded to become regular purchasers by this exercise.

Sales promotion? YES. The consumer was offered added value (free recipe and save 50p). Direct marketing? Almost certainly (in that recipients of the brand Y message were clearly identified and targeted and that a measurable response was obtained, followed up selectively by a telephone marketing programme). Thus we have another integrated campaign.

Real-world case histories are rarely 'textbook', however, and to my knowledge, except for the random sample that were telephoned, the names and addresses of the redeemers of the 50p coupon were never data-captured, far less used as the basis of an ongoing dialogue. The company in question might argue that the decision was based on a careful evaluation of the costs and benefits of investing in the construction and maintenance of a marketing database; others might point out that, in reality, the marketing manager in question had already overspent his budget for that financial year and that, for reasons that were mainly internal and short-term, the marketing director was not prepared to make an exception and divert the necessary funds into this project.

All this proves that, whether you specialize in direct marketing, sales promotion or advertising, the most brilliantly conceived marketing strategies will never be realized without a working understanding of the realities of organizational life.

CASE 3

A company we shall call 'Welloil' is a major player in the UK retail petrol (gasoline) market, selling fuel to private motorists, company car drivers and commercial vehicle drivers. By the early 1990s, their forecourt promotional activity had reached a crossroads. In common with their competitors, they had been running a series of promotions largely falling into one of two categories:

• Games – scratch-off instant win with 'theme'
• Free gift with purchase, for example, drinking glasses.

Research indicated that customers were, generally speaking, fed up with such promotions, sceptical about their chance of winning a major prize and disillusioned with the poor quality of the free items. Petrol was increasingly being viewed as a 'commodity' product; consumers were shopping on price, that is, buying the cheapest and ignoring the promotions, which were consequently becoming an expensive waste of time for Welloil as well as its competitors.

Welloil's dealers were increasingly negative about its promotions (which should have been a key tool to pull in customers on to their forecourts and keep them coming back) and motorists were tiring of filling (i) their glove boxes full of stickers and tokens, and (ii) their homes with low-grade glassware! Welloil also had some concerns about stock control and 'leakage' on the sites (enough said?).

Welloil's solution was to launch an electronic 'collector card' with a (non-competitive) partner whose retail outlets carried thousands of consumer products costing from £5 to hundreds of pounds. The driver purchased his or her petrol, presented the 'Welloil card', had the appropriate 'Wellpoints' credited to the card, and drove off. No voucher confetti in the glove box; no cheap glasses rattling in the boot. Full or partially full cards could then be redeemed at any branch of the high street retailer for an instant saving on any item in their range of quality branded products (no stock at Welloil sites, no time delays, no complex redemption procedures). 'Double points' on special days or special items for sale in the on-site shop provided scope for tactical promotional flexibility.

Other oil companies have since copied this long-running promotion and tacky forecourt freebies are now, largely, a thing of the past – testimony to this promotion's acknowledged effectiveness at building long-term customer loyalty.

So far, this looks like a nifty promotional idea built up into a long-term loyalty mechanism; but consider the following additional elements of this programme:

- *High mileage drivers.* By mailing selections from a database of fuel card users (that is, mailing company car drivers at home addresses), Welloil was able to target individuals likely to have a relatively high propensity to be heavy users of petrol (that is, to have higher than average consumption, particularly if they were an 'on-the-road' salesperson) and to tie them in to buying at Welloil (via mailing them half-completed cards and other promotional 'hooks'). Clearly one can justify

disproportionate allocation of available promotional budget to such 'high-value' potential customers, in order to capture their custom.
- *Fleet managers.* Those making decisions about fuel on behalf of their company's fleet of vehicles were also targeted by direct mail and made 'VIP' offers to encourage their drivers to refuel at Welloil sites. This was a sensitive area: the rewards were designed to be 'good business' for the fleet managers' company (for example, discounts on the overall bill, extended payment terms and so on).

Both Welloil and the high street retailer featured the Wellpoints promotion heavily in their advertising. The collector scheme became a key brand property of both organizations. As with all the best partner promotions (as we saw in Chapter 2), both players in the above case history contributed financially and profited commercially from the link-up.

At the time of writing, the feasibility of the fuller exploitation of the *data* on those collecting and redeeming Wellpoints is still being examined. It is certain, however that this is more than a classic sales promotion case history – elements of direct marketing and advertising brand building are integral parts of the programme. Interestingly, too, this is an example of a sales promotion being approached in a structured, long-term (dare I say even *strategic?*) manner – a long way from the traditional '10p off this week' or 'free fluffy duck'!

Brand building and marketing communications

Great brands win lasting customer
franchises because the product or service is
superior in quality, clearly differentiated
and is powerfully promoted
Robert Heller, 1994 Conference on Branding

In Chapter 3, we examined the role of advertising in building and maintaining brand values. A marketing communication is intended to motivate/influence a potential purchaser (either a consumer spending their own money or a business 'buyer' allocating their company's funds according to their judgement of the best 'value'). In this section, we consider the contribution of non-advertising marketing communications to this process. So what makes an individual choose a given product over another, seemingly identical one? As we concluded in Chapter 3, although the choice could conceivably be an entirely random decision – a whim – it is much more likely to have something to do with 'brand values', that is, the purchaser recognizes the brand name, or that of its manufacturer, and in some way 'feels good' about selecting that product (whether consciously or not). To a greater or lesser extent (depending on how serious a purchase decision we are talking about, which largely comes down to how much money is involved, that is, the cost of making the wrong decision), he or she is buying into the 'brand values' of that product or service. In other words, the decision process is partly rational, partly emotional. The choice of a new car, for instance, is an intensely personal one and, like it or not, we know we shall be viewed by others in a different light if we opt for a sporty Italian 'Supermini' as opposed to going for the basic 'sensible' economy of a Lada or Skoda, or even a second-hand Ford family saloon.

So how are the brand values of a given product or service defined and shaped? As discussed in Chapter 3, the main channel through which brand-building imagery is communicated and developed is that of advertising – mainly TV and press, although other media, including posters, cinema and radio, may all have a role to play. So too will the other elements of the marketing mix (price, distribution, packaging and so on). And great (that is, successful or effective and probably *famous*) advertising depends primarily on *great creative ideas*. We shall focus on these in Chapter 6.

If we are tempted to doubt the importance of advertising in creating brands, consider once again some of the brands cited in Chapter 3 and specifically what the following words mean to you:

- McDonald's
- Kellogg's
- Coca-Cola
- Kodak
- Marlboro
- IBM
- American Express
- Sony
- Mercedes-Benz
- Nescafé.

Each brand name conjures up a powerful set of images, some, admittedly, personal and specific to the individual consumer, but most created and carefully controlled by the brand owner, chiefly via a long history of brand-building advertising.

Suppose now that you are the worldwide marketing director of the company that owns one of the above brands. As 'guardian of the brand' or 'brand steward' (a term favoured by the Ogilvy and Mather Agency although perhaps applied to themselves rather more than to their clients), what are your concerns? What do your various 'paymasters' expect of you? In short, what are your key responsibilities? In most cases, they are likely to include the following (in no particular order):

- to safeguard the brand image/personality;
- to strengthen brand values;
- to maintain, and, where possible, improve product performance over the competition (exploiting new technology where appropriate), though in many companies this role will fall between New Product Development (which may be part of Marketing) and Production;
- to adjust pricing (versus competition) in order to maximize overall profitability (which will require the achievement of a certain sales volume);
- to promote the brand as powerfully and as cost-effectively as possible, and to communicate the brand values to the widest appropriate audience, thus generating incremental sales from new triallists, as well as securing repeat purchase and loyalty from existing customers.

. . . not much to ask for a marketing director's salary?

Given that the main responsibility of marketers is to contribute positively to the profitability of their organization, we can appreciate that the five concerns above together constitute the apparent paradox of (1) needing to stimulate sales via heavyweight advertising/promotional expenditure and (2) charging the highest sustainable price (to maximize unit profit), while at the same time (3) restricting spend on marketing communications (along with all other costs) to a minimum and also (4) keeping a close eye on competitor activity and market conditions in general.

This complex system is, of course, very difficult to optimize in any 'scientific' sense, since data are likely to be limited and controlled experiments impossible, so that in practice most marketing directors steer some kind of instinctive 'middle course' based on:

- 'historical' positioning (loosely defined as the way in which a product or service is presented to its market);

- 'historical' pricing;
- 'historical' advertising and promotional spend;
- sales performance/market share; and
- available research;

at all times watching, reacting to and, one hopes, attempting to *anticipate* the actions of the competition.

The charitable might describe the above approach as 'pragmatic', relying on 'gut feel' and professional judgement rather than any hard-and-fast 'scientific' rules. (After all, previous generations of marketers can't *all* be wrong, and surely one should learn from the wisdom of one's forebears?)

On the other hand, the more cynical observer might describe this policy as one of 'blindly blundering on', never daring to stick one's neck out (probably largely for personal career reasons) short-sightedly duplicating the over-cautious, uninspired practices of one's predecessors, basing one's decisions on 'the way we've always done things', so that no real breakthroughs in brand creation, brand building and other communications with the target audience are ever made and major opportunities for the organization are missed.

Be this as it may, one key task that all marketers (whether imaginative and risk-inclined or not) must address one way or another is that of allocating the marketing communications budget. Indeed, for most marketing directors, it is their primary job responsibility. Historically, this might have come down to one of the 'non-decisions' referred to above, that is, the media mix was effectively 'cast in stone' in the image of the previous year – certainly the power of inertia is mighty indeed.

As (hypothetical) examples, consider the three companies outlined below.

COMPANY A

A well-known brand of toothpaste *always* splits its annual advertising and promotional expenditure as follows:

- 70 per cent TV advertising
- 20 per cent women's press (colour) advertising
- 10 per cent on-pack promotions, trade incentives and so on.

COMPANY B

A life assurance company with a large 'consultant' sales force allocates its budget as follows:

- 60 per cent TV advertising
- 20 per cent colour press advertising
- 20 per cent sales force/intermediary commissions.

COMPANY C
A mail order company whose main products are fine porcelain 'collectibles' spends as follows:

- 50 per cent direct response ads in Sunday colour supplements
- 25 per cent loose inserts in selected magazines
- 25 per cent direct mail catalogues to database of previous purchasers.

The marketing director is responsible not only for *media* selection but also for the *creative* content of the various marketing communications. At this point it may be helpful to remind ourselves why we build brands at all – not so that we can stand back and admire the impressive edifice we have constructed, but rather so that we shall *sell* our product, in large quantities. This raises the interesting (and to many of my colleagues, past and present, no doubt deeply offensive) question – do we actually *need* pure brand building?

Indeed, should we instead simply adorn each and every packet of our product with exhortations to purchase such as the following:

- 'FREE ball-point pen with 5 proofs of purchase'?
- 'FANTASTIC PRIZE DRAW – WIN A HOLIDAY IN TORREMOLINOS!'?

not forgetting the classic technique for halving one's unit profit:

- 'BUY ONE – GET ONE FREE!'

Is such an approach the most effective way to guarantee long-term, profitable volume sales? Of course, the answer is – NO.

Such techniques, inappropriately employed, serve only to devalue the brand and the would-be purchaser's perceptions of quality and therefore rapidly erode any willingness to pay 'a little extra for a product that really delivers', undermining any previous hard-won success and probably not inconsiderable investment in building brand values. Indeed, depending on the profile of our target audience and how we position our brand to that audience, there is a danger that we are mortgaging our future sales by grabbing short-term volume and that sooner or later our brand will be damaged and eventually killed by such 'distressful marketing'. In such cases it would arguably be better to put the money in the bank, or maybe throw a mega staff party. Of course we want to sell lots of units of our product – not only now, but next week, next month next year *and for many years to come.* Thus it is essential that we build the brand, then nourish and continue to sustain it, so that people feel good (and happy and confident and reassured) about choosing our product rather than the competition. We must therefore create a platform of consistent communications messages, so that our customers will confidently buy our brand (Brandex), keep on buying it, and in due course teach their children that 'Brandex washes whiter', as their parents taught them. This is the essence of successful branding.

All this means that, as an example, we don't sell our Dinex Super Platinum card via small black and white ads in the back of local free newspapers; rather we choose to invest a six-figure production budget creating a beautiful 'mini-feature film' which we can, with minor adaptations and appropriate sound tracks, screen throughout Europe, hitting our core AB male aged 35–50 audience during peak TV viewing time. This is absolutely reasonable. The point is that branding is not, generally speaking, a manifestation of the extravagance and self-indulgence of the marketing department; it is a necessary investment, by the company, in its future profitability and therefore, if successfully planned and executed, branding serves to safeguard its very survival and to deliver profits to the shareholders.

Although we have established that there is indeed a role for pure brand building, this is not to say that the 'traditional' media mix will always be appropriate in the future. Let us revisit the media splits employed by companies A, B and C above. Shouldn't the marketing directors of these companies at least be considering whether 'the way we've always done it' is indeed still the most appropriate way? As integrated communications increasingly becomes the norm for major companies, it must be a key responsibility of each marketing decision maker to question ingrained prejudices and examine radically different ways of getting 'more bang for their buck'. This is part of their duty to their employer rather than evidence of their desire to be different; although, admittedly, if they are successful in challenging the media *status quo*, it is unlikely to do their careers any harm. For example, to revisit the three companies above (pages 77–78):

- *Company A* could test the water of *direct marketing*, siphoning off some budget into a mini-database of respondents to promotions, encouraging cross-purchase and 'member get member', and incidentally(?) cementing its relationship with its customers in the face of the increasing power of the grocery multiple retailers. TV may well remain the largest single medium in the communications mix, but as broadcast media fragment, the marketing director may well conclude that relationship marketing needs to be looked at (and preferably tested).

- *Company B* could switch 'routine' sales away from expensive face-to-face selling by intermediaries and consultants, establishing instead a 'direct marketing' unit employing direct response press ads and inserts, direct mail and telephone (outbound and inbound) to write policies remotely, with no sales visit, thus saving on intermediary commissions and freeing the company's consultants to concentrate on complex/high-margin financial products which do require face-to-face presentation and explanation in order to sell them fairly and responsibly. This could have major implications for the whole company, including possible downsizing/restructuring as field sales jobs are replaced by telephone operator jobs based at a call centre. However, the alternative might well be sharply reduced competitiveness, whose consequences for the company might be even less pleasant.
- *Company C* could test using TV in certain regions to create mass awareness and generate responses via an 0800 free telephone line (DRTV). This implies building a brand via traditional above-the-line media, a radical departure for this company which could even lead eventually to opening branded retail outlets (or at least 'stores within stores'), with major strategic implications.

The point here is that even something so apparently obvious as media choice should not be taken for granted. As integrated (direct) marketers, we must take the time to think laterally as well as linearly. For example:

- Need TV be expensive? NO!
- Need direct mail be tacky? NO!
- What about door-to-door?
- Or loose inserts?
- Or cross/partner promotions with another brand or another company?

These questions lead us to consider how the media decisions which marketers must make are becoming ever more complex as media fragment. At the same time new electronic media (that is, the Internet and specifically the World Wide Web) are revolutionizing the way that consumers and business decision makers obtain information and consume advertising, as we shall see in the next section.

The changing media landscape – the Internet and the World Wide Web

Change is spreading through the marketing communications world: media, clients, agencies. Change is a threat to some; an opportunity to others. Of course, the communications business has faced changes before: the arrival of commercial TV, satellite, cable, telephone marketing, and the reality of powerful low-cost marketing databases have, on their respective arrivals on the marketing scene, all challenged existing thinking and offered massive scope to those sufficiently open-minded to embrace them. The new 'interactive' media represent a new set of challenges – and opportunities. Fortunes are already being made from these new media; dinosaurs (both marketers and agencies) who refuse to embrace them may find themselves caught in their own Ice Age as extinction looms.

The Internet is, at the time of writing, the most 'high-profile' of the new electronic media and the most exciting new marketing communications medium to be launched since commercial TV half a century ago. Inevitably there is hype and overclaim. Some iconoclastic devotees are claiming that the rise of the Internet, or more specifically its 'submedium', the World Wide Web, herald the death of broadcast TV and direct mail, to name but two current media. This is not my view.

Certainly, the jargon is rife – the Web, the Net, online marketing, interactive marketing, surfing, hits, are all terms bandied about. There is much exaggeration: the new media have their evangelists and their rejectors; some see them as the media that will inevitably dominate the marketing of the future; others seek to dismiss them as a passing fad that offers little opportunity to any but a few 'con-merchants'; the majority of marketers are interested but display a healthy scepticism.

I believe it is important to be aware of what these new media can and can't do, and specifically what they offer to marketers.

It all started when the Internet, whose origins go back to the 1960s and the US Government's plans for communications in a post-nuclear holocaust scenario, was relaunched in 1992 as a commercial communications medium. In the period immediately before this it had been confined primarily to the distribution of academic research texts (an early example of electronic publishing which, it seems certain, saved a fair expanse of rain forest during the 1970s and 1980s). Today the Internet is a rapidly expanding network of computers scattered around the world, which can 'talk' to each other in an 'open communications' manner.

Currently Internet computers host some three million documents. These can be accessed, at least in the Americas and Western Europe, by simply getting hold of a personal computer and a modem (allowing transmission of data between computers via a telephone line), for the cost of a local 'phone call (there are good reasons to predict that local calls will in due course be free in Europe, as they are in the USA) and the monthly subscription charge levied by an Internet service provider (for example, Virgin Net, Microsoft Network, Demon or UUNET PIPEX) or alternatively via the original 'bulletin board' services such as CompuServe or America Online. Private consumers are currently buying around 20 million PCs per year, while the costs both of software and of high-speed data transfer are falling rapidly. These factors are contributing to what we may call without exaggeration 'the Internet explosion'.

Connecting to the Internet gives the user access to a previously unimaginable volume of information and enables him/her to exchange messages with fellow users around the world. Currently some ten million computers are estimated to be connected to the Internet, providing access to some 50 million individual users, of which some 70 per cent are from the USA and a further 20 per cent from Europe (mainly Western Europe). Of these, some 60 per cent are students or academics, some 30 per cent are business users and 10 per cent connect from home. In the UK, over two million users currently connect via around 500 000 computers. More than 50 000 new connections are currently coming on line each month. As I write, a growing number of the USA's Fortune 1000 companies have their own Websites and around 95 per cent of these companies are themselves connected to the Internet as users. Moreover, total annual worldwide Net *advertising* spend is estimated to be around $350 million. Among the current (early adopter) Web advertisers, the majority are in computers, especially Web-related products. Publishers, telecoms and cars are also represented, although the latter category currently represents only around $10 million total Web advertising spend. Moreover, if anything is certain about the Internet, it is that these numbers will be out of date before anyone (including my publisher) reads this. This is one rapidly developing medium.

As far as marketing is concerned, I believe the real opportunity is restricted (if that is a word applicable to a medium of such seemingly limitless scope) to the Internet's submedium, the World Wide Web. Any advertiser who wishes to lay out its product offering can do so by setting up a 'Website', which is effectively an address on the World Wide Web which customers and prospective customers can visit, and, as with a bricks and mortar shop, either browse or (in many cases) buy as the fancy takes them. Building these sites has become a specialist skill, and consultancies have sprung up to advise prospective Web advertisers on how to go about it. Agencies, seeing either a threat to their traditional revenues or, if we are feeling more charitable, spotting, via their far-sightedly established Media Futures Unit, a major opportunity to progress marketing communications and incidentally their own bottom line, have naturally been keen to get involved. A number of new offshoots termed 'Agency.com' or something similar and sounding suitably hi-tech have sprung up to guide the client through the jungle of advertising in 'cyberspace' (one of the few things apparently growing at a rate equal to that of the medium itself is the jargon relating to it). The advertiser can use the Website to 'set out their stall', display their range of products, offer more information, and increasingly provide opportunities for the visitor to 'jump off' to other, in most cases related, sites. This last development has been shown to have a drastic effect on the number of visits to the site (or 'hits'). In addition to the revenue a marketer may generate by setting up his/her own Website, there is also the option of selling space on that site to other (non-competitive) advertisers, either via banners (a horizontal strip along the bottom of the page) or via carefully situated 'hotspots' from which the surfer may jump off into a message (and possibly even into the Website) of the advertiser; how to make money out of buying and selling such 'online advertising' is currently a much debated issue.

As with all marketing communications, it is essential to define your *objectives* 'up-front' before plunging into the planning and construction of your Website. By way of illustration, there will be significant creative differences between sites intended for:

- *Mail order* – where the desired response is a *purchase*. Tesco and Sainsbury (the UK grocery multiples) have both set up direct wine-selling sites on the Web. Early concerns about the security of online credit card transactions have now largely been overcome.
- *Lead generation* – the prospect is delivered to another medium or location (for example, conventional telephone or a retail outlet) where the eventual sale is made (many car manufacturers, including notably Chrysler, have professionally constructed and highly successful Websites which operate alongside all their other marketing communications activity).
- *Awareness* (albeit with more involvement than via a conventional TV commercial).

There are also complex sites which offer more than one of the above types of communications in different places, including the electronic publishers such as the subscription-based online services (for example, America Online and The London Financial Times). In many respects, the overall communications task is akin to that facing a retailer, that is, to motivate visits (thus generating traffic and hence footfall). Moreover, since the site is the 'store' itself, its design presents challenges similar to those facing a retail merchandiser – in brief: display the goods attractively, draw people to the high-margin items, and make it easy for them to buy.

Looking at some of these Websites reveals an interesting variety of approaches. Just as there was a tendency among the pioneer TV advertisers of the 1940s and 1950s to create a press ad with a voice-over (or a radio commercial with a picture added), so many early Web advertisers have started, creatively speaking, from the media they know. This new medium (and I believe it deserves to be viewed as such) is, however, different from all others: neither the sound nor the picture quality currently compares with the best broadcast TV, but the interactive dimension offers exciting opportunities to involve the visitor/consumer/business buyer and establish a dialogue in a way that broadcast TV currently cannot.

Thus some of the best sites are far more than 'electronic ads'. Early pioneers include such FMCG products as Stolichnaya Vodka, Guinness, Grolsch Lager and Ragu Sauces. Perhaps unsurprisingly, several major advertisers have invested substantially in 'all singing all dancing' spectaculars and yet we may observe that, at the consumer's point of entry, their sites have no more prominence from a user's perspective than does, say, the site put together by Fred Bloggs in his bed-sit to advertise his own mail order computer games business. At least at present, the Web is a great 'leveller' – almost an advertising medium for the people. As *Media and Marketing Europe* put it: 'The global access offered by The Internet may be a problem for multinationals, but it is a good opportunity for small businesses . . . The Internet has democratized access to global markets.'

The trick in *creative* terms seems to be:

- gain *attention* (attractive graphics have a key role here); but also
- *involve* the audience (interactive techniques include competitions, quizzes and special offers designed to initiate *dialogue*); and, most importantly
- motivate a *return visit*. This requires regular updating of your site, keeping it fresh and interesting so that the surfer/shopper has a reason to visit it regularly to see what's new. As mentioned above, some Web advertisers have even attempted to establish their site as a natural

'jumping-off' point to other (often unrelated) sites, thereby gaining credibility and authority (not to mention visits) as a good place to start out – effectively a friendly and helpful guide for would-be 'Websurfers'.

The psychology of planning and creating such communications is fascinating and differs from other media, justifying the claims of specialist Web/Net consultancies that the advertiser in this medium needs to go to the experts. Whereas some of the early Web pioneer advertisers regarded it as a gateway to a global mass market, the current consensus would seem to be that Web advertising works best as a one-to-one medium – messages can be tailored to what is known about the visitor, that is, the Web should be viewed as less of a mass advertising medium and more of a direct marketing medium. Of course, as I repeatedly state in this book, all communications, including the Website, should be seen as a part of an integrated suite of messages, so the site should not only be true to the client's brand's personality, but may even be able to expose and develop it in a way no other media can. For instance the Stolichnaya site offers the visitor a chance to mix their own Stoli cocktails and have the resulting recipe 'judged' according to its taste.

In terms of the 'production costs' of constructing your Website, a crucial difference from 'conventional' advertising media is that there are no media costs, so that you can perhaps more easily justify spending say £50 000 per year on setting up and maintaining your site, given that this (when added to any costs of fulfilment which presumably you would need to pay, even with more traditional media) represents the total bill to the advertiser. In other words, from a *media* perspective, the fundamental thing to bear in mind about the World Wide Web is that there is no media owner: it's like a big (in fact, infinitely large) village green, on which anyone who likes can set out a stall selling anything people want to buy and there's no one to collect rent for the space. To marketers locked into the traditional economics of 'pay-per-exposure' media buying, this takes some getting used to. If you can make money out of the Web, then, provided your site is legal, decent, honest and truthful (and even apparently in some cases where it isn't entirely), no one will stand in your way. In other words: good luck to you! (This situation compares favourably with other communications media – consider for instance the spiralling cost of TV airtime or what one would pay the Royal Mail or other PTT for postage.)

In terms of measurement, the World Wide Web is a dream for the direct response advertiser. It is technically entirely feasible to measure not only who has visited (via a 'counter'), but when, how many times during a given period, what they have responded to, what they have revealed about themselves, and specifically what they have bought. Some Website owners invite visitors to 'register', thereby extracting even more data which can be used for marketing. It is also possible to obtain visitors' permission to e-mail them in the future (now *there's* one for the Data Protection Registrar to investigate . . .). In short, it is the ideal data-driven medium. Indeed, extremists might argue, if only all marketing were via the World Wide Web, all marketing would be classic direct marketing. At the time of writing, it is maintained by some that the World Wide Web is a virtuous circle which involves a fast-growing user base, rising access speeds, improving software and rapidly developing content.

As I have indicated, there is currently much overclaim surrounding the Web; it is important to examine carefully the claims of the 'missionary zealots'. Equally, just because something is being hyped doesn't prevent it from taking off in a big way and even becoming sensationally successful. Indeed, I believe that interactive media (and specifically the World Wide Web) will become an important part of the marketing communications mix. I do not believe, however, that the Web will replace or 'kill' broadcast TV or paper-based newspapers or direct mail any more than TV killed radio or radio killed the press as media by which companies and their agencies could communicate selling messages to prospective buyers of their products or services.

However, new media must inevitably steal a share of the total mix from somewhere, and I confidently predict that some messages which would otherwise be transmitted via paper-based direct mail will in future be sent electronically, and that some messages that would have been conveyed via a printed brochure will end up on CD-ROM instead. It is equally likely that instead of launching broadscale image-building TV campaigns, some advertisers will invest more money in their Website. In so doing, it is to be hoped they will bear in mind that this medium, despite its undoubted strengths (shoppers are searching it in the expectation of making a purchase; it offers immediate opportunities for dialogue including, in some cases, placing an order) also has limitations. For example, it offers advertisers little or no opportunity to 'ambush' the consumer when they are not expecting an advertising message; they are, indeed, looking for that message. In addition, the quality and speed of the graphics available for moving pictures are still inferior to broadcast satellite and cable TV; as yet not everyone chooses to subscribe to the Internet or even the World Wide Web, and the only time your Website can have any impact on the consumer or business prospective buyer is when he or she is sitting in front of their monitor actively surfing or looking for something specific. What seems certain is that the World Wide Web will offer advertisers an ideal *fulfilment* medium, and will therefore replace much current printed fulfilment material. It would appear to be less suitable in cases where it is necessary to catch the consumer unawares (which leads us again into the currently unresolved issue of how to advertise cost-effectively on someone else's site). Equally, despite the growth in home computing, it would appear that the Web will, for some time, offer more to business-to-business advertisers (especially those marketing Internet/computing-related products) than, for instance, to marketers of mass market FMCG brands.

Thus it is my belief that the Internet (or more specifically the World Wide Web) will be an important medium of the future marketing communications landscape, but that it will work alongside other, more traditional media, all of which also have their own strengths and weaknesses.

Let us remember too that there is more to the Internet than the World Wide Web; it is possible, for instance, to envisage outbound Internet e-mail messages serving as electronic direct mail, again possibly more appropriate for business-to-business than for consumer marketing. Indeed, there has recently been a serious backlash against transmission of 'junk e-mail' ('spamming') in the shape of 'flamemail' from 'Netheads' protesting at the unjustified commercial exploitation of cyberspace and some Internet access providers are helping their subscribers to avoid unsolicited e-postal services and the consequent mails. A comparable scenario might be the collapse or the death of direct mail, which would be the result of consumers' backlash when receiving, say, 200 unsolicited letters each day.

Another new medium, CD-ROM, offers the possibility of holding data that would previously have occupied several large books, on a single CD-ROM disk (exactly the size of the domestic audio CD), thus allowing the marketer to transmit moving colour pictures and large 'menu-driven' quantities of data or 'infomercials' for an ever-decreasing cost of duplication; moreover the penetration of CD-ROM drives into PCs in businesses and homes is increasing rapidly.

There are still some serious obstacles to the effectiveness of online communications – connections are frequently cumbersome and unreliable, and downloading graphics images from the World Wide Web is frustratingly slow. Moreover, the delays become worse for European Internet users in the afternoon, when the USA wakes up and goes 'Websurfing', especially in the early evening when the West coast joins in. Computers seem to go wrong much of the time; in general, hi-fi systems, TVs and videos don't. Moreover, it is clear that pure *information* is not a mass market consumer proposition, whereas *entertainment* is. Some people will continue to keep away from computers until they become cheaper to buy, easier to use and, overall, more *fun*.

Time will tell how great an impact all these 'new' media will have; it is certainly important to keep abreast of developments, since advances in these fields are taking place very rapidly at present, and their future direction is far from clear. Agency groups do well to keep a toe in the water since the cost of getting left behind may be very high.

By this stage in this book, I hope the reader will acknowledge that it has been established that the world of marketing communications is changing fundamentally and that there is an accelerating trend towards *convergence* of direct marketing, sales promotion, advertising and other marketing communications disciplines.

However, we are certainly not yet operating in a perfectly integrated marketing communications universe. We are, on the contrary, to a large extent, still dealing with organizational structures and, equally important, individual mind sets, that reflect the non-integrated world of advertising and its related disciplines in the 1960s and 1970s. This conflict is one of the reasons that the 1990s marketing communications industry is a volatile and exciting business in which to operate; the next century promises more of the same.

Advertising people have always been associated with glamour – the Armani suits, the Porsches, the lunches and dinners at The Ivy, Langan's, Le Gavroche, the Groucho Club or wherever else was fashionable and/or expensive at the time. Ad agencies have traditionally paid peanuts to workers at junior levels and fortunes to those at the top of the tree. Because the ultimate possible rewards (both salary and perks) have been so substantial, advertising has been one of those professions which has had no difficulty in recruiting the 'best' (that is, most intelligent and creative) graduates (along with merchant banking, stockbroking, the law, medical and veterinary sciences and client-side marketing). Such recruits have entered the profession mainly in account management and/or planning roles. Advertising people have thus, with some justification, felt themselves to be an élite within the business community in general and certainly with respect to those employed in the 'below-the-line' disciplines. By contrast, those working in promotions or direct mail houses have traditionally been looked down on. This attitude stems from a belief that advertising people, dealing with clients at marketing director (or managing director) level, act primarily as valued business partners, strategic thinkers, and guardians of the clients' brands, and that they create TV commercials, press ads and posters that not only confer the desired image and status upon the clients' brands and organization, but also (at least in the minds of certain admen) stand as works of 'fine art' in their own right, so that advertising is, for both business and aesthetic reasons, a 'worthwhile' profession, and a suitable career for talented and ambitious people to embark on.

Many of those subscribing to the above view would be of the opinion that the disciplines of sales promotion and direct marketing are, comparatively speaking, staffed by various forms of 'pond life'. Promotions people are seen as short-term thinkers (if they can think at all), more interested in whizzy ideas ('buy one get one free', 'free prize draws', 'free plastic daffodil' and the like) and both physically and intellectually dull, scruffy and lacklustre.

To continue this line of thought, the stereotypical promotions man would be in his fifties, fat, greasy and shifty. If he unbuttoned the overtight jacket of his crumpled, shiny suit, the observer would notice that, attached to the lining, was a collection of watches, imported (without troubling Customs officials) from the Far East. His own watch would be a (real) Rolex (how vulgar) with gold bracelet to match, and he would chain-smoke cheap cigars. In winter, a soiled sheepskin jacket, of the type favoured by less reputable members of the motor trade, would be added to his wardrobe. His opening sales patter would be along the lines of 'Boy, have I got a deal for you!'. In short, the above-the-line snob's view of *Homo promotionalis* is that of a cross between a spiv and a market trader. Successful? Certainly. But stylish? Never, and, by implication, incapable of strategic marketing thinking, and thus of any real partnership with his marketing clients.

'Direct marketing' was not a term recognized by many people before 1980. The equivalent view of a 'direct mail' practitioner would, at best, be that of someone supervising a warehouse full of women (*sic*) in nylon overalls (and perhaps hairnets) sitting at trestle tables and mindlessly stuffing letters into envelopes, before carefully licking a stamp and sticking it on to each pack.

No self-respecting university undergraduates would have dreamed (even in their worst nightmares) of being forced by economic necessity to earn their living in such occupations, even assuming their careers adviser had heard of sales promotion or direct marketing.

Today, of course, things are quite different. Direct marketing and sales promotion are 'respectable' careers in their own right (at least in marketing circles); salaries and calibre of personnel are equivalent; in the early 1990s recession, in which the advertising industry suffered more than most, losing an estimated 1 in 3 jobs, the extra accountability and measurable short-term effect on sales of sales promotion and direct marketing meant that these three branches of marketing communications at last assumed something approaching equivalent status, and certainly at least equal status to client-side marketers. Some admen would now even concede that 'style' has spread below the line.

Clearly, the marketing communications world is changing fundamentally and, it will be argued in subsequent chapters, irrevocably. The winds of change are blowing at a velocity approaching storm force. Marketers need to be prepared for what is to come.

5 DIRECT MARKETING AND SALES PROMOTION: ONE DISCIPLINE OR TWO?

> We're all recipients of those direct mail shots which repeat our names four times in an attempt to convince us that this really is specifically for us, personally . . . which offer a sales promotion inducement to respond . . . sales promotion is being used to try to increase response to a very expensive mail shot . . .
>
> Petersen and Toop, 1994

Definitions compared

We have established that *direct marketing*

> (the building and exploitation of a one-to-one relationship between one seller and many buyers, using a marketing database)

and *sales promotion*

> (the temporary addition of value to a product or service by making a special offer which gives an incentive to act)

have much in common.

In this chapter, we ask – 'how much?' – that is, are we really talking about a *single* field of marketing communications or are direct marketing and sales promotion genuinely *distinct*? This very issue has inspired many column inches in specialist direct marketing, sales promotion and other marketing periodicals (magazines, newsletters, and so on) and books (like this one) and the debate seems likely to 'run and run'.

There are 'hard-liners' in both camps. The two opposing views can be most clearly characterized as follows, using the words of an imaginary protagonist from each of the two schools of thought.

INTEGRATIONISTS

'Direct marketing and sales promotion are just two sides of the same coin – direct marketing is, after all, just promotions in an envelope. Promotions, in whatever medium, gather data, that is, produce a direct response which builds a database. It's only agencies which have artificially separated direct marketing and sales promotion. The two disciplines are most sensibly viewed as one: "direct promotions". One could equally well term it 'action marketing' but the principle is the same. To draw a distinction between direct marketing and sales promotion is to miss the point.'

TRADITIONALISTS/SEPARATISTS

'A client who knows s/he needs (for example) a direct marketing solution to a marketing problem/opportunity should be able to approach a specialist direct marketing agency and to commission them to plan and execute the activity in response to a clear, written brief. There is no need whatsoever for the agency to offer well-meaning (or, more likely, selfishly motivated) advice as to what sales promotion (or advertising) could bring to this particular situation – that decision rests with the client – in fact making this sort of judgement is one of the things marketing directors get paid for. The direct marketing agency should be a source of specialist knowledge and expertise in the areas of database, lists and direct mail creativity; it will not be thanked for getting ideas above its station and trying to do the client's job for him/her.

'By the same token, for a clearly defined formulation for an on-pack offer, the client's best bet has to be a specialist sales promotion consultancy which understands, and has in-depth experience of, the legal "ins and outs" of free prize draws and competitions, of forecasting redemption rates, of sourcing and buying premium items and of promotional response handling. Such an agency should be bursting with creative ideas for boosting sales of the product. Clients who know what they're looking for should be able to go out and buy it from an easily identified expert supplier.

'Direct marketing and sales promotion are as different from each other as they are from advertising; each has distinct, specialist skills which should not be mixed. Indeed by unwisely attempting to put themselves forward as "jacks of all trades", as some tried to do during the early 1990s recession, agencies risk losing even what credibility they originally had as specialists.'

Two diametrically opposed arguments; I believe each contains some valid points. In many ways direct marketing and sales promotion are, of all the marketing communications disciplines, the most natural candidates for merger/integration. They are viewed by many in marketing, especially in 'above-the-line' or 'image' advertising, as being part of something rather amorphous and faintly disreputable known as 'the other stuff', 'below-the-line' or 'marketing services'. This is deemed to involve a variety of activities, but to exclude TV, press, radio and poster advertising (which, by implication, are considered to be 'legitimate' advertising media). Some extremists would even argue that DRTV and direct response press ads were 'above-the-line' and therefore not direct marketing. Inaccurate and misguided as I believe these views to be, they none the less vividly characterize how direct marketing and sales promotion are lumped together (and not only by non-practitioners).

The two extreme views, as outlined above, will form a convenient basis for examining how direct marketing and sales promotion can work together, and indeed whether, as in the view of the most extreme integrationists, they are in fact the same discipline. At this point, I must show my own hand – I fall somewhere between these two camps. I believe that direct marketing and sales promotion have much in common, but require different specialist skills. Thus, in my opinion, the distinct terms are valid and can usefully be preserved in an integrated future. However, we are jumping ahead; first, let us examine the media employed by these two disciplines.

Direct marketing and sales promotion media

As made clear in Chapters 1 and 2, direct marketing and sales promotion are both marketing communications disciplines; they are *not* media (whereas direct mail, point-of-sale and press advertising, for example, are.) For this reason, when one reads, in a marketing magazine, or – perish the thought – in a book such as this one, a paragraph like the (artificially constructed) one below, one could be forgiven for adopting a sceptical attitude towards the author's credentials as a marketing communications 'expert'.

> Direct marketing is a highly cost-effective media, particularly if you can get a good database to mail to. The sales promotion media is also very effective. Mailers and sales promotions are targeted and therefore lower cost, so that they are attractive to clients compared with say TV advertising

which is expensive, wasteful and sometimes doesn't even contain a memorable 0800 phone number. In short, direct marketing and sales promotion are measurable and pay for themselves . . .

Of course the savage misuse of the word 'media' is only one of the numerous heinous crimes perpetrated by the (fictitious) author of this particular piece; others include an over-reliance on the sweeping generalization and a basic lack of understanding of the indisputable benefits to be gained from image advertising. Indeed it is outbursts of this type from 'below-the-line' practitioners which have helped to reinforce some of the negative views of direct marketing and sales promotion held by 'above-the-line' people. Clearly I exaggerate to make a point, but the above is not a million miles away from some of the less well-informed material which appears in print.

The following are the main media employed by the discipline of direct marketing:

- *Direct mail.* Generally regarded as being 'what direct marketers do', although, as we have seen, it is only one advertising medium used as part of the system of marketing we call direct marketing. Direct mail can be used to communicate a message (which can certainly involve an element of 'brand building') and also to make an 'added-value' offer, particularly as an incentive to respond. To this extent, direct marketers have been employing sales promotion techniques since direct marketing began and are certain to continue to do so.
- *Press 'advertising'* (that is, paid-for sales space). Although a double-page spread in full colour in, say, *The Sunday Times* magazine, with beautiful photography and a few, carefully crafted words of copy, is one of the most 'above-the-line' of image-building communications, the same medium (that is, 'press', meaning newspapers and magazines in any of their many forms) is one of the most cost-effective (and consequently important) direct marketing media. Off-the-page ads, either for mail order sales or lead generation, along with inserts (loose or bound in) are important weapons in the direct marketer's arsenal. An offer may certainly be employed (for example, a life assurance company offering: (i) 'a free travelling alarm clock when you ask us for a personal illustration' *and* (ii) 'a free weekend break for two or a free 5-piece luggage set when your first premium is received'), but few would call this activity sales promotion. Rather, it is direct marketing with a response incentive.

However, advertorial features and reader offers are generally viewed as sales promotion (we are even in danger of straying into the field of PR at this point – more on all this later).

- *Door-to-door distribution.* This much misunderstood (looked down on unfairly by just about everybody) medium presents us with another rather controversial classification task; traditionally, it has been employed more by sales promotion managers and their agencies than by their direct marketing colleagues (and *their* agencies). Indeed, even some direct marketing practitioners have been known to sneer at this unaddressed medium, regarding it as a poor man's direct mail and considering it more akin to an untargeted mass medium (and, even worse, one lacking the glamour of the broadcast media). However door-to-door has come a long way in the last decade or so; major advances in profiling and targeting techniques have made it a highly cost-effective alternative to direct mail, particularly in cases where suitable lists are simply unavailable, and/or where the task is to hit a wide audience cost-effectively (for example, to get a sample of a new FMCG product into consumers' hands along with the trial-gaining/response-generating mechanism of a money-off coupon/reply device). So perhaps door-to-door *is* a poor man's direct mail – or maybe a careful (non-extravagant) marketing director's direct mail. The Royal Mail itself offers a deluxe (premium-priced) door-to-door service for unaddressed items, where the delivery is made by the regular postman/woman as part of the daily delivery round along with the normal (addressed) mail; what could be more reliable? Thus door-to-door can be used to hit a carefully (geodemographically) profiled audience with a one-to-one communication which generates a measurable response – surely a perfect example of effective direct marketing activity?

  Consider, on the other hand, the alternative view of door-to-door: that it is primarily a trial-gaining mechanism for packaged goods (via money-off coupons), that is, a conduit of sales promotion activity and thus undeniably a sales promotion medium.

  Clearly we are running into considerable difficulties of classification with door-to-door – this will not be the last such occasion.

- *Telephone marketing.* Whether inbound or outbound, use of the telephone for marketing purposes is generally agreed to fall under the umbrella of direct marketing. However, certain promotions employ premium-rate telephone lines (0891 and 0898 numbers) for consumers to phone in their entries to a competition, for example; typical promoters would include the brewers (beer/lager on-pack promotions) and newspapers (in-paper promotions). Telephone marketing (or, infuriatingly for the diminishing subset of marketers who at some time in the distant past studied Greek, 'telemarketing') is an increasingly important marketing tool which may account for the current ownership disputes between direct marketing and sales promotion practitioners.

These are the main media of direct marketing, especially direct mail, direct response press (space and inserts). Door-to-door and telephone marketing are also employed by sales promotion practitioners.

So what of sales promotion media? As we have seen, there are very few marketing communications media which are the exclusive preserve of a single marketing communications discipline. Consider, however:

- *On-pack.* We are speaking here mainly about an FMCG product (that is, a 'packaged good'). This is the nearest thing to a 'pure' sales promotion medium. With an offer communicated on-pack, the sales promotion manager is in complete control of the medium (at least there is no media owner trying to increase the cost of the space). He/she is also guaranteed 100 per cent reach of regular users of the product, and if a trial mechanism is featured on-pack, then at least one purchase is guaranteed, with no danger of misredemption. The on-pack medium is free to the owner of the pack, although compromise of the on-shelf impact (carefully created by the pack design team) is a valid concern: certain luxury goods, in particular, have a policy of eschewing any on-pack activity, in the belief that it detracts from the brand identity communicated by the packaging.
- *In-store* (point-of-sale). By this we mean the Aladdin's Cave of materials including window bills/posters, take-one leaflets, shelf wobblers, and the like, and also the activities of 'in-store demonstrators' distributing samples, money-off coupons, and so on to identified target individuals, either in a store or in a shopping mall. These activities typically accost the consumer (almost, in some cases, ambushing them), grabbing the attention of, say, a supermarket shopper 'cruising the fixture' and making a powerful and immediate extra benefit offer to motivate purchase at the point of sale. Sales promotion? Few would disagree.
- *Press: reader offers and advertorials.* These are a typical feature of women's magazines. Partner promotions are often executed through this medium (a link between a manufacturer of branded FMCGs and a media partner); costs are shared; extra value is delivered to the magazine's readership; and the advertiser gains valuable exposure (and implied editorial endorsement) sometimes for less than the cost of equivalent advertising space, although total cost to the advertiser may be greater than that for the space if the publication supplies editorial and

production (so that the piece blends smoothly into the editorial environment of the publication). In other cases a 'contra deal' may be put together, for example inviting readers to call in for free trial samples of a new product, or offering a big prize ('Win a car every day this week, only in the Daily X').

Unquestionably sales promotion, although the media departments of certain full-service ad agencies, as well as media independents (organizations which plan and book advertising space/airtime as their main activity) and even PR agencies, have developed specialist skills in this field.

So much, then, for direct marketing and sales promotion *media*. Some are shared, whereas some are fundamentally the preserve of one or other discipline. Others verge on the territory of advertising or even PR. Indeed when we consider a list of communications media:

- direct mail
- press (space, inserts, advertorial features/reader offers)
- door-to-door
- telephone
- on/in-pack
- in-store

as well as:

- TV
- posters
- radio
- cinema
and so on,

we may reasonably conclude that the medium is less important than the *nature of the communication*: the objectives of the activity, what data are generated and, crucially, what is done with them.

Direct marketing and sales promotion as distinct disciplines

Integrationists would have us believe that direct marketing and sales promotion are essentially the same discipline. This is a fashionable, but in my opinion, fundamentally flawed view.

Either knowingly or, let us hope, ignorantly, those who argue for uniformity miss an important point: certainly, any number of communications disciplines can be forced together in a marketing 'shotgun wedding', even to the extent of making the same executives in client marketing departments (and their agencies) responsible for both disciplines, but this is not (and never can be) integration. Direct marketing and sales promotion are distinct: it's a mistake to try to mix them.

Take an extreme example. Suppose Joe Smith, the head of direct marketing at Readers Life Associates (RLA), a leading mail order publishing company, finally tires of 'kowtowing' to his MD and finance director and, in an admirably grand gesture, throws his resignation letter on to the boss's desk. He is leaving to set up his own consultancy. Suppose he has enough contacts in PR and the marketing press to contrive a relatively high-profile launch. He sets up as 'Smith Integrated Communications' (SIC) in a business centre with a shared receptionist and secretary – effectively a one-man band. Low overheads, plenty of contacts and promises of business – it seems the world is his oyster. Suppose, however, that Joe had originally joined RLA as a junior product manager some ten years earlier, having earned his marketing stripes first as a graduate trainee and subsequently as an account executive at a leading direct marketing agency. Suppose further that John Brown, Brand X's marketing director, reads in 'Promotions News' that SIC is up and running, and likes the look of what Smith appears to be offering – after all, why brief two or three agencies when one will do? One 'most enjoyable and informative' lunch later, Brown has awarded SIC a 12-month contract to handle all Brand X's on-pack and in-store promotional campaigns over the next year. The rest is predictable, when we consider Smith's background and experience. Of course, he now has to recruit – to build a promotions team from scratch. No sooner has the euphoria (and inevitable press/PR bonanza) subsided, than Smith is forced to confront the cold harsh reality of what he's taken on: a major chunk of business of which he has absolutely no experience. To misquote Oscar Wilde, 'For an agency, there's only one thing worse than not winning business, and that is winning business you can't handle.'

So now Smith desperately tries to hire 'some good promotions people'. But the odds are stacked against him: he has never worked in sales promotion; he doesn't understand how the business operates; he lacks relevant technical/production knowledge; and, perhaps worst of all, he has no passion for the promotions business. Because he knows nothing of this world, the CVs which land on his desk mean little to him; he makes some recruitment mistakes, SIC fouls up several times on the Brand X account, and after 12 difficult months, the account is awarded to another agency – specialists in sales promotion. SIC nearly goes under. Smith has to make all his newly-employed sales promotion executives redundant and of course the ladies and gentlemen of the press – those fair-weather friends – have a field day. Smith resolves that, in future, he will 'stick to his knitting' and renames the agency 'Smith Direct Marketing'. Moral: don't bite off more than you can chew. Direct marketing and sales promotion are distinct disciplines: you can be an expert on one and an ignoramus about the other. (An alternative moral from this tale, for agency people, might go something like: 'Don't misrepresent your agency to potential clients, as this will only lead to grief for all concerned.')

In summary: if your pipes burst, consult a plumber (quickly). If your car breaks down, it makes sense to approach a trained auto-mechanic. If you need advertising, try an ad agency (as your first port of call, at least). For direct mail, a direct marketing agency. For an on-pack offer, a specialist sales promotion consultancy. And so on.

The 'take-off' of integration in UK marketing communications certainly owes much to the pressures of the early 1990s recession, but it is certainly very much here to stay; however, that is not to say that direct marketing and sales promotion are the same discipline, any more than that, say, PR is the same as advertising. All these disciplines have their own specialists who understand and can practise them better than self-styled generalists. *Vive la différence!* (and this is from someone who believes fundamentally that all these disciplines can and should work together, that is, an integrationalist).

Why not 'one discipline'?

Having declared that I *do* believe there is a distinction between direct marketing and sales promotion as marketing communications disciplines, I shall now put forward the arguments for the opposite point of view, that is, that there is advertising, and then all other communications, so that 'below-the-line' is best viewed as a single discipline. We shall examine the arguments one by one. This point of view is typically expressed in the following terms:

> Direct marketing is about getting people to
> do things – to mail back a reply card, to
> phone an 0800 telephone number, to visit a
> retail outlet. So is sales promotion. Sales

promotion adds value to a product or service by making a special offer and giving the respondent something extra if they take the required action within the appropriate time-frame, exactly like direct marketing; did you ever see a successful piece of direct mail which didn't offer an incentive to respond? Direct marketing and sales promotion thus share a dependence on making an offer to the recipient which is additional to the fundamental brand proposition as communicated by above-the-line, 'image' advertising.

Of course this argument conveniently ignores the substantial *differences* between sales promotion and direct marketing. Whereas the former discipline depends almost entirely on offers, the latter may employ them as an extra inducement to action, but is fundamentally about *relationships*.

Direct marketing and sales promotion also share a common role as regards their contribution to the success of the company (whether manufacturing or service) that uses them, that is, they boost sales. It's as simple as that; if they fail in this, their primary role, they cannot justify their place in the company's marketing mix. Many direct marketers (and the more pretentious sales promoters) make out that what they do has a long-term, brand-building effect, but they are, fundamentally, fooling themselves (and even worse, in some cases, others). Direct marketing and sales promotion are sales tools – they generate short-term sales advantages, and should be regarded as tactical weapons in the marketer's arsenal. This is their great strength; it is the reason they work so well alongside image advertising and indeed why they can never replace it; advertising builds brands, giving emotional reasons for consumers to choose a product or service (for example, become more attractive, successful, happier and so on). Direct

marketing and sales promotion, on the
other hand, give tangible (albeit in some
cases relatively minor) reasons to make the
relevant selection/purchase decision (for
example, 'save 10p', 'free plastic daffodil/
fluffy duck', '10% extra free' and the like).
Both advertising and below-the-line 'action
marketing' are important tools which can
help achieve the overall result of convincing
the maximum number of consumers (or
business decision makers) to purchase the
product.

This view fails to acknowledge that all communications disciplines are
designed to boost sales – there is no other possible justification for their
(often substantial) cost. Direct marketers tend to be 'experts' who
understand the importance of long-term relationship building, driven by
marketing data. They specialize in accountable communications, whether
employing direct mail, press inserts or telephone marketing. Typical client
companies employing direct marketing include mail order, charities and
insurance, *whereas* sales promotion experts are more likely to be 'ideas'
merchants'. They specialize in coming up with whizzy creative ideas to
give sales a quick boost – whether it's 'Win a car a day' or 'Free Our-Price
CD voucher with every student bank account opened' or 'Double the
cleaning power – *2* bottles of Scrubbo for the price of 1'. These people
can certainly calculate redemption projections but they're not boffins like
the 'database/statistical number crunchers' doing their multivariate
regression analyses at the *Reader's Digest.* Sales promotion experts also
understand FMCG and are comfortable working with heavily advertised
consumer brands – unlike some old-school 'purist' direct marketers.

As I believe I have just demonstrated, the hard-line 'integrationalist' view
just doesn't stack up. Direct marketing has specialists in database, creative
work and fulfilment; and sales promotion has experts in thinking of creative
themes, skilled designers of on-pack flashes and fix-a-form promotional
labels, and specialists in printing latex scratchcards. A direct marketing
creative has little in common with a sales promotion designer. A direct
marketing account manager may have quite different skills from a sales
promotion account manager – and neither knows much about TV advertising or public relations, which are of course quite different disciplines
again.

None of this is to say that the disciplines of direct marketing and sales
promotion cannot coexist happily, either within an integrated below-the-

line agency or even an integrated through-the-line operation, just as they have coexisted within client marketing departments for years. However, in my view, the only credible 'below-the-line' or, for that matter, 'integrated' agency is one that recognizes the differences between direct marketing and sales promotion and employs a full complement of direct marketing and sales promotion experts, including database, creative and production, so that for each below-the-line marketing challenge, the appropriate solution (on-pack, in-store, direct mail, telephone marketing or whatever) is delivered professionally and cost-effectively by people who have learned and perfected their specialist craft. Chapter 8 deals in more detail with how to structure such an agency.

Conclusions

Direct marketing and sales promotion have long been viewed as distinct disciplines within marketing. A certain folklore has grown up around each; gurus have emerged and starred on the lecture circuit; books and magazines have been published (and in some cases read); specialist careers have been built. Experts in direct marketing have viewed their counterparts in sales promotion with suspicion/contempt and vice versa.

In this chapter, we have examined both the integrationist and separatist extreme views. Certainly, each has been presented with a certain degree of exaggeration – few members of either camp adopt quite such radical positions as the stereotypes presented here. Nevertheless, the debate is a real one and is certainly more than a topic of 'academic interest' to MBA students and their lecturers. It does matter to those whose work involves any aspect of 'below-the-line' communications. It affects the structure of marketing departments, and of their agencies. It influences the way that marketing budgets are allocated and apportioned. Above all, it helps to shape the attitude that direct marketing and sales promotion practitioners bring to their work; how they view the role of below-the-line within the marketing mix, and consequently the decisions they make about the campaigns they conceive and implement.

My own views on this debate are drawn from experience of working in various agencies, some integrated, some non-integrated (and at least one pseudo-integrated). I believe direct marketing and sales promotion are fundamentally distinct disciplines, with their own specialist skills (and, as a result, a need for specialist personnel – clients, agencies and suppliers), but that there are significant areas of overlap between the two.

Sales promotions can be communicated by direct mail, door-to-door and press (response ads and inserts), as well as the more traditional 'sales promotion' media of on-pack and in-store. Most direct marketing activity involves making the recipient an offer – many such mechanisms are also found in sales promotion. Sales promotion activity generates data which can be captured to form a marketing database. This can then be used as the basis for data-driven or *direct* marketing.

In other words, as the title of this book suggests, it is my opinion that direct marketing can, and indeed should, be integrated with sales promotion and other marketing communications disciplines, but that the two are certainly sufficiently distinct to be viewed as separate branches of marketing.

One consequence of this view is that there is and will continue to be a genuine need both for 'craft specialists' who are experts in direct marketing and for others who specialize in sales promotion and in sub-branches of these, such as telephone marketing and scratchcard production techniques. There is also a need for generalists, whose task it is to understand the two disciplines and knit them together into effective marketing solutions. These generalists (whether they work in an integrated agency or in a client marketing department) will be increasingly in demand as we move further into the new era of integrated communications, and I believe such a move is inevitable. Their role will be to coordinate the activities of the various experts/specialists, and (most difficult of all) to make rational, even-handed marketing judgements about the allocation of limited marketing resources between them, in the best interests of the brand, its manufacturer and its shareholders.

I hope that any readers who consider themselves to be hard-line integrationalists will not, at this point, conclude that this book is worthless and toss it away in disgust (much as one would an unwelcome item of 'junk' mail or an unattractive promotional take-one leaflet). Such readers should be aware that I do not maintain that direct marketing and sales promotion have nothing in common, any more than I believe that they are interchangeable or indistinguishable – I merely point out that they require different specialist skills, which are frequently found in different individuals and even in different agencies. However, if you are determined to part company with the rest of us at this point, please at least find a more open-minded friend or colleague to whom this book might usefully be passed.

As a consequence of the above discussion, we shall start the next chapter from the premise that direct marketing and sales promotion are *distinct* disciplines but that they can and should be *integrated* so that they work in tandem to give the optimum overall results (although this implies no hard and fast rules about clients' agency arrangements) and broaden the discussion to include 'above-the-line' or image advertising.

To illustrate companies' use of direct marketing and sales promotion in combination, the following case histories are offered.

Case history

Company	Shell UK Limited
Background	Shell, the joint market leader in retail fuels, required a long-term consumer loyalty programme to increase consumer loyalty and market share in the increasingly competitive retail fuels business
Marketing objectives	• To gain and sustain a strategic competitive advantage over a minimum five-year period by creating a new unique selling point. • To maintain and increase volume sales while still maintaining a premium pricing policy • To increase consumer loyalty to Shell.
Solution	Shell and its agency, Option One, London, came up with a loyalty scheme to embrace all motorists with an overriding strategy of specifically targeting high-mileage competitive users. The promotion needed to maintain interest for a minimum of five years by still being able to offer tactical promotions within the long-term scheme.
Promotional concept	A personalized Smart Card was chosen because it:

(a)   is able to store electronic points, which are the basic currency of the scheme;

(b)   is a totally secure reward system (unlike magnetic strip cards) and has the ability to store unlimited value on the card – plus the ability to redeem for high-value items instantly;

(c)   enables Shell to build a database with actual transaction history, giving the company the ability to track and target best potential customers;

(d)   allows a paper-free redemption instantly and securely at third-party partners (away from the Shell service station).

Plate 5.1 Shell – loyalty scheme
Source: Option One for Shell UK

*Campaign
execution*

- Cardholders were recruited at Shell service stations and through third-party partners including UCI Cinemas, TicketMaster, John Menzies, RSPCA, Motability and The British Heart Foundation.
- Customers who had previously taken part in Shell promotions were sent cards.
- The third-party partners allowed instant redemption of points at their sites.
- A catalogue of merchandise was sourced, ensuring that the best-quality brand names were chosen but also at a points advantage or at least equal with all competitors.
- The range of merchandise was selected to appeal to all types of motorist: male and female, old and young, and their driving habits. The minimum entry level was one fill (5 points for free blank audio cassette); long-distance truckers could 'earn' TVs, camcorders and so on.
- Shell included the ability to collect *Air Miles* points on the Smart Card as an incentive for long-term and high-mileage collectors.

Communication media
- 1800 forecourts with full POS and five million catalogues.
- Promotional assistants actively recruiting on forecourts (particularly motorway sites which get high-mileage competitor users).
- National TV advertising.
- Door-to-door around specific sites.
- POS and application forms in all partner outlets including screen slides at the start of films within UCI cinemas.
- Local radio promotions.
- Direct mail to *Air Miles* database.
- Inserts and ads in charities magazines.
- Direct mail to encourage maximum activation, particularly targeting high-mileage motorists. Data on activation and loyalty were received through transactional data download from the Smart Card on to the database.

Results
- The target for recruitment for the first year of cardholders was achieved within the first four months. Three million cardholders within a year of national launch.
- Volumes in the test region of Scotland saw an increase against the rest of the country in excess of a staggering 20 per cent, which considerably exceeds all payback criteria and smashed all targets set.
- Similar results were subsequently achieved nationwide while Shell maintained a premium pricing policy.

Case history

INTRODUCTION

Microsoft is one of the world's leading developers of software for personal computers. Established by Bill Gates in 1975 as a major force in the software market, it has developed operating systems and a number of applications that have captured the imagination (and budget) of a new generation of computer users.

The UK company was founded in 1983 and by the time of this case study, had gained a strong position in the market and had built an enviable reputation for high-quality, innovative PC-based software solutions.

However, the UK senior management met late in 1993 following the results of a research survey, part of an extensive ongoing research programme carried out over several months.

The research identified that Microsoft had a potential problem in one particular market sector – the home and small business sector (less than 50 PCs). The survey showed that these 'small users' often felt neglected by parts of the software distribution chain. Manufacturers, dealers and retailers all had a tendency to overlook this group because their spending power was small when compared with large corporate buyers. However, the needs of this group of customers were greater than others' for two reasons:

1. They lacked the resources of an in-house IT infrastructure (as often found in large companies) to turn to when software support was required.
2. Their use of computers was, generally speaking, 'mission-critical', that is, any problem actually stops them functioning, so that the lack of support is a major threat to their success and constitutes a continual source of stress.

Microsoft's concern about this situation was based on the belief that the small business market was set to grow at double the total market rate. In addition, research had established that small business users of PCs were remarkably influential within their peer groups when it came to PC software purchase.

Microsoft therefore agreed to allocate a substantial budget to a programme to address the needs of this key market segment.

The PC software market is highly competitive and is characterized by rapid innovation and, in recent years, short product life cycles and diminishing margins both for manufacturers and for resellers.

Some large dealers have their own databases of end-users and are known to operate direct mail programmes of varying degrees of sophistication – Microsoft have thus far largely confined themselves to building a strong and credible overall brand image.

One effect of the speed of change in this market has been end-user confusion and (as with hardware) a fear that the state-of-the-art software purchased today will be obsolete tomorrow. Indeed, there is evidence that would-be purchasers avoid making purchase decisions for fear of buying badly. There is a considerable degree of anxiety and dealers/resellers are in a powerful position to reassure and influence this market.

The case history that follows is the story of Microsoft's response to the above market opportunity.

Company	Microsoft

Background
- Microsoft is the world's leading computer software company
- Founded by Bill Gates in 1975
- 1994 turnover was $6 billion
- Microsoft software runs on 80 per cent of all PCs
- Microsoft identified the need for an end-user loyalty programme
- Key audience was small businesses (no IT support)
- Neglected but powerful *and growing* sector of the overall software market

Marketing objectives
- Identify and recruit an 'army of champions' for Microsoft
- Achieve incremental product sales
- Make the whole programme self-funding in Year 1

Solution

The 'Microsoft Plus' programme

- Launched April 1994
- Designed to help users get more from their current Microsoft software
- Targeted at users in:
  - Small-/medium-sized businesses (< 50PCs)
  - Working from home
  - Customers with limited access to a formal IT department
- Subscription-based: £34.95 per year

Microsoft *Plus* magazine

- Sent direct to Microsoft *Plus* members six times per year.
- 56 pages of:
  - Advance news, information, new products
  - Q&A, helpful hints
  - Special offers, member benefits

Microsoft *Plus* Hints &Tips

- Sent direct to Microsoft *Plus* members six times per year
- 12 pages of invaluable 'how to' hints and tips on:
  - Word (Windows & Mac.)
  - Excel (Windows & Mac.)
  - Works
  - Windows

Microsoft *Plus* Bulletin Board

- Allows online communication with other members and Microsoft in:

  - UK, France, Germany and USA
- Includes:
  - free 30 days of connect time to the forum
  - free 30 days of CompuServe basic services

Microsoft *Plus* discounts

- Discounts to help members get more from their software, including:
  - 30 per cent off Microsoft hotelmen support
  - 25 per cent off training courses at participating Microsoft training centres
  - 20 per cent off Microsoft Certified Professional examinations

Microsoft *Plus* rewards programme

- Ongoing loyalty bonus for continued registration of:
  - New Microsoft products
  - Microsoft upgrades/trade-ins
- Members earn points, exchangeable for free Microsoft products
- Members receive points statement six times per year

Membership profile:

- > 20 000 members in UK
- 97.5 per cent influence the purchase and use of software within their organization
- 73 per cent are in small-/medium-sized businesses (the target audience)
- 68 per cent use a PC at work *and* home (70 per cent of those have a separate PC for home and work)

Increased customer satisfaction:

- Microsoft *Plus* members are 76 per cent more satisfied than average Microsoft customers
- 78 per cent will recommend Microsoft *Plus* to others (43 per cent already have)
- 73 per cent agree programme will make them more likely to purchase Microsoft software in future
- Programme is 100 per cent self-funding

Case history

Company	Alfred Dunhill
Background	Alfred Dunhill is a world-renowned retailer of luxury goods with a very 'English' pedigree. Christmas is an important time of year for retail sales, but nowhere more so than in Japan.
Marketing objectives	To increase foot-traffic to the Alfred Dunhill outlets, ensuring existing customers visited for their Christmas shopping but also prompting 'hot' target customers to visit the outlets for the first time.
Solution	Alfred Dunhill and its agency, Marketing Principles, developed a mailing mechanic which directs known customers to the Alfred Dunhill outlets; visits to the outlets resulting in the customer being rewarded with a gift – without making a purchase.

Taking the essential 'Englishness' of Alfred Dunhill as the creative impetus, the mailing was designed around the traditional English Christmas.

The mechanic had to be arresting, quirky and intriguing – the Japanese direct mail industry not being famous for its creativity.

Plate 5.2   Alfred Dunhill – the Christmas pudding mailing
Source: Marketing Principles for Alfred Dunhill

Promotional concept/ campaign execution	'The Alfred Dunhill Japanese Christmas Pudding Mailing' – the mailing told of the tradition of placing an old-fashioned English threepenny bit into the Christmas pudding. If one was lucky enough to find the 3d bit on your slice of pudding then one would have good luck for the rest of the year.
	An original 3d bit was affixed to a leaflet and included in the mailing package. Customers were invited to bring their 3d bit to an Alfred Dunhill outlet and in return would receive an original English Christmas pudding, as well as being able to view the Christmas merchandise.
	Also included in the mailing was a special edition of the Christmas gift catalogue and a personalized letter.
Communication media	The piece was mailed to the existing Dunhill database and also tested on 'hot prospects' derived from magazine enquiries and two bought-in lists – famous company executives' wives and luxury-brand buying females.
Campaign results	Overall, the campaign was very successful.
	Average response rate 15 per cent across all outlets with over 65 per cent purchasing whilst in the outlet. Purchases were at a high unit value – one lady purchasing 90 pairs of socks!

6 THE CREATIVE PROCESS

Nowadays the underlying role of everyone
in an advertising agency who doesn't create
advertisements – the only important thing
they do – is to ensure that the
advertisements the agency creatives create
are perfectly tailored to their task.

Winston Fletcher, 1994

The only purpose of advertising is to sell: it
has no other justification worth mentioning.

Raymond Rubicam, founder of Young and
Rubicam Advertising

The communications strategy should not
be considered a straitjacket by the creative
writers and art directors . . . it is just the
opposite because it narrows the parameters
of creative experimentation. The strategy
allows the creative people involved more
time to experiment and break rules.

Don Schultz, Stanley Tannenbaum and
Robert Lauterborn, 1993

Creativity is not painting the Sistine
Chapel, it is shifting gear on a wet night in
Crewe.

Ian Shirley, Roar Marketing And
Promotions, *Marketing* Magazine, 1994

It is generally thought that artists are
interested in art. Nothing could be further
from the truth. Artists are interested in
money. It's the rest of us who are interested
in art.

Howard Gossage, as quoted by
Winston Fletcher, 1994

Response versus creativity

I shall use the word 'creative' in this chapter to refer to what creative people (copywriters, art directors and creative directors) *do*, which primarily means 'generating advertising ideas' (although we shall also discuss alternative views of who is allowed to be 'creative'), that is, they start with a 'Creative brief' (or at least an 'Advertising proposition') and a blank sheet of paper. Figure 6.1 shows an outline for a creative brief.

The creative team comes back (after minutes, days, weeks or months) with something like:

'ALWAYS COCA-COLA' or

'AMERICAN EXPRESS – don't leave home without it' or

'HEINEKEN REFRESHES THE PARTS OTHER BEERS CANNOT REACH'

with the appropriate accompanying pictures. Sometimes the idea is more visual (like David Ogilvy's 'man in the Hathaway shirt' or the creation of the 'Nicole' character by Renault in the UK for its Clio car, or Howell Henry Chaldecott Lury's UK TV campaign for 'Tango' soft drink). To these famous campaigns we could add hundreds of other 'classics', including the original Doyle Dane Bernbach Press ads for the Volkswagen Beetle, Chiat/Day's stunning '1984' commercial for Apple Computer (directed by Ridley Scott) and Saatchi and Saatchi's work for the Conservative Party and British Airways in the 1970s and 1980s.

More often, however, the creative team comes back with something workmanlike and brief, but far less memorable than the above examples – not all or even many campaigns are destined to become truly 'famous'. But, generally speaking, great brands require 'great advertising' (let's argue about definitions elsewhere), which in turn depends on great ideas, that is, *creativity*. Indeed for many people in and outside the communications industry, the *creative process* is what advertising is in essence – all the other actors (account management, media, production, finance and even the client) are merely playing supporting roles. It is also the process imbued with the most mystique; many highly creative people like to encourage the view that they operate as a 'black box', inexplicably turning base inputs into pure gold, in a manner those on a lower plane could not possibly hope to comprehend. This at the same time serves to enhance these individuals' salaries, bonuses and prestige, of course.

A1 AGENCY CREATIVE BRIEF

Client:

Job title:

Job no:

Date issued:

Issued by:

Requirement:

Target audience:

Objectives:

Communications:

Business:

Positioning:

Proposition:

Substantiation:

Action required:

Tone of voice:

Mandatory inclusions:

Media/sizes:

Budget:

Timing:

Approved by:

Planning Director   Date
Account Director   Date
Creative Director   Date

Figure 6.1 An agency creative brief

Now let us consider the following questions:

1. Must the use of certain media (however skilful the creative treatment) inevitably devalue the brand?
2. Must volume response always be gained at the expense of creativity and brand values?

In other words, are there two extremes:

- brand-building creative communications (which make people feel good about the product or service); and
- response-generating communications, shouting 'WIN!', 'FREE!' and 'ACT NOW!' (which make people actually *buy* the product or service)

with little or no middle ground available?

Read on, to explore these and other related issues!

Let us start by posing a question. In marketing communications, is brand-building, imaginative advertising implacably opposed to hard-working response-pulling activity? If the answer is 'Yes', we must conclude that what the US direct marketing guru Stan Rapp has described as 'double-duty advertising' (that is, brand-building communications which also pull response) is a chimera, so that one must choose: response or creativity? In holding a debate 'Response versus creativity', we assume 'response' is self-explanatory. However, what exactly do we mean by 'creativity'?

> **Create** *v.* Latin *creare* – bring forth, produce. To bring into being, cause to exist, 'to form out of nothing'.
> *The Shorter Oxford English Dictionary*, 1972

Few words in the sphere of marketing communications produce such extreme reactions; for some, 'creative' means all the things that are bad about advertising in general and advertising agencies in particular, as in 'Yeah – my agency is creative all right; creative at finding ways to spend more and more of my money and win themselves a sideboard full of awards.' (A. Client, Anytime, Anywhere)

Volumes have already been and no doubt will in the future be written on this subject, even if we confine our attention to creativity within the field of marketing communications. For a start, should creativity be regarded as the sole preserve of those employed as so-called 'creative' people, that is, those whose job title is one of the following list:

- Copywriter
- Art director
- Visualizer
- Designer
- Creative director?

Alternatively, can anyone, including account management ('suits'), or planners, media people or even (shock, horror!) *clients*, be, in the right circumstances, described as 'creative' (albeit perhaps only with a small 'c')?

In sales promotion circles, where copywriting is not the dominant discipline (and account executives tend to be awarded the task of writing the copy for, say, an on-pack offer), an account handler (of any level of seniority) would be delighted to be described by colleagues as 'creative', meaning in this context one or more of the following: 'imaginative', 'full of ideas', or even 'having a sound grasp of marketing strategy with a strong empathy with the client's brand/market and communications objectives'. In other words, for many sales promotion professionals, the epithet 'creative' is nothing more or less than a general term of approval. In direct marketing and advertising circles, 'creative' applies only to the 'Ideas Department' (that is, the Creative Department) and few other members of the agency would have any pretentions or even desire to be considered 'creative' (as compared with 'strategic' or indeed 'insightful', to which they are more likely to aspire). Cynics would in any case point out that in many agencies the only truly creative people are to be found in the Finance Department where their jobs afford them ample scope to apply their talents.

In any case we shall employ the 'communication ideas' definition of creativity – these generally come from the Creative Department. Certainly, no one could deny that the extremes of each genre of marketing communication are very different as regards their creative content.

At one end of the scale, therefore, we have full-colour, lavish production values, big budgets, heavy exposure in peak time, long commercials, early double-page spreads in the most 'up-market' colour magazines featuring beautiful photography, short copy and lots of white space. These communications are all about *image, awareness, attitude shift*.

In short, we are dealing here with advertising (almost) as fine art, to be admired largely for the beauty and the excellence of its execution. The desired consumer 'take-out' would be 'Wow!' or rather something much more sophisticated, but along the same lines.

At the other end of the scale, we have small spaces in the black and white press, featuring such proven attention-grabbers as:

- FREE!
- WIN!
- SAVE!
- MONEY OFF!

often displayed within the much dreaded 'starburst' or featured as a dramatic 'flash' across the corner of the ad.

These communications are also noted for the prominent display of large, bold, memorable 0800 free telephone numbers, for near frantic exhortations to 'CALL NOW!' or 'REPLY TODAY!' and for an emphasis on minimizing costs at every stage of the creative and production processes. The end product of this approach is, generally speaking, a communication which looks cheap and comes across as aggressive, brash, crass, clumsy, crude and, at the extreme, even downright *rude*. Anyone who had been to art school (and a fair few who hadn't) would feel distinctly queasy in the presence of such work. And, of course, much of the time, such communications generate large numbers of responses/ redemptions and sell large volumes of product very rapidly. In this case, the desired 'take-out' would be 'Great – I'll buy some, now!' or something similarly action-oriented.

So is there any common ground at all between the two extremes? Must every marketer, whenever planning any communication, choose between them? Consider the graphical view of the 'axis' described above – shown in Figure 6.2.

This continuum is a neat and convenient way to consider communications of varying degrees of responsiveness. But why should work based on genuine *creative ideas*, which achieve 'cut-through' and 'touch the

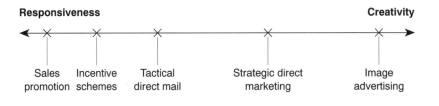

Figure 6.2 The response–creativity continuum

consumer's nerve endings' preclude the simultaneous generation of volume *response*? Indeed, surely engaging the consumer's attention is a necessary first stage in the process of getting them to *do* something? Can't imaginative communications ideas also result in large numbers of enquiries and orders direct from the end user?

The answer, of course, is 'Yes'. Indeed one of the major breakthroughs of the direct marketing and sales promotion industries in the 1980s which effectively marked their 'coming of age' as fully fledged elements of the marketing mix was their success in achieving 'brand literacy' in 'below-the-line' marketing communications; that is, such communications no longer had to look tacky and cheap. Indeed the condition imposed by major above-the-line advertisers (including Kodak, Ford, GM, American Express, British Airways and latterly Heinz, Nestlé and Procter and Gamble) for dipping their toe into direct marketing in particular was an insistence that their long-established, carefully (and expensively) crafted brand values would in no way be compromised. Such had always been a concern with sales promotion, which had despite this become a staple of most FMCG marketer's communications mixes by the 1970s; now direct marketing was also embraced with increasing confidence by companies which had traditionally relied largely on advertising to build the brand and generate sales. (It should be noted at this point that, in addition to excellent design, copywriting and production, vastly improved list maintenance and enhanced targeting and profiling skills have played a crucial role in direct marketing's recent achievement of respectability/ coming of age – more of this in Chapter 7).

To state my own position on this 'hot' and much debated issue: brand-building communications are *not* incompatible with response generation and sales stimulation, that is, you can achieve a *balance* of the two within one campaign or even one communication. Thus 'double-duty' advertising can work, but that is not to say that the two duties could not be better achieved by two separate communications – in many cases, I believe they *could*. It is certainly vital to decide in advance where your priorities lie – clear objective setting is essential to successful integrated marketing communications. This is a theme to which we refer throughout this book.

In the remainder of this chapter, we shall seek to establish that 'creativity' should refer to the *power* of marketing communications *ideas*, and that in cases where a piece of marketing communication is intended primarily to generate *response*, the work is creative if and only if it produces bucketloads of the right sort of *replies*; whereas *image-building* communications are creative if and only if they grab and hold the consumer's attention and convey a powerful brand message, in the process *raising awareness* and *changing attitudes*.

'If the idea's big enough . . .'

It seems safe to conclude at this stage that the only generally agreed thing about creativity in marketing communications is that it is all about *ideas*.

We are talking about intelligent, imaginative, *different* ways of communicating, of engaging people's attention, of capturing their imagination and of retaining their interest long enough to sell them something. That's all, and this might appear to be a relatively simple task; but of course in a cluttered 'overpromoted' world it becomes an increasing challenge. Our would-be viewers, listeners and readers see us coming and 'tune out' our promotional messages; we've got to be cleverer still – certainly just shouting loudly is unlikely to work these days. We are more likely to be successful if we seek to charm, to intrigue, to amuse and/or to entertain. Certainly if mere repetition of an advertising message was ever enough, it isn't any more. This issue was highlighted in the 1970s and 1980s by the contrast between US and UK advertising – the former brash, pushy, 'sales'-oriented, the latter subtle, entertaining, and perhaps at times even a little self-satisfied. Certainly, as Drayton Bird, the UK direct marketing guru has said, you can't *bore* people into buying your product! Most practitioners would these days add that neither can you 'beat them over the head' as a sales technique; you've got to earn and win first their attention and ultimately their hearts and minds. Excellent marketing communications creativity (in any medium) is that which makes *contact*, captures *attention* and only then *persuades*. The best communications do not deceive or hoodwink the unwitting consumer, as famously suggested by Vance Packard in his 1957 book *The Hidden Persuaders*, in which he propounded a 'conspiracy theory' of advertisers as evil manipulators of a hapless and innocent public. Even were it not for the elaborate apparatus of controls regulating the marketing communications industry (notably the BACC, the ASA and the various codes of conduct drawn up by the DMA, the ISP and others) which seek to ensure that its output is legal, decent, honest and truthful, tricking people into buying a product which doesn't deliver what you claim for it is just downright bad business. (Not only do such customers never come back, but they are unlikely to be enthusiastic advocates for your brand when talking to friends, relatives or colleagues.) Mr Packard flattered the advertising industry with his (unsubstantiated) claims about its powers of manipulation.

At this point, let us look at the headlines of some classic ads. As it happens, all are cited as examples of advertising creativity at its best by John Caples, in his classic book, *Tested Advertising Methods*. As it happens, all were press ads. However, if we discount the inevitably dated sound of some of them, and consider the appeal of the headlines, we shall see that they touch a nerve now as then, and speak to the consumer in all of us, across the years and regardless of the medium in which they were originally executed:

- 'Here's an extra $50, Grace – I'm making real money now' (for international correspondence schools)
- 'How to win friends and influence people' (by publishers Simon and Schuster for Dale Carnegie's book)
- 'Do you make these mistakes in English?' (Sherwin Cody School of English)
- 'They laughed when I sat down at the piano. But when I started to play!' (US School of Music)
- 'At 60 miles an hour, the loudest noise in this new Rolls-Royce comes from the electric clock' (David Ogilvy for the Rolls-Royce Silver Cloud).

If marketing communications creativity has to do with coming up with ideas that *persuade*, it is but a small step to conclude that this process need not be tied to any particular communications *medium*. In most cases, an idea which communicates the benefits of a product strikingly and persuasively on TV can surely (with minimal adaptation) do a similar job in a press ad, on the radio, in a point-of-sale leaflet, or in the shape of a direct mail pack; and indeed if a campaign incorporates two or more of these media, the effect can be that of mutual reinforcement (invariably called 'synergy' in the 1980s).

As Kevin Morley, founder of the UK-based integrated agency KMM (more recently part of Ammirati Puris Lintas, London) has said,

> if the idea's big enough it will carry
> through . . . you've got to keep going back
> to the drawing board to come up with an
> idea that is absolutely so big it works
> everywhere.
> *Business Age*, January 1994

So the only problem is the one that has always existed – having the 'big idea' in the first place, which is exactly what the creative people (especially the copywriter/art director team and their creative director) get paid for. It is also necessary to distinguish between good ideas and bad, and to recognize the strengths and limitations of the various media as regards which executions will be most effective where (for example, 'That would make a *great* cross-track poster' or 'That would work really well as the first spread in the direct mail leaflet'). And of course every great idea needs great execution (photography, illustration, TV direction and post-production) to result in truly excellent marketing communications; most clients will admit to having been sold an idea at one time or another which looked better as an agency art director's rough than it ever did on TV or in the press. Similarly, the finished colour visual (with 'Greek' copy) looked so beautiful when the creative director presented it that the finished printed product was a disappointment by comparison. In any case, an increasing number of international advertisers are now orchestrating genuinely 'integrated' campaigns embracing a number of media (irrespective of their differing agency arrangements) which are clearly driven by a single central creative theme or idea.

Such campaigns, incidentally, disprove many of the misconceptions traditionally advanced by above-the-line-based critics of the 'below-the-line' disciplines. Indeed these campaigns exhibit true integration of all elements of the marketing communications mix – no discipline is inherently deemed to be superior, although there is generally a lead discipline which needn't be advertising. The message, theme and tone of voice are all carried through so that, for example, the direct mail is not tacky, cheap-looking or in any way damaging to the brand image; blue-chip clients such as those featured above would hardly be likely to accept any other state of affairs.

My own view is that few, if any, brands can be adequately built solely by 'below-the-line' techniques but that creative synergy and integrity through-the-line is entirely possible (and highly desirable). The above-the-line components of the campaign achieve awareness and attitude shift on which the below-the-line draws to build enduring one-to-one relationships and achieve measurable increases in sales – all disciplines coexist harmoniously. It is interesting to note that few marketers would be able to defend a complete disparity between TV and press advertising for a given brand, while at the same time their point-of-sale material, trade incentive scheme leaflet and sales presenters might appear to follow a completely different corporate identity manual and few would even question it. One somehow expects TV and press to integrate; but this is largely a product of the above-below-the-line division which, as I argue throughout this book, is largely an artificial one.

An analogy sometimes drawn by advertising account planners is that of the brand as 'friend'. You expect your friends, by and large, to exhibit consistent and relatively predictable characteristics. You don't expect them to be a completely different person from one day to the next (hence the need for consistency of brand communication over time).

Nor do you expect them to behave differently when you meet them in the street from how they behave as a guest in your home, or when they write to you, or speak to you on the telephone (hence the need for consistency of communication across media). There is certainly ample evidence that the consumer makes no differentiation between messages emanating from a brand depending on how they are delivered; tone of voice and message must be recognizably similar. When properly constructed, such multi-media campaigns can indeed achieve synergy, that is, the whole becomes more than the sum of the parts (1+1 = 3).

A typical example campaign schedule for the integrated launch of a new product might be:

- *Week 1*   Pre-launch 'sell-in' presentations to key retailers/wholesalers
- *Week 1*   Forty-second TV commercial breaks; 96-sheet posters go up
- *Week 2*   Press ads break in Sunday colour magazines
- *Week 3*   Direct mail/door-to-door to generate store traffic
- *Week 4*   In-store displays/featuring as full distribution is achieved
- *Week 5*   Follow-up direct mail to non-respondents. More press to build mailing lists.

Experience suggests that the heavy-duty brand-building awareness advertising (TV and colour press) should be used to 'kick-start' the campaign, after which the more hard-hitting response-oriented below-the-line activity can be used to turn awareness into action (sales).

As we have touched on elsewhere, planning, creating, researching, fine-tuning and executing a campaign in a *single medium* (for example, TV, press or direct mail) is a challenging and demanding task at the best of times.

Multimedia campaigns present whole new challenges in terms of creative 'translation' from one medium to another, production schedules (for example, point-of-sale material production takes longer than the procedure for press ads, so that the photography schedule should be driven by the lead-times required for the former, say) and, most fundamentally, the apportionment of the available budget between the various 'candidate' media. Still, these challenges are there to be tackled and overcome and, as many campaigns illustrated in this book show, it can be done.

Although this book is primarily aimed at those concerned with strategic issues in marketing communications, it is appropriate at this point to address creative issues, and specifically the various techniques required to create effective brand-building and response-generating communications.

As argued previously, it is undoubtedly possible to approach all the elements of the communications mix from a holistic viewpoint. However, it must be recognized that specific creative approaches will be most appropriate in certain media to fulfil particular communications briefs.

Next we examine the techniques used by creative people to achieve certain communications goals. First, the universals:

- Attention
- Interest
- Desire
- Conviction
- Action

This list, which may already be familiar to some readers, constitutes what is termed, especially by advertising planners, as the 'buyer behavioural model', which seeks to break down the process by which purchase decisions are made into stages; at each stage we are dealing with a different mental process and thus a different creative challenge.

The model can be used as a checklist against which to assess the effectiveness of a marketing communication in any medium. An understanding of how and why people buy is naturally fundamental to the creation and targeting of any such communication, which must, as a minimum, sequentially grab the target's attention, convince them of the desirability of the product and lead to the desired action (which could be anything from experiencing 'a nice warm feeling' to placing an immediate telephone order).

Retaining this breadth of approach, we examine each stage in turn.

ATTENTION

Our communication must achieve an immediate engagement with the consciousness of the consumer (the prospective purchaser of our product/ service). In the first five seconds of our TV commercial, the picture and headline of our press ad, the introductory two lines of our telephone script, and in the envelope 'teaser line' of the direct mail, we are fighting the creative's worst enemy, which can kill all our creative efforts stone dead – Inertia. Human nature adopts the line of least resistance – we are all to some extent lazy, and assimilating someone else's selling communication is, generally speaking, hard work. To minimize the effort required, to somehow inveigle the reader into participation, needs real creative skill, based on an instinctive (or learned) grasp of how people consume advertising communications. It is not impossible – after all, most of us watch films or read for interest and pleasure at one time or another.

Not far behind the dreaded Inertia comes another foe – Distraction. This takes the shape of 'competitive noise'. Our precious target consumer is certain to have other things to do and people to see, and of course we must allow for the plethora of competing communications messages, all fighting for the consumer's attention. As consumers of advertising (and indeed of any external information) we are all *editors*. If something fails to interest us, we ruthlessly switch off (mentally, and in some cases literally) and turn our precious, scarce resource of attention towards something more attractive.

For all these reasons, we 'have a job on'; we need 'stand-out' (and indeed 'cut-through'). It is absolutely essential that our communication gets off to a powerful and attention-grabbing start, so – shout, amuse, arouse (?), entertain, stop the audience *but don't lose them – if they switch off now, you're finished.*

INTEREST

To have any chance of selling to our audience, we must first interest them. As we have noted, 'You can't *bore* the consumer into buying your product!' Having grabbed the consumer's attention with our explosive start, we must now harness that attention by turning it into a real and growing interest.

To interest your prospect, talk about something that matters to them. Tell them news. Make a powerful offer; suggest you're about to make them richer, more attractive, happier. Engage their attention by starting a story in an intriguing way (learn from newspaper journalists how to do this – they're fighting a similar battle to win readers).

Work hard on the detail of your communication: prune surplus words ruthlessly, use the language your audience speaks; make it relevant. Above all, keep them hooked, or everything you've achieved so far will be wasted. Consider the analogy of the door-to-door salesperson; you're now in the customer's living room and they're making you a cup of tea – get your samples case open quick and start showing them something they'll like the look of; drive home those benefits. Turn on the charm, turn up the charisma. Above all, don't let up – you're on a knife-edge here, the minute you get boring you'll be 'gonged', that is, shown the door. So choose every word carefully, keep it pacy, unfold your story, introduce a new twist, tell them something interesting – hang on to them!

DESIRE

It is now time for you to make the prospect *want* whatever you're selling. You must create desire. As evidenced by many film stars/sex symbols/pin-ups, this emotion need not have any firm basis in reason – somehow something you tell them, or show them or even better don't show them but rather suggest (that is, make them imagine) must produce a want. The desired 'take-out' (however arrived at) is:

'I want that – I must have it.'

This is the ideal; in certain cases, you may instead be prepared to settle for

'Mmmm . . . that might be nice . . .'

This emotional stage of the buyer behaviour model/selling process is essential and cannot be bypassed. The key is to turn product or service *features* into *benefits*. A common mistake among trainee sales executives (and junior copywriters/art directors) is to stop at the *features* without spelling out the *benefits*. Consider the effect of doing this, for example, in selling to a grocery retailer:

'This soap powder contains our fantastic new titanium accelerator' (FEATURE)

which means that:

'You'll sell more at a premium price and generate more turnover/ profit' (BENEFIT)

or to a consumer:

'the new Zeta 500 is fitted with our own L series engine' (FEATURE)

which means that:

'You'll be able to accelerate effortlessly from 0 to 60 mph in 7.8 seconds' (BENEFIT)

The most likely reaction when the salesperson stops at the features is: 'So what?'

Use this as a 'check' for your selling copy. Don't allow your buyer to say or even think 'So what?' Sell the benefits and create *desire* – this emotion can be experienced by *any* individual, given the right communication (honest) and is an essential stage in the selling process.

CONVICTION

Although emotion is important, we all have a rational side as well, and purchase decisions are about spending money, which, to a greater or lesser extent, is a limited commodity for each of us. We must convince ourselves that we can *afford* whatever we want to buy; we must in effect give ourselves 'permission to purchase'. Without this, the emotional longing will be overridden by the rational conscience: 'I can't really afford that this month.' Thus the creative work of our marketing communication must supply this *justification*, effectively convincing the consumer that 'they deserve' to make this purchase and that they should yield to the desire we have just created and move on to the next stage of the purchase process. This step may not be purchase as such; we merely seek, for the moment, a request for more information, so that the buyer reaches the 'conviction' stage. So desire must be followed by conviction, or our communication will not succeed.

ACTION

This is more relevant to 'below-the-line' action-oriented communications (as in 'CALL NOW') but is applicable to all marketing communications to some extent – we want some 'take-out' and, in many cases, specific action. This could be a telephone order or information request, or a trial purchase in a supermarket, or even a decision to test-drive a particular car when a change of vehicle is due next year. In any case, we must do what all salespeople are trained to do – close the sale. We must leave the consumer of our communication in absolutely no doubt about what they have to do. Spell it out without apology; the call to action (coupon, reply card, TV response end-frame) is no place for coyness or over-cleverness. If we do not urge the response we are seeking right at the end of our communication, we are missing a vital opportunity and may even fall at the final hurdle. The novice salesperson may miss getting the order from a buyer who is both willing and able to buy because he/she is too inexperienced, too faint-hearted, or even too *shy* to close, so take your courage in both hands and – *ask for the order.* You may be surprised how readily it is given, once you summon up the courage.

John Caples, the famous US copywriter, offered five rules for writing headlines:

1. Get *self-interest* into the headline
2. Get *news* into the headline
3. Merely to *arouse curiosity* is not enough
4. Be *positive*
5. Offer *quick and easy reward.*

His advice is as valid today as when it was written and applies as much to the Internet and DRTV commercials as to posters or press ads.

Finally in this section, let us recognize the role of pictures as opposed to words, of design and art direction as compared with copy. A picture does indeed in some cases paint a thousand words. Most of us think visually some of the time; some of us, most of the time. Illustrations and photographs can work with words to evoke strong emotions from deep within us. Hence the power of TV as a medium, combining sound with moving colour pictures. The skilful expression of imaginative ideas using a combination of words and pictures is the essence of a truly creative marketing communication.

Creative people in communications agencies

The very word 'creative' evokes in some people's minds images of out-of-touch, scruffy, surly, massively overpaid individuals (traditionally, it has to be said, males) who favour long hair and long lunches, the former generally in pony-tails, the latter in Soho/Covent Garden wine bars. During the few short hours they are actually in the agency, they sit about in their offices reading *Campaign*, drinking coffee and Soave from the creative director's fridge, and making 'phone calls, either to arrange elements of their complex and demanding social life or to their headhunter to discuss their next (even more overpaid) job at the agency across the road.

Occasionally, however (so this extreme view has it), the Muse descends on them (generally around 3.30 p.m. as they are returning from the pub to drink a (free) double espresso before heading for home); an idea strikes and they scribble down something like:

'Heineken refreshes the parts other beers cannot reach' or

'Happiness is a cigar called Hamlet' or

'The world's favourite airline'

Anyway the idea 'flies'; it is even deemed to 'have legs', and thus exhibits the magical property of 'campaignability'. The account director loves it. The client loves it, and equally important, can convince his/her finance director to spend $X million on it. This of course, makes the client's brand famous. It makes their agency famous. It also makes the creative people individually (and personally) famous. And more expensive. They are consequently promoted to be directors on the agency board. Then the group board. Then they are made international vice presidents. The agency is fast running out of sufficiently grand titles to award them. Their already ludicrous salaries are hiked yet again (since the agency now desperately wants to keep its newly discovered 'stars' and anyway, it's the client's money). Their company cars are upgraded from Porsche 911s to Ferraris. They now spend even less time in the office, getting in later and taking even longer lunches – sometimes (especially in the spring and summer) they fly off (business-class, *naturellement*) to review the creative work in Paris or Rome. However, as long as the 'big ideas' come sufficiently often, their agency is happy, their reputation continues to grow, no one puts them under any undue pressure and the gravy train stays firmly on the rails, with all the above excess cheerfully funded by the agency's shareholders. Nice work if you can get it – oh to be 'creative'!

So much, then, for the cynical view of agency creative people – most often expressed in terms similar to those used above, by those who have never even set foot inside a communications agency of any sort. It is, of course, a gross distortion of reality; it contains a germ of truth in describing a very small number of creative superstars in above-the-line London agencies in the boom days of the mid–late 1980s, but this was, even then, a tiny minority, all but killed off by the savage recession that followed. The vast majority of creative people in all sorts of communications agencies have always worked hard, under considerable pressure; rewards have admittedly been significant for the few who rose to the top of the tree, as in most professions, but even they are generally regarded to be 'only as good as their last ad', and even superstars have been made redundant as a convenient way of achieving a sizeable saving on the salary bill when times became hard.

A contrasting (but equally inaccurate) view of agency creative people is held by those for whom the very word 'creative' conjures up mysterious and intoxicating images. For them (often aspiring art school students, would-be copywriters or envious junior clients) to be 'creative' (and specifically, to be the creative director of a major agency) is to have arrived – to be gifted beyond the dreams of mere mortals, to be possessed of that magical ability to sprinkle 'Disney Dust' over everything that one touches, and to be able to draw on some mystical inner force to literally *create* award-winning advertising out of nothing!

Needless to say, these gods, these leviathans of the pen and magic marker (or in these days, the word processor package and Apple Macintosh) must, in the opinion of their disciples (both inside and outside agencies), never be gainsaid. However ambitious, however expensive, however apparently ridiculous their ideas might appear, the creative director always knows best and must be obeyed without hesitation and, above all, without question, particularly about costs. (Admittedly the recession reduced the size of the group who espouse this view of creativity!)

'Creative' is an overused word in the marketing communications industry. In its most general sense, it is used to indicate that a concept (or a person) contains an *idea* – this is the crux of creativity in this chapter. It also connotes imagination, vision, lateral thinking and empathy with the target audience – their wants, needs, concerns, hopes and aspirations (and perhaps also their fears, paranoia, greed and even lusts). On this basis, anyone involved with marketing communications (client, account handler, media planner, art director) can contribute creatively to the effectiveness of the communications material (TV commercial, press ad, direct mail pack and so on). More specifically, as we saw in the first section of this chapter (page 114), the description 'creative' is applied to certain job functions within an advertising (or sales promotion or direct marketing) agency; we have, in the modern agency structure, a 'creative department' headed, generally, by a single 'creative director'. In this context, 'creative' describes the job task, rather than implying anything about the value of that individual's contribution. A typical structure might be as in Figure 6.3.

The creative department structure shown in Figure 6.3 and prevalent from the 1970s to the 1990s, assumes that each creative team consists of:

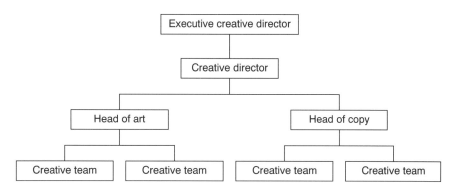

Figure 6.3 Creative department structure

1. An art director, broadly responsible for pictures, visuals and the overall 'look' of an ad; and
2. A copywriter, broadly responsible for the words

(This is admittedly a pretty small 'team' in any normal interpretation of the word.)

These two individuals typically have a very close, often long-term working relationship, having worked together as a team at several different agencies on a variety of accounts. In some cases, there is such a meeting of minds that a communications idea is somehow *created* between them, with the copywriter often contributing visually and the art director coming up with copylines. Such is the mystery of the advertising (or direct marketing or sales promotion) creative process, which is very exciting when it really works well – the ether crackles, sparks fly and genuine imagination is brought to bear on an often seemingly mundane task of selling a product or service. This is what it is about, of course, and perhaps partially explains why the best agency creative people do command substantial salaries; in general they pay back several times over in terms of the business they *attract* to the agency and the business they *keep* by their communications ideas which is, effectively, what clients are buying from the agency.

The copy/art team arrangement is a relatively recent one, however; in the agencies of the 1950s and 1960s, different structures were found, as David Ogilvy has related when discussing his early career in his book *Confessions of an Advertising Man*. For example, a copywriter might receive a brief from a 'rep' (a job title from which most modern-day account managers/directors would undoubtedly recoil in horror). The writer would then toil away in his office, and when he finally emerged with a finished ad, he would take it up two floors (say) to the art department for 'finishing off' (that is, attaching a suitable picture and making it 'look pretty'). Today the creative process is much more a team effort, with ideas coming first, and the words and pictures being arrived at via a fusion of two (or more) people's creative brainpower.

Modern-day creative directors have sometimes introduced 'non-standard' methods of working. For instance Dave Trott, in his massively successful creative department at Gold Greenlees Trott in the 1970s and 1980s, operated a much less formal structure, with 'teams' being made and unmade on a project basis, and often a free-for-all on a pitch, with many throwing in their ideas and 'The Man' arbitrating and decreeing which ideas merited further development, and which made it to the final presentation. Famous campaigns to emerge from this process included 'Hello Tosh Gotta Toshiba?' and 'Ariston and on'. (Dave Trott's 'school' of none-too-subtle creativity has been likened to 'a brick through the consumer's window with the client's name attached to it'.)

It is also important to note the differing attitudes to creativity between specialist advertising, direct marketing and sales promotion agencies. Whereas certain ad agencies have placed creativity on a pedestal as their unique selling proposition (particularly prevalent where one or more founding partners is a creative person by background), direct marketing agencies have tended to be more hard-nosed, response-oriented, dominated by copywriters, and generally more suspicious of what David Ogilvy described as 'The Big Idea' and of what they might consider to be self-indulgent ad agency hype/waffle. Traditional specialist sales promotion agencies, on the other hand, have, generally speaking, grown up by fulfilling the needs of FMCG manufacturing companies for on-pack promotions and in-store/point-of-sale material. Admittedly, such activity needs a degree of 'creativity' in terms of coming up with ideas (for example, whizzy gadgets as free gifts, themes for prize draws and competitions, and novel ways of persuading consumers to 'trial' a given product), as well as a strong design/visual element, but sales promotion typically requires less input in terms of copy (that is, well-reasoned sales arguments). For these reasons, sales promotion agencies tend to be well stocked with art directors, designers, visualizers and Mac operators of varying degrees of conceptual and manual ability, but to have few, if any, specialist copywriters. The limited number of words which are required tend to be supplied by the junior account management (who in any case are more familiar with the legal terms and conditions applying to a free prize draw or a competition/contest of skill). The relatively diminished role of the creative function in (some) sales promotion agencies, compared with advertising and direct marketing shops, also puts more onus on sales promotion account management to supply *ideas* (that is, to be 'creative'). Thus, as we have noted in the first section of this chapter, whereas an aspiring advertising or direct marketing account executive would hope to convince potential employers that he/she was well organized, capable of strategic thinking, persuasive, charming, they would certainly lay no claim to being 'creative' (that being someone else's job!). By contrast, a sales promotion account manager would be expected to exhibit 'creativity' in abundance.

Thus, although creativity means different things to different people, there is certainly no doubt that it is a vital ingredient of any successful marketing communication. Many individuals' successful careers have been based on real or perceived 'creative talent'. Creativity has launched and sustained famous and successful agencies. Knowing where to find it, recognizing it when one sees it, and judging how much to pay for it are arguably the most relevant skills any marketing director can possess. For an agency, hiring, motivating and getting the best out of creative talent is a crucial determinant of profitability, that is, success.

Creativity in 'other' disciplines/media

This book has so far dealt with direct marketing and its role within a 'twenty-first century' integrated communications mix alongside advertising and sales promotion.

We now move on to discuss what Kevin Morley, the founder of the UK integrated agency KMM (now part of Ammirati Puris Lintas in London), has termed 'the other stuff'. We could also call them the forgotten media. But hang on – haven't we covered them already? What's left, after all, given that we've already dealt with direct marketing, sales promotion and advertising (in Chapters 1, 2 and 3)? OK – so suppose we include telephone marketing and door-to-door distribution, advertorial features and sales force/dealer incentive schemes within an enlarged direct marketing/sales promotion bucket (covered in Chapters 1 and 2). Surely that's it, now? Well, no – what about:

- PR
- Design (packaging/new product development/corporate identity)
- Sponsorship (and product placement on films and TV)
- Conferences (for employees, dealers, distributors and so on)
- Exhibitions

• New electronic/interactive media (already touched on in Chapter 4)?

The answer, of course, is that all these media can act as part of the communications mix, and that imaginative and powerful creative ideas can shine through from each and every one. To conclude our examination of the creative process, let us examine each of these 'other' media in turn.

PR

Cynics have dubbed PR professionals 'spin doctors', reflecting the view of their role as that of putting a spin (gloss) on the product, to minimize its downside/drawbacks and accentuate its strengths.

Following this line of thought, PR could be defined as 'the art of making your organization/product/service look good'. However, this not a wholly satisfactory definition of PR, as the same could be said to apply to most other communications disciplines (including advertising, direct marketing and sales promotion).

Thomas L. Harris, in his 1991 book, *The Marketer's Guide to Public Relations*, ventured the more comprehensive, albeit somewhat wordy definition:

> Marketing Public Relations is the process of planning, executing and evaluating programs that encourage purchase and consumer satisfaction through credible communication of information and impressions that identify companies and their products with the needs, wants, concerns and interests of consumers.

Philip Kotler, famous for his widely accepted framing of what marketing is and what marketers do, has suggested, more concisely, that PR helps a company to achieve its objectives by 'serving as protector and promoter of the company's image among its various publics'. These publics, or 'key stakeholders' can be considered to include:

• customers and potential customers
• employees and potential employees
• shareholders (and potential shareholders)
• others (legislators, journalists, opinion formers and the like).

If all these parties can be kept happy and positive, then the organization's PR machine is indeed working successfully.

So much for definitions. To get down to practicalities, it may be more useful to explain what is included within PR, as set out in what follows.

Media relations

This is the area of greatest PR activity: putting one's case to the aforementioned key publics via TV, press and radio in an editorial context, ensuring the 'right' things are said by spokespersons whom the public believe and, it is hoped, digested by the viewer/listener/reader in the right media. Favourable editorial coverage can often be far more credible and persuasive than obviously 'paid-for' advertising space. Indeed, some PR agencies do little other than media relations. We could also stray into the area of advertorial features here, a potential area of overlap/conflict between PR, sales promotions and even advertising agencies. The skills required here are various: having a clear understanding of which are the key media; knowing who controls what goes out in a given medium; and understanding how they make their decisions as to what will interest their viewers/listeners. Successful media relations needs a combination of marketing understanding and practical know-how in terms of the day-to-day logistics of securing column inches/broadcast minutes. It is much more than the relatively simple matter of sending out a stream of press releases to a list of journalists.

Stunts/events

Skilful PR agents can actually go out and create 'photo opportunities', that is, they can get secure free column inches of media coverage by engineering an occurrence which the news media lap up because they believe it will interest their readers/viewers. As with other aspects of media relations, a thorough grasp of what the media want, and how to control what they are given, is essential to successful exploitation of these opportunities.

Crisis management

Every organization dreads the day when it faces a major PR crisis, for example, the oil company whose tanker leaks, the food company whose product is contaminated, the political party whose leader is the subject of a personal scandal. It is crucial to have a plan ready in advance to handle this, and specialist crisis management PR agencies have carved out a highly lucrative niche for themselves. Setting up 'crisis lines' for consumers to telephone for 'the facts' and handling the media (appearances on TV, radio and timely dispatch of positive press releases) are vital ingredients of these damage limitation exercises. It is, generally speaking, too late to start considering a plan when the crisis has already struck. Examples of successful crisis management include Procter and Gamble's rapid and complete withdrawal of its 'Rely' tampon when it was linked to 'toxic shock syndrome' in the late 1970s, and Nestlé's handling of the 'benzene in Perrier' scare a decade later. Shell Oil had a less happy PR experience in 1995 with its on–off plans to sink its Brent Spar platform in the North Sea. Prompt, decisive and responsible actions in these situations can, paradoxically, actually enhance a company's market position since it thereby comes across as responsible, well organized and concerned for the welfare of the public – a classic example of turning a negative into a positive.

Parliamentary lobbying

This is a sensitive and difficult area. At its most ethical, it means acting as an advocate to ensure the client's voice is heard in the forum where decisions are taken, that is, fairly putting a case, as is one's democratic right. Difficulties arise when questions are asked about the extent of the pressure being brought to bear/encouragement offered to those in a position to change the law in order to smooth the path of the activities of the client organization. Ex-government ministers are frequently recruited into these organizations, arguably less for their marketing skills than for their 'little black books' of influential contacts who will always be happy to meet them for a chat/a bite of lunch.

Nevertheless lobbying is a legitimate practice: MPs are responsible to their constituents who have a right (and arguably a duty) to make their views known on issues that are of concern to them. Some highly professional and highly ethical organizations operate in this specialized field, which requires a detailed knowledge of how government/parliament functions and of who the key decision makers/policy influencers are.

DESIGN

This used to be done by the client in-house, or by a junior art director at the ad agency, but no longer. Design reached its zenith in the 1980s, spawning various specialist sub-categories (retail, point-of-sale, packaging/new product development design, corporate literature/annual reports and so on) and despite massive cut-backs during the early 1990s recession, has recovered strongly and is generally now recognized as a discipline in its own right. Certainly the importance of the overall corporate identity to the coherence of an organization's integrated communications is these days beyond dispute. A common overall *look* to all communications is a necessary, but not in itself sufficient condition for truly integrated communications. A properly conceived and carefully implemented corporate identity (CI) can be one of the key determinants of corporate image. The CI manual (laying down all aspects of design from use of logos to typefaces and colour schemes) should be an essential reference work for all those involved in the design, creative and production aspects of all marketing communications.

SPONSORSHIP

This can be variously considered as a branch of sales promotion, a subset of PR, or a discipline in its own right. It is certainly big business in the US and European markets, and is growing everywhere. The main areas are sports and arts, and the objective is the simple one of linking the sponsor's name/brand with an event/property which has positive connotations for its customers/potential customers and which thereby confers a 'halo effect' on the client. For this benefit, the owners of the events are learning to charge serious money, and the whole discipline is becoming increasingly sophisticated and competitive. Specialist sponsorship agencies are appointed to secure suitable sponsors for their client properties (football teams/championships, Formula One motor racing teams, athletics championships, rock artist tours, ballet, opera and so on). Such agencies may also offer to handle PR/merchandise, communications/advertising as part of an overall package. A growing area in the UK is that of educational sponsorship, as state schools increasingly seek outside funding for computers, books and other course materials. Undoubtedly this area is one where creativity, both in terms of imaginative sponsorship ideas and in communicating the linkage between the event and the sponsor, has an important role to play.

CONFERENCES

These are, in a sense, the 'odd discipline out' in that they are essentially inward-facing media; they are concerned with internal audiences (employees, dealers/distributors) rather than customers, that is, they are not 'marketing' disciplines at all. However, such internal audiences are crucial to the success of any marketing programme. They should, ideally, be fervent advocates of a given planned marketing initiative so that they actively merchandise and promote the product/service to the target (marketing) audience – this applies especially to those employees who face customers, either in person or over the telephone.

Hence many major blue-chip organizations are now assigning substantial budgets to sales force/dealer conferences and employee training/motivation programmes, and finding that they more than pay for themselves in terms of increased efficiency and productivity and an enhanced overall marketing/sales orientation throughout the organization, particularly the crucial customer-facing staff. These events generally work best when they achieve real 'business theatre', which makes a powerful impact and leaves an impression which will be retained for months and even years to come. Creativity in internal communications, harmonized with that of the customer marketing programmes, is a vital component of these communications.

EXHIBITIONS

For most business-to-business marketers and a significant proportion of consumer marketers, this area is an important part of the marketing mix. It has the advantage of being one of the few ways in which a company can contrive to have its customers and prospects come to it; they will seek it out without any need to be chased, pursued or hunted down. In just three days (say) an office equipment manufacturer (say) could have 300 of its key (potential) customers visit its stand, meet the sales manager, hand over a business card, have their key requirements logged (for later follow-up), watch a corporate video, drink a complimentary glass of wine and walk away with a handful of professionally produced (and highly relevant) company brochures. Great!

However, few decision makers who pay for the design and building of a company's site and stand at exhibitions are entirely comfortable about the extent of the pay-back from this activity. There is a disturbing element of 'our competitors are always here, so we have to be too', and there is a recognized phenomenon of 'stand one-upmanship', whereby competitive companies vie to outspend each other and thereby presumably out-impress the customers. Incremental sales derived purely from presence at exhibitions are hard to measure precisely and the costs extend beyond the space and the stand to supporting literature (much of it wasted) and the significant opportunity cost of the (normally senior) personnel whose week is devoted to manning the stand and glad-handing the attendees. One of the problems is the 'time-waster' syndrome. Staff time and promotional literature are scarce resources, and the most effective exhibitors are those who successfully minimize wastage of each. Resources must be allocated as far as possible to key prospects, and a good system for separating the wheat from the chaff (such as qualifying enquiries) is essential. Many exhibitions go through a recognized cycle: slow initial take-up, followed (in subsequent years) by increased attendance (often for defensive reasons), then disillusionment, with one key player staying away, then widespread drop-outs, and eventual death of the event (only to be relaunched under a different banner the following year).

Despite this, many companies rightly regard exhibitions as a necessary and cost-effective element of their total marketing mix. Creativity, especially in stand design and communications, will be needed to secure the highest-value attendees and deliver them into the hands of key sales personnel at the exhibition.

NEW ELECTRONIC/INTERACTIVE MEDIA

What has been called the 'information superhighway' is already with us, although what we mean by the expression is far from universally agreed. A full discussion of all the new media opportunities is beyond the scope of this book. We have touched on the Internet and the World Wide Web in Chapter 4 above. What is clear is that these media are changing so fast that fresh predictions appear to be needed each month, and even expert media 'futurists' publicly disagree about the shape of the future. Certainly it would appear that cable TV (with two-way images and electronic messages transmitted to and from every home) will be part of the future at least for the next 20 or so years. Home entertainment will be revolutionized by 'video on demand' (dial a movie on a pay-per-view basis) and there will be a rapid convergence of the technologies of home computers/TV/video/audio and telephone. Telephones will be personal and portable: within the first half of the next century, the offices of the twentieth century, cluttered with a forest of cables, leads and wires will be an amusing anachronism. Mobile, wireless communications will progressively dominate, and consumers will be able to access a plethora of TV channels and other electronic information sources at will. Messages will be transmitted increasingly by electronic means. Facsimile and e-mail will progressively replace printed mail, as electronic publishing partially substitutes for printed newspapers.

All this technology already exists. The specific shape of the future will be determined by a combination of economics and consumer preferences – what will people be prepared to pay for and what will they reject as an extravagance? Will people dominate the technology and succeed in editing their own consumption (like disciplined TV viewers who today use their VCR to consume exactly what they choose and nothing else), or will the competing messages produce consumer overload and confusion? There is certainly a role for programme and event sponsorship in a future where identifiable advertising messages are simply 'tuned out' by sophisticated consumers. In situations where people are willing and able to buy, the right message, conveyed via the right medium, will always make the sale. The challenge for marketers, creatives and media planners will be to exploit the strengths of these media of the future to take the product to the consumer in new and imaginative ways. In any case, it seems certain that, as the media available to the marketer continue to multiply and mutate at sometimes bewildering speed, the need for creative communications ideas that catch and hold the target's attention, cutting through the competitive clutter, will be as great as ever.

So much, then, for these 'forgotten media': each can play a valuable role in a company's communications mix. It would, of course, be ludicrous to suggest that they all need to be used in every situation – budget realities alone preclude this – but these media/disciplines should always be considered. Integrated media planning must be dispassionate and wide-ranging. The dictum 'no lead discipline' should be the motto of all true marketing communications integrationists.

'Creativity sans frontières'

This book has made a case for viewing direct marketing as working alongside the other, complementary communications media, within an integrated marketing communications mix.

However, we have not so far considered the geographical context of such activity: must each country represent its own marketing microsystem, or should we be thinking, and acting, on a broader scale? In other words, should integration of marketing communications go 'through the line' but still stop 'at the border', or should integrated campaigns cross national boundaries?

In this electronic age, the world certainly seems much smaller than it did even 15 to 20 years ago. With broadcast TV, satellite, cable and newer 'interactive' media, including electronic mail/the Internet and so on, more and more consumers are exposed to more and more images and messages originating many miles from the location in which they receive them. No allowance is made for national boundaries and variations in language, culture and currency.

In addition, an increasing proportion of the world's population is travelling more and more regularly across international frontiers. Many companies are now trading across continents and a number even on a global scale. In particular, many packaged goods manufacturers are now marketing similar or identical products to consumers in many different countries.

So should marketing communications, from advertising to direct marketing to promotions, be planned, created and implemented internationally? Certainly there is much evidence that, by and large, people the world over, both as consumers and business decision makers, are similar in terms of their wants, need, motivations, ideas and beliefs, and that in terms of marketing communications, what works in one market will generally work in another.

Consider the range of benefits that can be derived from, say, creating a single pan-European advertising campaign:

- one set of agency fees for creating a single set of ads;
- one commercial to be shot;
- one photographic shoot for press ads, direct mail, point-of-sale and so on;
- aggregated media-buying muscle applied to cross-border media sales points; and hence
- significant economies of creation, production and delivery of advertising messages.

Moreover, consider the benefits of consistency (remember 'a brand should be as dependable as a friend') and of maintaining strategic and creative integrity across boundaries, so that a consumer in Wolverhampton watching an Italian League football match on TV will recognize the logos of Kodak, Nike, Mobil and Xerox around the perimeter of the pitch in Naples, say, as representing the same brands s/he chooses in the high street or at the office the next day. Similarly the Danish businessman relaxing in his Frankfurt hotel notes the satellite TV commercial for American Express and makes a mental note to pay his bill with his card the next morning – same name, same logo, same imagery, same ad and, above all, the same brand values. Car commercials can work in a number of countries, with the film 'flipped' between left- and right-hand drive markets and with different sound tracks, as can soft drink or fragrance commercials, for a fraction of the cost of originating individual (and idiosyncratic) ads on a country-by-country basis.

So much for the case *for* cross-border integration, but we must be equally aware of the arguments *against* rushing into it:

- *Language and cultural differences.* There are famous stories of the pitfalls of international branding from the damaging (for example, Krapp toilet tissue and various products branded Fanny) to the potentially amusing (like the Mitsubishi Starion – Japanese stable-mate to the Colt, perhaps?

– and the Volkswagen Sharan). Some international brand names may make a lot more sense in languages other than English, and of course this works between any two languages in the world, which gives plenty of scope for getting it wrong.

- *Variations in the legislation.* What can one advertise, what can one say about it, where can one say it? This is more of a factor in some specific markets, for example, pharmaceuticals, alcoholic drinks and toys. Germany has, generally speaking, the most restrictive regime in this respect.
- *Data protection and promotional legislation.* Laws in this area can affect 'cold calling' by mail or telephone and can effectively outlaw gift with purchase offers, incentive schemes and list rental in certain countries.
- *Variations in branding and distribution between countries by a given advertiser* (often a perfectly rational response to the above factors).

Let us also consider how valuable the benefits suggested above actually are to a real-world trading company. Unless your product is available and consistently branded and positioned wherever the ad is received (say in its 'footprint' on a pan-European satellite channel) there will inevitably be some wastage at best, and at worst consumer confusion or even a negative impact. Achieving consistency between markets can be expensive (compare Mars's Marathon/Snickers, and Daz/Tide/Ariel/Persil across Europe).

Then there is the issue of the actual value of achieving consistency of image across borders. The proportion of the total population who are regular consumers of advertising messages in more than one country (in more than one language) is small indeed, so what is the actual benefit of having consumers in a number of discrete geographical markets feeling the same about a brand which they can buy and consume locally? In some cases, one suspects the benefits are more *perceived* (by the European marketing director in Brussels/Paris/Amsterdam/London or the president of the holding corporation in New York, say) than *real*, in terms of marketing effectiveness, as measured by incremental sales.

Orchestrating pan-European campaigns can also pose problems in respect of your agency partners: if you retain a pan-European (or even global) agency network, there is likely to be one lead office, where strategy and creative input is controlled centrally (typically between the agency office and the client head office) and the satellite offices are reduced to translators/adapters of someone else's ideas in line with the maxim: 'Think global – act local'.

This state of affairs is not particularly motivating or fulfilling for the staff of the various local offices, particularly the creative department, which, if it is any good, will always have a vested interest in arguing 'It's different here in Xland; you don't understand our market; we must be left alone to create our own country-specific ads which will save money overall, since they will be so much more effective.' The client's local office, if it has some national pride, may have a vested interest in backing the local agency office's protestations (or in some cases will even argue for appointing a local independent creative 'hot shop' which 'has a unique insight into how to sell to citizens of that region/country'). One way to organize pan-regional campaigns is to have a client company so structured that local offices follow, without question and to the letter, the instructions of the head office, namely to work with the local office of the (equally well-disciplined and also staffed and managed by 'corporate soldiers' who do as they're told) multinational agency appointed by the centre. This approach will be efficient, consistent to the point of uniformity, but, at the end of the day, not guaranteed to result in the most creative or effective marketing communications.

As we have discussed, creativity in marketing communications means *ideas*. A good creative department can make the difference between average, workmanlike, derivative communications and brilliant, famous, memorable campaigns; this applies regardless of media.

I believe that, generally speaking, since the early 1960s, the most talented (imaginative) creative people have resided in the creative departments of large above-the-line advertising agencies, with TV commercials generally showcasing the finest in the industry. The 30-second film (or if the creative director could swing it, 40- or even 90-second) has, for more than 20 years, been the ultimate for those on the creative side of the marketing communications business. Indeed, some of these epics have been closer to mini-feature films (in scope, imagination and sometimes budget) than to their predecessors, the early 1960s product demonstration soap powder/confectionery commercials. (Directors including Alan Parker and Ridley Scott have successfully combined the two genres within their careers.)

However, things are changing, fundamentally. The next phase in the history of marketing communications, and of marketing creativity, is already here. As we have noted, so-called 'below-the-line' disciplines are not only becoming recognized as commanding significant client budgets and attracting 'reasonable' account management personnel, but even as offering scope for genuine creative inspiration. Thus most working in marketing now believe that true creativity can these days also be found in specialist direct marketing, sales promotion or integrated agencies (see Chapter 9), and indeed, as media other than TV and colour press lose their stigma, top creative talent will increasingly be on show in below-the-line and integrated campaigns. Thus we join with Kevin Morley, founder of KMM when he says:

**If the idea's big enough, it will work
anywhere.**

With truly through-the-line communications, response versus creativity is a non-issue. The two should, and indeed must, go hand in hand.

7 THE MARKETING DATABASE

The relationship between a seller and a
buyer seldom ends when the sale is made.
In a great and increasing proportion of
transactions, the relationship actually
intensifies subsequent to the sale. This
becomes the critical factor in the buyer's
choice of the seller the next time around
. . . The sale merely consummates the
courtship. Then the marriage begins. How
good the marriage is depends on how well
the relationship is managed by the seller.

Theodore Levitt, 1983

A database should be designed actively to
achieve goals . . . Names should be
collected and transcribed into electronic
formats only if they will produce a profit. A
database is a marketing tool, and should be
designed to achieve marketing goals.

Edward Nash, 1994

As a general rule, the most successful man
in life is the man who has the best
information . . .

Benjamin Disraeli

If the real cost of manufacturing
automobiles had declined, since 1950, at
the same rate as the real cost of processing
information, it would be cheaper today to
abandon your Rolls Royce and buy a new
one rather than put a dime into a parking
meter.

Don Peppers and Martha Rogers, 1993

> Every 20 years the computational power
> that can be bought for one pound, has
> increased a thousandfold. There is more
> computational power in a new passenger
> car today than there was in the Apollo
> Spacecraft that went to the moon.
>
> Graeme McCorkell, 1990

Definitions/what can a database do?

For the purposes of this book, we shall use the following definition:

A marketing database is a collection of names and addresses of individuals (customers or prospects) together with relevant data about them.

As with many areas of marketing, much nonsense has been talked (and written!) on the subject of marketing databases. In the early days of direct marketing in the UK, the question didn't arise: databases were things that computer boffins tinkered with (generally on a mainframe computer that occupied a building about the size of a small factory). What honest, hard-working, unpretentious direct marketers were interested in was mailing lists! These, of course, were something everyone could understand, not much different from any other list (shopping, New Year's Honours, Civil, Christmas card and so on), except that these were names and addresses of people one might like to write to with the specific purpose of selling them things.

Great skill and not a little showmanship went into the art (or was it craft? – it certainly wasn't science) of compiling, maintaining and selecting from these lists. People actually began to find mailing lists interesting and some went so far in their enthusiasm as to set themselves up as list brokers, often acting as a cross between a quack doctor and a conjurer, taking a brief from a would-be direct mailer and, by some mysterious sleight-of-hand, producing, with a flourish, *exactly* the right list of people desperate to purchase the product or service the client was hoping to sell.

The lists that list brokers offered (some their own, some sourced externally from other brokers or from list managers employed by list owners) were from a variety of sources and of variable quality. The normal deal was for a 'one-off rental fee' to be paid by the client (the person or company wishing to do a mailing) which allowed them to mail the whole list once only. Any responses were the property of the mailer, and could be used as the basis of a new list of enquirers whom the client might wish to mail in the future.

One of the few costs in the whole area of marketing communications that is currently on a long-term downward trend is the cost of computing power. With each year that passes, it is becoming massively cheaper to store and manipulate data. This is over and above any short-term or cyclical recessionary/boom factors and is due to seemingly ever-accelerating technological progress. The computer, mentioned above, that filled the factory 20 years ago had computing power greatly inferior to that which now sits on most office desk-tops. Many of us now carry around electronic organizers which, had a soothsayer predicted them as recently as 15 years ago, would have amazed computer scientists. Our children regard computers as a completely normal part of everyday life and eagerly embrace each new electronic gadget (whether video game, home entertainment device or learning technique used in their school). The Internet and World Wide Web are rapidly becoming part of the media landscape. Computers are increasingly penetrating every aspect of our business and home lives and their presence is being felt in direct marketing more than in other areas of marketing.

These accelerating changes in our society go a long way towards explaining the almost incredible rise of the marketing database in modern marketing, as well as the meteoric rise of direct marketing as a marketing communications discipline during the 1970s and 1980s. Suddenly data were relatively cheap to store, manipulate, enhance and exploit; information about customers (and increasingly competitors' customers) became not only desirable and interesting, but increasingly affordable and easy to use.

Partly as a result of these factors, people in all fields of business and commerce have become much more comfortable about using computers (despite having generally no idea about their detailed workings or how to programme them – neither of which is any more necessary for a computer user than it is necessary to be a qualified mechanic in order to pass one's driving test). Data-driven marketing or database marketing has arrived.

These factors have been made even more relevant by the simultaneous trend towards segmentation in most of the previously mass consumer markets, so that media have fragmented, niches have proliferated, and it has become not merely desirable but more and more necessary to treat each customer as an individual, with distinct needs, wants, tastes and (yes) even dreams. In short, marketing information has become gold-dust and a whole industry has sprung up around the need to obtain it, improve it and use it with maximum cost-effectiveness as an essential marketing tool. The mailing list is dead – long live the marketing database.

In other words, a marketing database is just a fancy mailing list – and ignore anyone who tells you different. Take a mailing list, add some rudimentary facts and figures about each customer or prospect, perhaps 'overlay' some additional data from external sources (for example, one of the geodemographic market segmentation systems such as ACORN or MOSAIC, which operate on the premise that 'birds of a feather flock together', that is, we are – largely – where we live) and hey presto – you've got yourself a marketing database. The constituent data may have come from any one of a variety of sources – customer records, sales force records, branch records, dealer/retailer supplied data, responders to mailings or ads. When these data are put into a computer, assembled in a format in which they can be analysed and segmented, with extractions made according to any relevant criterion, then they become a powerful marketing tool and far more than a mailing list – a true marketing database.

In this chapter, we examine the planning, construction and exploitation of the marketing database. Ironically – although, as I shall demonstrate, it is fundamental to the new integrated (direct) marketing – the database has become perhaps the biggest barrier to the full integration of direct marketing and its exponents into the world of seamlessly integrated marketing communications planning, which is the subject of this book. For there is a perception that, unlike their colleagues in the other specialist communications disciplines, direct marketers 'know about computers'.

Non-direct marketing experts react to this misconception in two ways: either they are contemptuous of direct marketing exponents, viewing them as nothing more than a bunch of database boffins; or they are totally psyched out by such apparently cerebral, scientific types. In fact, as will become clear, with the exception of the (relatively few) technical experts in the hardware and software of marketing databases, direct marketers know little more about computers than do the traditional experts in advertising or sales promotion. The average account director in a specialist direct marketing agency couldn't write a computer program to save his/her life.

What direct marketers *do* know is, generally speaking, what computers can do for them in marketing terms. They should also have an overall understanding of the value of data and how they can be profitably employed in targeted marketing communications, but this, as they say, is hardly 'rocket science'. Indeed, understanding this much is important for all of the new generation of integrated marketers, for it is clear that database costs can only continue to fall and that database marketing can only gain in importance as a key part of the new integrated marketing mix.

So why build a marketing database at all? At the simplest level, there are two reasons. A marketing database can:

1. Help you to *understand* your customers and prospects better (ANALYSIS).
2. Help you to target appropriate *selling* messages to individual customers and prospects (COMMUNICATION).

No other possible uses for a marketing database are as valuable as these. (Few others are of *any* value.) Both are designed to help you to *sell* (as of course all your marketing activity should be – it's just a question of how soon you see the sales and of how patient you can afford to be).

Understanding your customers and prospects can include using your database for analysis and research of particular segments of your customer base, or of those prospects who have repeatedly enquired, but never converted to purchase. You can go on to identify your best (usually the most profitable) customers and examine what it is about them that makes them so right for you, that is, predisposed to purchase your product or service, and keep on doing so. This technique is known as *profiling* – it enables us to paint a picture of the sort of people most likely to be good customers for us. From here it is but a small step to finding others like them, using geodemographic segmentation tools (ACORN, MOSAIC and the like) and/or by purchasing or renting external data ('cold lists'). The location process is shown in Figure 7.1.

Figure 7.1 Location of customers and identification of new customers

Much has been written and said about databases, data-driven marketing, database marketing and so on. Much of it is unnecessary and unhelpful. The key reasons for subjecting yourself and your organization to the cost and effort of building and maintaining a marketing database are to know your customers and potential customers better, and to help you to sell more to them via one-to-one communications, that is, by direct marketing. Of course, many great minds are employed in building, enhancing and maintaining these beasts once the decision has been taken to take the plunge, but we should never lose sight of the underlying reason for the undertaking: a marketing database should *never* be an end in itself.

Building your database

In what follows, we shall tackle the key aspects of embarking on the process of database marketing in stages, as illustrated in Figure 7.2.

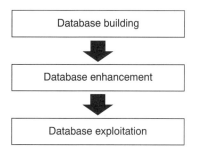

Figure 7.2 Database marketing

It is important that the right data are not only collected and stored, but stored in such a way as to be available when you need them, and in the form you need them. This means that technical people have a crucial role to play. Involve them early, explain what you want to be able to do with the database (that is, detail the desired 'functionality'), empower them to do what you need doing, and then watch them like a hawk. Bear in mind that in the real world of databases in real organizations, just because something is indisputably a good idea, technically possible (and probably even straightforward), none of this in any way implies that the organization will necessarily *do* it. Indeed, the interconnected processes of database construction, enhancement and exploitation, involving as they do many different individuals in various departments of the company, bring out some of the worst aspects of interdepartmental company politics and throw into sharp relief the inadequacies of communication between the various parties. Embarking on a programme of database marketing may represent a fundamental process of change within an organization; and change can represent threats to certain parties who will, out of suspicion or self-defence, oppose it, and in some cases actively attempt to sabotage the entire process. To compound the problem, companies are notoriously bad at communicating internally, requiring as this does time, effort and perseverance in activities for which one is likely to receive little or no credit or reward.

For all these reasons, the way that data are collected, assembled and then deployed for communications purposes may, to say the least, be 'suboptimal'. The effects on the perception of the company by the outside world are frequently dramatic and sometimes disastrous. Consider as an example the well-known (even today) scenario of the major financial services organization (let's call it Natleys Assurance) with four and a half customer databases and one prospect file, all held in different locations and all stored in different formats, with no interconnectivity and substantial (it is strongly suspected) overlap between them, and the five main Natleys marketing departments competing for marketing funds and never talking, far less integrating their efforts. Comments such as 'Don't start me on the politics of this place; and as for the IT department, they're a law unto themselves . . .' are still alarmingly common in this age of apparently integrated database marketing.

This scenario implies a number of potentially lost opportunities and an equal number of genuine threats: not only will the customer whose endowment policy pays out not be invited to apply for the new Natleys 21st Century Investment Bond, but a customer who has been paying into a Natleys whole-of-life policy for the last 15 years could receive a rather cold communication, treating her like a complete stranger and trying to sell her home contents insurance; even worse, the next day she might receive two separate mailings from Natleys selling motor insurance, one to her husband who passed away nearly three years ago (she quite clearly remembers telling her local Natleys branch at the time).

To minimize the occurrence of incidents such as the above, it is essential that the data on the marketing database are stored in such a way as to be accessible and available, with maximum speed and convenience (cost-effectiveness), for the marketing tasks to which we shall refer throughout this chapter. Also, support for the installation and exploitation of a marketing database must go right to the *top* of the organization, in order to rise above petty interdepartmental rivalries and sectional vested interests. So if you're responsible for implementing a programme of database marketing within your organization and you're not at the top yourself, find a sponsor or 'champion' who is.

Database structure or 'architecture' is an area for specialists: it is necessary to determine at the outset the key tasks the database will be required to perform; although flexibility is always built in, certain routes may be inadvertently sealed off at the earliest stage, unless those building the database are fully aware of the objectives and probable requirements of the intended users.

Let us now move to specifics. Suppose you have decided that a marketing database is appropriate for your organization, and that you have defined, in broad terms, the tasks you require your marketing database to perform (its 'functionality'). You are going to need certain data about each individual on the database, which will be held on that person's 'record'. A typical record structure is shown in Figure 7.3. The data are logically segmented into the following broad categories:

(A) DEMOGRAPHICS
• name
• address
• telephone number
• age
• married/single
• spouse name/age
• children sex/name(s)/age(s)
• occupation
  etc.

(B) PSYCHOGRAPHICS
• education
• hobbies
• interests (wine/gardening/football/clothes/literature etc.)
• holidays
• product preferences indicated.

(C) TRANSACTION HISTORY
• customer/prospect status
• communications received/responded to
• products enquired/purchased/dates/value/payment method
• competitive products purchased/dates
• salesperson/dealer/retailer/branch (contacts/dates)
• any other contacts ('member-get-member'), complaints, correspondence etc.

Figure 7.3 Marketing database – sample data record structure

• demographics (facts and figures about them, their households, their situation);
• psychographics (their hobbies, interests, lifestyles, wants, tastes and aspirations);
• transaction/communications history (what they've bought from us and from others and what contacts there have been between us and them, with what result).

The idea is that, for every individual on the database, all the fields indicated are filled (or 'populated'). If you have no immediate use for some of the data fields you have built in, fine; you are allowing yourself some flexibility you may be glad of later. However, beware the trap of building in too much flexibility and (worse) collecting and storing data you will never use: storing useless data clutters up your database, wastes time, and costs you money (like most data, they are also likely to go rapidly out of date). 'Nice to know' may be a luxury in this case; 'need to know' makes a lot more sense in terms of designing your database and planning your direct response datacapture vehicles (reply cards, coupons, competition leaflets, inbound telephone scripts and so on). At any rate, think about it and share your objectives with the technical people – find one who is bilingual (computer-speak and English, or whatever your native tongue is).

Thus it is essential that the functionality of the marketing database is borne in mind from the outset if it is to be suitably constructed. It is necessary to decide, as far as possible, what sort of selections you will wish to make (for example, 'all male customers between 25 and 35 years old, who are not in arrears and have indicated that they are likely to repurchase sometime in the next six months'), and what sorts of reporting you will require (the boffins will be happy to provide you with half a rainforest-worth of printout every day, so think carefully!). There will certainly be a cost involved in building in extra functions up front, but the alternative – suddenly deciding, two years after your marketing database has gone live, that you want to do something different with it – will certainly be either far more costly, or even impossible. Plan ahead, and don't let the boffins bully you into accepting compromises with which you are unhappy; there are few things in corporate life more frustrating than realizing that two years ago you invested a large amount of your company's money in a marketing database which cannot deliver what you demand from it, owing to inadequate original design.

But where are all these rich lovely data going to come from? The answer is, pretty much anywhere and everywhere. Customer and prospect data are all around us. Your organization is probably bursting at the seams with them. Consider Figure 7.4, which shows the various sources of data.

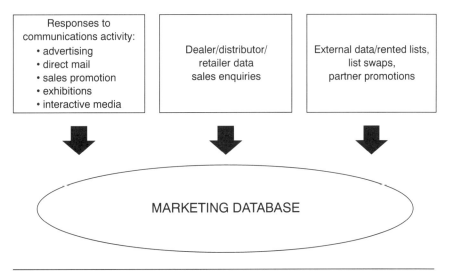

Figure 7.4 Database data flow 1

Knowing your customers

Think of your customers, who are represented by their names and other data on your marketing database, as a collection of friends and acquaintances. As with any such group of people, your relationship with each will be at varying stages of development and varying levels of intimacy, ranging from bosom buddies through casual acquaintances to relative strangers. To this extent, it is appropriate to talk to each in a slightly different manner, depending on how well you believe you know them (and how well they believe they know you). What is certain is that if you do not communicate with them, the relationship, however well developed, will be endangered and, with sufficient neglect, will inevitably wither and ultimately die. The blanket one-way messages put out by your advertising will, it is true, at least preserve name awareness and keep your company in your customers' minds, but it is an inescapable fact that healthy, mutually satisfying relationships, in commerce as well as in life generally, require dialogue to sustain and nourish them. Without two-way communication, customers will, consciously or subconsciously, feel neglected and will be vulnerable to a predatory approach from competitive organizations who appear to take more interest in them. Hence the importance of the marketing database and of its intelligent usage and constant updating. One of the burdens of building a marketing database is the responsibility of having to update the records continuously if the value of the data held is not to deteriorate, which it will naturally do as the information is made irrelevant by events (new purchases, deaths, moving house, changes of postcodes and so on).

Current business wisdom suggests that it costs between 7 and 10 times as much to acquire a new customer as to retain an existing one. This sort of thinking partially explains the 1990s craze for 'loyalty marketing' with air miles, the airlines' 'frequent flier programmes' and a seeming myriad of other customer retention/collector schemes, some embracing new technology (swipe cards, electronic point-of-sale equipment in retailers, and the like) and sophisticated database manipulation techniques to make appropriate offers to customers depending on their value and estimated current loyalty score, others relying on the good old-fashioned mechanism of sticky tokens on a collector card. All these schemes are focused on locking in the customer, encouraging them to adopt a habit centred around the purchase process, so that there is no reason to approach the competition. This is customer loyalty. Companies such as Heinz, Nestlé, Unilever and Procter and Gamble have made headlines in the marketing press by embarking on (generally speaking small scale and carefully constructed) test direct marketing activity, generally involving a mechanism by which they could capture their customers' names and addresses (since they have none of the advantages that financial services companies, say, have in this respect).

All excellent initiatives, and exciting for direct marketing practitioners who have watched FMCG companies ignore direct marketing for so long but, in strategic terms, most definitely nothing new. We saw in Chapter 2 how retailers have been running customer sales promotions since people first sold things to other people; the baker's dozen as a quantity discount was an early (albeit slightly apocryphal) example. Let's face it, 'Look after your customers' is the most elementary rule of business (if only direct marketing agencies practised it a little more assiduously there might not be so many clients chasing round among their competitors). We are here once again (as frequently in this book) in the grey area of overlapping terminology between direct marketing and sales promotion, since the main ingredient of an ongoing customer loyalty programme is likely to be a range of special privileged added-value offers to motivate and reward valued customers, that is, sales promotions.

Whatever the description of the activity, there is no doubt that customer care is not merely desirable, but essential. If you have retailers or branches, training customer-facing staff is certainly a priority. However, in addition, and especially if you do not have a 'public face' (for example, if you are an insurance company rather than a bank or a building society), the customer database offers you a wonderful opportunity to build and sustain a profitable direct relationship with these 'friends' (in an entirely mercenary sense of the word). The marketing database is the key tool for planning and executing a made-to-measure suite of timely, relevant communications, selling product, generating leads, disseminating information and generally sustaining and developing the relationship with each of these many customers on a one-to-one basis (see Figure 7.5).

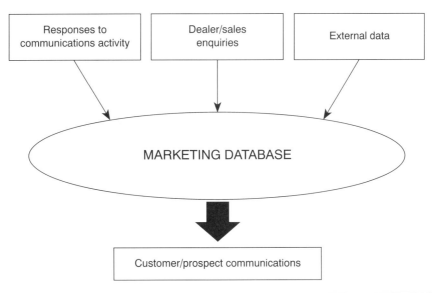

Figure 7.5   Database data flow 2

Hence its central role in the new integrated direct marketing – the subject of this book.

The database as an integrated marketing resource

In this section we examine the crucial role of the marketing database as a tool for driving integrated direct marketing. As such, this section concentrates on the central theme of this book: direct marketing, driven by a marketing database (or databases), is not only a key discipline of marketing today, but will increasingly become the dominant discipline in the marketing communications of the future. As media fragment, as consumers and business audiences become more heterogeneous and difficult to reach by traditional 'mass marketing' techniques, and at the same time the cost of holding and storing large quantities of data on individuals continues to fall dramatically with every year that passes, the arguments for constructing and intelligently exploiting a marketing database become more and more compelling.

In the old specialist full-service advertising agencies, there was a department called Media. This was broadly split between two different sorts of individual:

- the media planner, an 'intellectual' who thought deeply about media and was an expert on allocating clients' money between the various media options to achieve the desired 'frequency and coverage', working closely with the planning department (referred to in this context as 'account planning' in an attempt to minimize confusion); and
- the media buyer, who was generally a complete animal and whose job it was to negotiate (intimidate, maul, bully, pressurize, but never cheat) the media owners into selling the best possible exposure for the lowest possible price. Like all buyers, their goal was value for money; some took this to extremes.

Of course both these groups of media specialists still exist in advertising agency media departments today; they are also increasingly present in organizations called 'media independents' set up as specialists in media planning and buying, offering no creative or production facilities, but claiming to deliver 'more bang for the media buck' by virtue of their specialist expertise, low overheads and media-buying muscle.

It would be fair to say that the majority of these old-style media specialists, when faced with the question: 'How do you feel marketing databases assist you in your work?' would either become disoriented and spit on the floor in contempt, or take to their heels, hurling a copy of BRAD (*British Rate and Data*, a weighty tome which is the standard UK media reference book) at the questioner in the process. There are a number of information/ research databases including the National Readership Survey (NRS), the Target Group Index (TGI) and the Financial Readership Survey (FRS), as well as the wealth of data available from BARB (British Audience Research Bureau, dealing with ITV station viewing habits), but the client's customer database is not a natural place for the traditional media specialist to start.

The point of this section is that for a media planner to operate like this is to miss an opportunity. The new integrated media planner will certainly employ all the above planning tools and more; however these are openly published data and are by their very nature generally available – media specialists can only add value by using the data more intelligently than their competitors (or the client themself). The client's competitors and their media advisers have access to exactly the same data. But look at the in-house marketing database. It may well contain prospects as well as customers, and there is a wealth of actionable data attached to each record. We can look at our customers'/prospects' reading habits, their TV viewing patterns, their purchases linked to particular promotions or other communications in specified media. We can isolate a sample of customers with a given profile, or selected to be generally representative of a cross-section of the customer/prospect base and then telephone them to explore a particular issue in more detail; we can make different offers to different segments of the database by direct mail (if done properly, no one cottons on to what's happening here, least of all your competitors). This is a private source of data and intelligence; your competitors have no access to it.

In short, the marketing database is potentially a very valuable media planning tool and at this point in the late twentieth century, must go down in history as one of the biggest missed opportunities in UK marketing so far.

Even companies who have large marketing databases are still under-exploiting their potential for planning the deployment of the marketing budget between the various candidate media. Certainly, the external information will continue to be important, but the internal data are unique – no one else has them. In most cases they refer to actual behaviour rather than research-based 'predicted' behaviour, which makes them even more valuable: there's no substitute for specific information about what consumers actually do (particularly when it relates to how they spend their hard-earned cash).

We have seen that a marketing database can contribute much more to an integrated marketing programme than merely acting as a mailing list: it can assist in the complex and difficult process of media *planning*, deployed, by the media specialist, alongside the other tools available. But the marketing database can do still more; as indicated above, it can be used as a base for market research, both qualitative (mainly focus groups) and quantitative (for example, telephone surveys). In much of such research, finding sufficient numbers of individuals of a suitable profile (meeting specific criteria of age, credit rating, transaction history, and so on) can be a big difficulty; in these situations, the marketing database is an unrivalled source of names and addresses of suitable people.

Moreover, the marketing database can be employed as a test-bed for controlled experimentation with your product range and pricing strategy. It can be segmented, and particular groups offered the same product at different prices (normally by direct mail); or asked to complete a questionnaire about possible new communications initiatives, say. No one needs to know that these communications are tests; successes can often be rolled out rapidly and with minimal extra origination cost, while failures can be quietly laid to rest and put down to experience.

Much has been, is, and undoubtedly will be written about the increasingly important role of the marketing database in marketing communications. Much of it is true. Major FMCG marketers, including Procter and Gamble, Unilever and Heinz, are believed to be investing substantially in large-scale consumer databases, albeit under an even thicker cloak of secrecy than is usual even for these organizations. They are not thinking in terms of building the world's largest mailing list; rather they are witnessing and reacting to the increase in retailer power, the accelerating fragmentation of mass media, and the consequent increase in the cost of reaching every individual whom they need to influence if they are to continue to sell their products at a profit. This is the reason that the marketing database is becoming increasingly important to a large number of major companies' marketing strategies.

Finally, a word of caution. Do not move into database marketing just because everyone else seems to be doing it. In particular, if your business does not naturally generate or depend upon a marketing database, think carefully before taking the plunge and embarking on what is likely to be a significant construction project. There are some similarities between certain marketing databases and Frankenstein's monster. Feeding this creature will not be cheap, and it is highly unlikely that it will pay back within two to three years. Data costs money to acquire, and are becoming out of date from the day they are loaded on to the marketing database. Updating ('cleaning') your data can become an onerous task; the more so because the alternative is that your expensively built database rapidly becomes useless. Set objectives. What do you want your database to help you achieve? By when? In this situation, the recommendation for all your development activity is:

- learn the rules;
- plan carefully;
- use judgement; then
- test.

You may find that you have built into your database functions you never use or slots for information you never obtain; 'switching them off' may cost little and save you much. As we have seen, direct mail is an *evolutionary* medium, so test, refine and test again. Play tunes on your telephone scripts; check everything is working before you extend your database to the next level of sophistication – don't try to run before you can walk!

Database marketing is here to stay; the marketing database lies at the heart of the new integrated direct marketing. As we have seen, it can be much more than a mailing list. However, it generally represents a major investment and clear thinking is needed before embarking on construction. On average, a three- to five-year view is appropriate when considering potential pay-back timescales.

To illustrate companies' use of database marketing the following case history is offered.

Case history

Company	BMW (GB)
Background	'The ultimate driving machine' campaign had been in force for 15 years, underlining BMW's core values of quality, technology, performance and exclusivity.
Marketing objectives	In 1994, BMW management wished to introduce a very select audience to their pride and joy – the new 7-Series. Of course there would be advertising (in the successful, established style that was already inseparable from the BMW brand), but there was also a need to reach key prospects for the new car on a one-to-one basis and expose them to it individually.

The target audience was drivers of competitive executive/luxury cars (Mercedes, Audi, Porsche and the like) and therefore very select (the car cost between £40 000 and £70 000) and very discriminating. They would not be heavy TV viewers, and more than a little cynical about marketing 'hype' and sales 'gimmicks'. Hard to reach, and harder to impress. None the less BMW were certain that the best way of persuading them to buy the new 7-Series was to show it to them at first hand, in a favourable environment, and allow them to experience it for themselves.

Solution BMW decided to stage an exclusive event. They booked a superb venue – Packington Hall in Warwickshire (the stately ancestral home of Lady Guernsey) for the three consecutive preview days of the motor show at the nearby National Exhibition Centre in Birmingham.

They then proceeded to target key prospects by direct mail, inviting them to an exclusive reception at Packington Hall, from which they would be taken to the motor show in a top-of-the-range 7-Series and be able to view the new 7-Series in a calm atmosphere. The highly creative (and highly BMW-branded) mailing also featured a powerful device – a 'member-get-member' (or 'bring a colleague') mechanism. Thus a sales director could bring his fleet manager; a managing director could bring his finance director; a successful entrepreneur could bring his/her business partner; and a retired captain of industry could bring his wife.

The whole event was also something of a logistical challenge; to succeed it needed a certain number of the right sort of attendees, but they shouldn't feel crowded or rushed.

BMW estimated the total UK universe of potential buyers of this car to be as few as 40–50 000 people: there were approximately $3 \times 550 = 1650$ places to fill. They had run somewhat similar events in the past, but this was of the order of three times as big; nothing could be allowed to go wrong.

The solution was a carefully controlled dispatch of the direct mail (with new phases being released as responses came in), combined with an equally careful telephone follow-up to confirm attendance. It was also necessary to estimate the level of 'no-shows'.

The event was a complete success. All three days were full, but not oversubscribed. A few cars were sold at the event itself; a substantial number of genuine serious sales leads were obtained, and in the weeks following the event a high proportion of these were converted to sales.

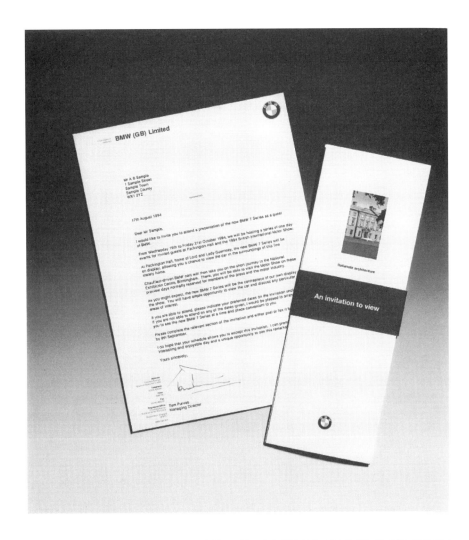

Plate 7.1   BMW – an invitation to view
Source: BMW (GB)

Perhaps the best proof of the success of the event and the associated direct mail/telephone marketing campaign is that BMW repeated the process at subsequent motor shows.

This case history shows how 'below-the-line' disciplines can successfully draw from, and build on, the firm foundation laid by strong brand advertising:15 years of consistent brand building in the UK under the 'ultimate driving machine' banner has created a brand that commands a considerable price premium and retains a high degree of exclusivity, despite the fact that there are now approximately six times as many BMWs on UK roads than at the time of the establishment of BMW (GB) in 1979.

Note: The role of the database was key to the success of the campaign. BMW used records they had already compiled from previous campaigns, from response data and some external data they had purchased. The list was carefully qualified by telephone research and the attention paid to the invitation lists was justified by the quality of those attending the event – a major contributory factor in the overall success of the whole campaign.

8 THE INTEGRATED COMMUNICATIONS AGENCY

As direct marketing continues to expand in scope and to mature as a discipline, a trend seems to be developing to include direct marketing in a total loop along with general advertising, sales promotion and PR. Hence the term *integrated communications*.

Bob Stone, 1994

For years there was a wall between the disciplines of general advertising and direct marketing. Today those walls have come tumbling down . . . a total assimilation that retains the strengths of both . . .

Ed Nash, 1994

But if integrated communications is to be the bright future for direct marketing, . . . then both advertising agencies and direct marketers must begin to look at direct marketing in a different way . . . the late 1950s to the 1980s saw direct marketing enjoy fantastic growth as a stand-alone discipline and as a separate profit center. Integrated communications dictates integrated budgets . . . this situation leads to turf battles . . .

Bob Stone, 1994

Leading Trade publications have bluntly called attention to the existence of a serious problem with headlines like 'What Ails Ad Agencies?', 'Agencies, change or die' and 'Raising Agencies from the dead' . . . It must be understood that these changes are not the result of business cycles. We are in the midst of an irreversible restructuring

... that will require a fundamental
reinventing of agency/client relationships
... These changes involve nothing less than
a reinventing of the existing agency
organisation and the way agencies work
with clients.

Robert M. Viney, 'Solving the agency –
client mismatch', *Advertising Age*, 1993

Advertising, sales promotion and direct marketing agencies – a brief history

For me, now, Carburton Linex & Self is
another kind of waiting room. But what a
place! You should see how much money we
pay each other, how little work we do, and
how thick and talentless many of us are.
You should see the expenses claims, the air
tickets that lie around in here, and the girls
... We all seem to make a lot of money.
Man, do we seem to be coining it here ...
The car is free. The car is on the house.
The house is on the mortgage. The
mortgage is on the firm – without interest.
The interesting thing is: how long can this
last? For me, that question carries an awful
lot of anxiety-compound interest ... We
estimate that Keith Carburton spent
£17,000 on lunch in fiscal '80, service and
VAT 'non compris'.

Martin Amis, *Money*, Penguin, 1984

The 1980s are dead. Gone are the days of Thatcher and Reagan, yuppies,
Dire Staits and the worst excesses of the City of London and of
advertising agencies. The early 1990s recession took a heavy toll on the
advertising industry as agencies cut costs and staff to the bone. Below-the-
line was hit later, but ultimately equally hard. There is certainly no doubt
that the arguably over-enthusiastic expansion of certain marketing services
groups in the late 1980s was savagely punished; in several cases the banks
simply pulled the plug on basically highly successful organizations which
were trading profitably but which had made perhaps one acquisition too

many. While advertising and design agencies probably suffered the most, no sector of the marketing services agency community emerged unscathed.

Today's intake of determined and talented graduate recruits into advertising and other agencies find themselves in a different world from the halcyon days of champagne and long lunches of the 1980s; even university careers advisers have at last got wise to the new austerity which arrived with the 1990s. Much of the glamour has gone and many junior agency people work under extreme pressure with little job security – hardly the optimum atmosphere to foster creativity. But the changes are not all for the worse: in today's agency, there is certainly much less waste; people work harder, and fewer liberties are taken with client's budgets; agencies' efforts are more focused – clients demand it. And they also, increasingly, demand *accountability* – is it working? Having established how much bang they're getting for their buck, clients have now set about getting more – pushing their agencies harder, just as they, as marketing people within large organizations, are themselves being pushed harder by their own managements. These factors helped direct marketing, in particular, to recover from recession, although they did not boost the profitability of direct marketing agencies in proportion; canny buying by hard-pressed clients would seem to be one lasting legacy of the early 1990s slump and, historically, margins recover from recessions more slowly than turnover.

Whereas the 1980s were the decade of corporate supremacy of the *marketing* function, the 1990s have seen a return of the *accountant* to the top of the tree. Marketing has lost people, lost budget, and lost corporate clout; it is under pressure, and is passing some of that on to its various suppliers. In this chapter, we shall focus on how agencies can adapt to this challenging new world; specifically, we present a model of an integrated agency which can deliver the integrated communications, and particularly the integrated direct marketing, which is the subject of this book.

ADVERTISING AGENCIES

So what do agencies do, and how are they structured? Let us start with the traditional 'full-service' advertising agency.

Agencies generally aspire to be more than a supplier of advertising to their clients; rather, they would like to be a *strategic marketing partner*. To achieve this, they formulate advertising strategies (in line with their clients' *business objectives*, from which flow *marketing objectives*), and then execute them via imaginative (and ideally original, powerful and enduring) creative ideas, produced to the highest standards (generally on TV, or in the press, but also on posters/billboards, radio, cinema and other media). Such an agency is likely to be structured as in Figure 8.1.

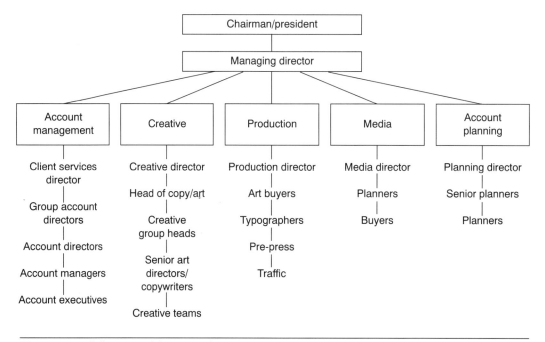

Figure 8.1 Full-service Advertising Agency

It is instructive to compare the structure shown in Figure 8.1 and the roles of the various people within the integrated agency analysed below (page 173). For now we take each department in turn.

Account management

The 'salesmen' of the agency. The account director (and his/her junior colleagues, the account manager and account executive) represent the client to the agency and vice versa. They take the brief from the client, go back to the agency and communicate the requirement to the creative people, and finally 'sell' the agency's creative product to the client (it is, of course, rarely this simple and the foregoing is inevitably an over-simplification). They are also coordinators within the agency, tapping into the specialist expertise of the other departments. As such, they risk being branded 'jack of all trades and master of none'. At the same time, the job requires a wide range of skills (diplomacy, tact, persuasiveness, organization, administration and prioritization – the ability to juggle several projects simultaneously).

Creative

The ideas generators. This is what most people who don't have any personal experience of advertising agencies think everyone in advertising does. It's the job of starting with a blank piece of paper (or increasingly a blank computer screen) and finding the right combination of words (often as a soundtrack) and pictures (often in colour, and moving) to catch the attention of the consumer and drive home the advertiser's message, leading to the purchase of the relevant product or service. It's sometimes scary, sometimes supremely satisfying and, at the highest level, very well paid. Crudely speaking, copywriters write the words and art directors do the pictures, although, in practice, a creative team often works in a more complex way, at best achieving a kind of alchemy which leads to the strongest ideas. The creative department was tackled in detail in Chapter 6 above. For its most successful practitioners, and the thousands of aspiring youngsters seeking to follow them, it is the most important (and perhaps even the only) department in the agency – it's the area where the talent resides and which pays everyone else's salaries. Arguably, without it we don't have an ad agency. It is possible to source Creative from outside 'freelancers', but many clients would prefer to see the relevant people in-house. Agencies with a reputation for being 'highly creative' can take great liberties in terms of client service and financial control (but of course it doesn't do to rely on this).

Production

If the creatives are artists, production people are technicians, which is not to belittle their craft – great advertising requires great execution as well as great ideas. This department specializes in crafting the final images in TV, print or other media and ensures the right 'artwork/mechanicals/film' arrives at the right publication/TV station at the right time (and that the right price is paid to the various suppliers). This is self-evidently a crucial role and it will be equally vital in our integrated agency, as we shall see.

Media

These people are the targeting and placement experts. Media *planners* are the *strategists* (experts on the allocation of funds between TV, press, radio and so on) and the *buyers* are the *tacticians* (somewhat unfairly once dubbed 'gorillas with calculators'). Whereas advertising agency media planners require a good working knowledge of the strengths and limitations of many media, much more will be asked of integrated media departments – see below (page 177).

(Account) planning

This is the discipline generally agreed to have been 'invented' in the early 1970s by Stanley Pollitt of the London agency BMP (now BMP DDB Needham). It seeks to understand the consumer better as regards his/her wants/needs/attitudes and motivations, so as to fine-tune the communications strategy, the creative product and the media plan. It embraces qualitative research (especially focus groups) as a technique and attracts 'intellectual' entrants to the advertising profession and a high proportion of women graduates. During tough times, of course, it has been a soft target for cuts, but the best advertising agencies in the UK and increasingly around the world have used planning to build a strategic and high-level relationship with their clients, cementing their role as 'brand guardians' and fighting off the incursions of the large management consultancy firms.

So much for the various jobs in the traditional ad agency. In the early 1990s, recession meant that agencies trimmed the fat, then cut it, and in some cases went too far and lost muscle too (cost cutting only works if you can reduce expenses with minimal negative effect on revenues; otherwise the organization simply implodes, collapsing in on itself until you have no costs, no revenue – and no business). To some extent, staffing peaks and troughs in the agency world are largely cyclical and, by 1995, rebuilding was already under way. Something far more fundamental had happened this time, however – something which should be distinguished from recession-related factors. This was the start of a large-scale move by agencies to provide a broader range of marketing communications services: one indication of this is that sales promotion and direct marketing agencies have started to overlap in terms of their output, and in some cases to merge. Examples include the major US-based international communications group, Young and Rubicam, merging its direct marketing and sales promotion agencies worldwide to form Wunderman Cato Johnson. IMP and DMB&B Direct combined throughout Europe under the name of the former, offering a broad range of below-the-line disciplines. Other multinational agency groups including Bozell Worldwide launched a network of integrated below-the-line operations, offering direct marketing and sales promotion without any bias, as part of a 'media-neutral' overall offering which includes advertising.

In addition famous long-established 'pure' advertising agencies like Collett Dickenson Pearce (CDP) and even the mighty (old) Saatchi and Saatchi have 'reinvented' (or is it 're-engineered'?) themselves as integrated agencies. They have been joined by some of the newer wave of advertising agencies, notably Howell Henry Chaldecott Lury, which has imported heavyweight below-the-line talent into an existing and already very successful above-the-line operation. Kevin Morley (ex Managing Director, Commercial, of Rover Cars) did the unthinkable at the start of 1992 and set up his own agency, KMM, from scratch, to handle the £100 million pan-European Rover business, initially on a five-year contract (plus any other clients he could attract). It was unusual at the time in that it was, from the outset, an *integrated* agency.

Indeed, as this book goes to the printer, it is becoming increasingly rare to find an agency which does *not* claim to be integrated – it has become almost a mandatory positioning. However, it should be noted that much of this 'integration' is more of a fashion pose than a genuine capability, and also that there is no absolute guarantee that this situation will endure; indeed, some expect the cycle to swing back towards specialists. It is certainly possible that a mix of different sorts and sizes of agency could thrive. And it should be noted that, even in this 'integrationalist' climate, certain major players are not following the herd: the Ogilvy Group has chosen to keep its three main UK agencies – Ogilvy and Mather (advertising), Ogilvy *One* (direct marketing) and Promotional Campaigns (sales promotion) – quite separate; Abbott Mead Vickers/BBDO owns controlling interests in Barraclough Hall Woolston Gray and Craik Jones (direct marketing) and Clarke Hooper (sales promotion) without apparently fostering any close affiliation between the four agencies. Integration of agencies is currently widespread, but it is not universal.

Looking back into agency history, the traditional way was that of specialized skills. In the UK, advertising agencies grew up first. They were, at the beginning, true agents of their clients; they bought space from the various newspapers/journals on their clients' behalf, produced an advertisement to fill it, and received a cut of the cost of the space (or commission) from the publication for their trouble. This commission eventually settled at 15 per cent for consumer press and 10 per cent for trade and technical/business press and was for many years inflexible. In addition, these early advertising agents would add a mark-up (normally of 17.65 per cent, as this was equivalent to retaining a commission of 15 per cent of the gross price to the client) on to their production costs (illustration, typesetting, 'paste-up', 'bromides' and the rest).

Such agencies employed copywriters and designers of various descriptions, but at first in separate departments. There was apparently no question of two minds working together to crack the creative challenge. The current format of the copywriter/art director team really started in the USA after the Second World War and came to the UK in the 1950s. Up until 1956, advertising agencies concentrated their efforts on press advertising, mainly relying on illustration and often given tremendous creative freedom to make extravagant and sweeping claims for their clients' products (cigarettes gave you a clear throat, Guinness was good for you, Andrews Liver Salts and Beechams Pills would ward off all manner of nasties and so on). It is interesting to note that these early agencies did not turn their noses up at other media, including handbills, posters (especially on railway platforms, trains, trams and buses) and even, on occasion, 'direct mail advertising'.

An event that revolutionized the UK advertising scene in 1956 was Unilever's commissioning of the first TV commercial shown in the UK, for Gibbs SR toothpaste. Other advertisers rushed to follow SR into this exciting new medium, offering as it did the powerful combination of sound and moving pictures (even if colour was still some way off at that time; indeed, for that milestone the UK had to wait until Lintas's colour commercial for Bird's Eye peas in 1969). Suddenly more and more advertising budget was being poured into TV advertising, and agencies realized that they had to get into TV commercial production and book airtime if they were to retain their powerful position between the advertiser and the media owner. So agency media and creative departments started up a very steep learning curve with emerging specialist TV media planners and TV media buyers, along with creative teams (at times supplemented with US ex-pats) who excelled in the new medium. Interestingly, though, no famous agencies ever positioned themselves as 'full-service TV only' or 'full-service press only' – that degree of specialization never arose. However, TV production companies and TV directors now emerged as a new class of specialists, some within agencies, some operating as external suppliers to agencies.

SALES PROMOTION AGENCIES

So much for advertising agencies. Sales promotion agencies started later. In the postwar period, sales promotion (already becoming known as 'below-the-line') was, true enough, something of a refuge for those admen who were either not good enough, or were getting too long in the tooth, to 'cut it' above the line. Since client organizations were only slowly beginning to recognize that a planned approach to special offers and free gifts could benefit the brands they were building via advertising, the normal route was for them to have a junior brand manager buy the 200 000 fluffy ducks (say) to give away to customers sending in four proofs of purchase. If they needed a promotional leaflet for the reps or the retailers to give out, a junior team at the ad agency would knock something up in a spare hour. As we have seen in Chapter 2, in the 1950s, the promotion pioneered in the USA for Getty Oil, 'Matching Half Notes' came to the UK via the Glendinning Company (mainly led by ex-Procter and Gamble executives). A new breed of sales promotion consultancies sprang up in the UK over the late 1950s and early 1960s, doing the 'below-the-line' things that ad agencies had little experience of and less enthusiasm for, doing them well, adding tangible value to the client's marketing mix and making a good living along the way.

At first, they worked almost entirely for FMCG clients (for example, Heinz, Kellogg's, Nestles (*sic*) and Cadbury) often alongside the client's in-house below-the-line department. Their remuneration was normally a combination of agreed project fees and mark-ups on print and premium items purchased. It was this latter area that made many sales promotion agency founders' fortunes: four shillings profit per Fairy Snowman (sourced from a factory in Taiwan) across 5000 units = £1000 – not bad for two days' work in 1965. This was the heyday of the (now infamous) 'free plastic daffodil', along with such classics as the 'free storage jar' which doubled as the packaging for the coffee it was promoting. Famous UK sales promotion agencies of the 1960s, 1970s and 1980s included Kingsland Lloyd Petersen (KLP), International Marketing and Promotions (IMP – now the below-the-line brand of multinational agency group DMB&B), Clarke Hooper and Francis Killingbeck Bain (FKB), now part of Carlson.

DIRECT MARKETING AGENCIES

Direct marketing agencies arrived on the UK scene later. Most of the early entrepreneurs learned their trade in the dog-eat-dog world of mail order where, if your ad didn't pull, you didn't eat. This environment, naturally enough, concentrated the mind wonderfully and creative skills became focused exclusively on getting response, generally employing off-the-page press to build a list of hot prospects/first-time customers, which was then 'milked' remorselessly via direct mail.

Many of these mail order experts were copywriters/businessmen, who learned the economics of sourcing products, buying space and mailing lists, writing and designing the ads and mailings and running fulfilment operations by *doing* all these things. They lived on their wits and they paid the mortgage with the proceeds from the last ad they wrote; in the process, they naturally enough developed very firm views as to what 'worked' and what didn't (which was not always a recipe for harmonious relations when those they employed brought their own ideas to the party). Some of these gurus noted the rise of direct marketing as a 'respectable' marketing communications discipline and, when they started agencies to cash in on this trend, their clients were mostly from the fields of mail order catalogues/off-the-page selling (collectibles, book and record clubs and so on), along with charity fundraising and some business-to-business lead generation (for example, office equipment).

In those days, the business was 'mail order advertising', 'direct mail advertising' or 'direct selling'. Famous UK direct marketing agencies and their leaders during the 1960s, 1970s and early 1980s included Amherst (led by direct mail 'giant' John Fraser-Robinson), Wunderman (the UK office of the US-based network founded by the eponymous Lester), later to become Wunderman Cato Johnson (Young and Rubicam's below-the-line network), Trenear-Harvey, Bird and Watson (three gurus in one agency!) and, of course, Christian Brann Ltd, conceived, managed and fronted by the man himself, Christian Brann – the Anglo-Danish mail order entrepreneur who founded, close to his home in Cirencester, the direct marketing agency that survives and thrives today as Brann. Other successful agencies of this time have since lost their independence (including Halsey, Leigh and Young – now part of Grey Integrated – Minors Hankin, an excellent full-service direct mail shop founded by Ian Minors and Mark Hankin which became MHA and is now part of Carlson. Also part of Carlson is Smith Bundy and McCorkell Sidaway Wright, which became MSW Rapp and Collins and has now been transformed into WWAV Rapp Collins). These are famous agencies, led by some giants of the UK direct marketing business, and contain lifetimes of experience of how to 'make the tills ring'.

Today's large direct marketing agencies are a far cry from the shops set up by the hands-on entrepreneurs referred to above. Some employ 100 or more personnel. They are similar in structure and business philosophy to their ad agency cousins. They have creative and account management departments; they exist to add value to their clients' businesses, and their client lists include not only 'traditional' mail order clients, but nowadays also various branches of the financial services industry (banks, building societies, insurance companies, finance companies, credit card companies and so on), retailers, travel, automotive, and even FMCG companies. They are more aware than ever of brand values, but they are still specialists – the focus is still on getting a response and they are staffed by direct marketing professionals. They coexist with other types of specialist agencies, but compete, to an extent, with integrated agencies, to which we next turn our attention.

So much for the development of the specialist advertising, sales promotion and direct marketing agencies. We have also noted that there has been a trend in recent years towards the establishment of integrated agencies. In the next section we shall examine various possible models of such an agency.

The model integrated agency

The traditional 'full-service' ad agency (one which handles strategy, creative, production and media) is structured as was shown in Figure 8.1 (see page 166). Direct marketing and sales promotion agencies have traditionally structured themselves in a similar way, although 'Media' and 'Planning' might be replaced by 'lists/database' and 'Production' could include premiums/merchandise sourcing and buying, telephone marketing, response/fulfilment management, lettershop and coupon handling, among other specialist areas.

However, if one were to set out to establish an integrated agency, planning and executing, on behalf of clients, campaigns which include any or all of advertising, direct marketing, sales promotion (and design, conferences and exhibitions, publications, PR, training and motivation/incentives and the like), what structure should one ideally choose? Suppose one has the enormous luxury of setting up such an agency from scratch, and suppose, further, that one has sufficiently secure and large clients already signed up to enable one to build a structure with confidence – how should the various departments be organized for maximum efficiency, optimum client service and the greatest overall profitability (which is, of course, ultimately also in the clients' interest)?

One solution appears in Figure 8.2.

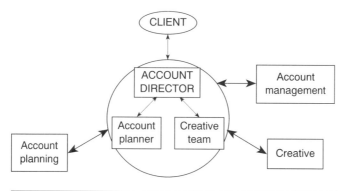

Figure 8.2 The integrated communications agency, Model A

The agency is built around the core functions of Account Management, Account Planning, and Creative. These roles are similar to their equivalents in the traditional ad agency. For each piece of business (for each of the agency's clients) there is a designated account director, who is the main point of contact with the client. The account planner helps with the overall strategic approach, developing a thorough understanding of the client's business and market, getting 'under the skin' of the client's customers and ensuring the agency's creative output is perfectly tuned to the relevant communications tasks. The creative department is the 'ideas factory'. Far more than words and pictures, it generates the imaginative (hopefully 'breakthrough') ideas which make the agency's communications effective and the client's business successful, which of course leads to more business and greater profits for the agency – a virtuous circle of spiralling success. So for each piece of business we have the core team of three experts who draw on the strengths of their respective departments. However, given that this is to be an 'integrated' agency, the demands of the client may be many and varied. The agency must have the resources (preferably in-house) to meet these requirements. It will be appropriate to equip the core team with a number of additional resources. Consider the structure illustrated in Figure 8.3.

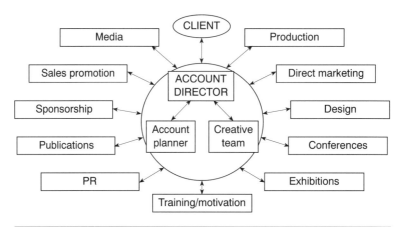

Figure 8.3 The integrated communications agency, Model B

Now we have equipped our core team with an impressive array of resources such as only the finest and *largest* integrated agencies would be able to boast. And what resources, what serried ranks of experts, in everything from the skills of balancing the features and newsy stories in a customer magazine (publications) to sourcing an expert printer who can handle the intricacies of security printing of latex scratchcards (sales promotion) to the experts on exhibition stand design and build (exhibitions) and the maestros of multiple slide carousel AV, with cars flying in from the sky amidst clouds of dry ice (conferences/video). An expert for everything, and each expert in their place. Whatever field of marketing communications the client wants, it's here – at the account director's fingertips.

However, this model contains certain anomalies. The key one is this: note that there are specialist departments for direct marketing, sales promotion, publications and so on, despite the possible overlaps between them (sales brochures, promotions communicated by direct mail, mailing leaflet production and the like). There is a significant absentee from the chart – the advertising department! Where are the specialists in communication via TV, posters, radio and image press? For the answer we have to look more deeply into the way such an 'integrated' agency might operate.

Each client has an 'account team' of account director (part of the account management department), account planner (part of the planning department) and creative head (part of the creative department), with the account director as the client's key point of contact, with responsibility for orchestrating the most appropriate solution to the client's particular marketing problem/opportunity, regardless of whether the need turns out to be for a 'shelf wobbler' or a 90-second pan-global TV commercial. So far so good. But in some 'integrated' agencies, the account directors are *not* such super-generalists, with sufficiently broad experience truly to justify the title 'experts at everything', but advertising people who are 'Road to Damascus' converts to integration (this was a factor in the early 1990s – recessions are powerful motivators). Thus the theory is that *they* supply the advertising expertise, in their spare time, from organizing no-lead-discipline integrated communications solutions. This can never be pure integration, since these allegedly dispassionate, unbiased, honest-broker coordinators are really nothing but 'foul-weather integrationists' and still, deep down, in love with the TV film and the glossy double-page spread. Moreover, they have to run to a specialist 'boffin' whenever a client threatens to start talking about sales force motivation schemes or (perish the thought) database segmentation.

Even worse, if traditional advertising has a stranglehold on the senior management of such an agency, this can result in a method of operating that mistakenly regards direct marketing and sales promotion (say) merely as media, or channels to distribute the core message alongside TV, press, radio, cinema and posters (and implicitly as second-rate media at that). This whole approach to integrated communications fails to recognize that direct marketing and sales promotion are fully fledged *disciplines* in their own right, so that to plan and execute them successfully one needs planners and account managers who are steeped in these approaches to marketing and who will be credible in front of senior clients – not just a few 'bolt-on junior specialists' who can implement the mechanics of a mailing or a fix-a-form on-pack leaflet, while the 'brand guardians' make the important decisions!

The idea that direct marketing (say) is too important to be left to direct marketers is a one-way ticket to disintegration and a suboptimal communications mix. Indeed, unless the power base (that is, the board) of such an agency consists of a balanced team of people with above-the-line and below-the-line backgrounds, it cannot be genuinely true to the philosophy of 'no lead discipline'; its recommendations will always be biased and are highly unlikely to be in the client's best interest. Another anomaly in Model B (Figure 8.3) is the lack of communication between the specialist disciplines. For example, sales promotion and direct marketing don't appear to talk to each other except via the account director (and perhaps in the pub after work), whereas their work must have large areas of overlap and there is presumably much to be gained by their liaising closely.

A good try, then, and, with the right accounts, likely to be profitable, but ultimately not what is required by clients who genuinely seek *impartial* advice about marketing communications backed by the *specialist skills* to deliver it to the highest standards.

Let us turn, instead, to a different model (see Figure 8.4).

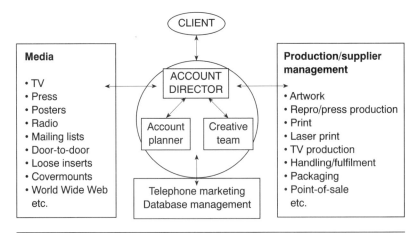

Figure 8.4 The integrated communications agency, Model C

This appears to go right back to the traditional ad agency structure, but let us look more closely at who does what.

The first question is: 'What's happened to the specialists?' The answer is that nothing's happened to them; they haven't been dispensed with – on the contrary, they have been deployed more effectively. In this structure, they are categorized by what they do – their function – rather than by any advertising, direct marketing or sales promotion specialism. In other words, expert advertising/direct marketing/sales promotion people will be found *throughout the other departments*, that is, media specialists will be found in:

- TV (image and DRTV)
- press (image and direct response)
- radio (awareness and direct response)

but also in:

- direct mail (lists)
- press inserts
- database
- sponsorship
- partner promotions; and
- advertorials.

Of course we're not saying that any one person in the media department has to be an expert in all the above, but there needs to be sufficient expertise within the department as a whole, and the media director must have a broad understanding of all available media choices.

Similarly creative and production departments will contain all the specialists who used to work in traditional direct marketing and sales promotion agencies. Indeed, all these three departments will need to be managed by individuals who are able to take a broad overview of advertising, direct marketing and sales promotion (at least), so that we shall have a head of media, a head of creative, a head of planning, and a head of account management who have a genuine interest in, and experience of, a number of media and communication disciplines. These departments will be staffed by individuals with particular discipline-specific skills (just as traditional ad agencies have expert TV creatives or expert press media buyers). There are no specialist departments; all are fully integrated. Thus this new model integrated agency will certainly employ a hotshot TV airtime buyer (who knows their direct response infomercial buying from their ABC1 attitude-shift/rapid-awareness-build buying), and also a skilled direct mail copywriter as well as someone in production who could write the book on latex scratchcard printing technology in the late twentieth and early twenty-first centuries).

We do not have a head of direct marketing, sales promotion or advertising – these are merely tools or techniques used to communicate selling messages according to their appropriateness in any given situation, but since they are much more than media, experts in them are to be found in *all* agency departments and, crucially, *senior management genuinely has no discipline-specific axe to grind*. The planning department, in particular, seeks to optimize the communications mix from the point of view of maximum effectiveness for the client and regardless of any personal preference or previous career history of individual agency personnel. This structure avoids the stigma suffered by many below-the-line specialists in allegedly 'integrated' agencies or agency groups, for instance the token direct marketing expert, wheeled into the pitch, and left with ten minutes at the end of the presentation (after creative and even after media – 'above-the-line' media, that is, except that once again the meeting overran – 'don't worry, the direct mail stuff's all in the document'). With the above structure, there is no lonely, shiny-suited, ever-so-humble 'specialist' begging for a slot on the above-the-line agenda. Instead, integration, while strategically driven by Planning, is the responsibility of all departments and (implicitly or explicitly) part of the agency's contract with its clients. Recruiting the right people into the right roles in this agency will not be easy; individuals with specialist agency backgrounds are likely to find themselves in unfamiliar departments with unlikely job titles. However, the concept of the agency, and the logic of this structure, appears almost too obvious to require justification; clients increasingly demand it and agencies must, as was ever the case, adapt to meet their needs.

Model C is, I believe, the structure most likely to lead to a genuinely 'integrated product'. It is also essential that the agency can actually deliver, when in competition with the 'non-re-engineered' specialist agencies.

Kevin Morley, Chairman and founder of KMM, said of his pitch to the Rover Car Company Board in 1991:

> I said to them – I've been seeking
> integrated communications, and they said,
> yes, we know that . . . they listened
> patiently because they knew I'd been an
> advocate of Integrated Communications for
> many years . . . This is not Rocket Science,

> it makes sense, it's extremely logical . . . If
> the idea's big enough, it will carry through
> everywhere, and part of the problem/
> opportunity with integration is the idea's
> got to be big enough . . . We've got the best
> direct marketing agency in the world in
> KMM . . . We had to have the best people
> so that I can go to other clients and say,
> 'you want direct marketing, we'll give you
> direct marketing and we're doing it very
> successfully'.
>
> *Business Age*, January 1994

Of course, the central and crucial role in this new model integrated agency is that of the integrated account director (IAD). These individuals need to be very talented operators; much will be demanded of them. Below-the-line account directors, lacking a planning and a media department, have always needed to be more versatile than their above-the-line counterparts, delivering strategy, creative ideas, supplier management and client service. Our new model IAD has to be an exceptional individual indeed; able to incorporate the best of the predecessor specialists and supersede them; to be the client's key point of contact, and the orchestrator of the integrated marketing communications solution, understanding all the relevant (and irrelevant) marketing communications disciplines, representing the client to the agency and the agency to the client. Look again at the Model C structure (Figure 8.4). We are looking for a new marketing communications Renaissance man or woman.

WHERE DO WE FIND OUR IADs?

Finding the right IADs is likely to be a determining factor in the success of 'integrated' agencies structured as in Model C, and possibly a brake on their growth; without the right individuals in this key role, truly integrated communications cannot be delivered, and the whole promise falls down. There are several potential sources of candidates for the role:

(i)   account directors currently working in advertising, direct marketing or sales promotion agencies;
(ii) account directors in integrated agencies;
(iii) marketing managers in client companies.

- Category (i) people are likely to have problems adapting/learning new skills in disciplines where they never did the 'spadework' as account executives/account managers.

- Category (ii) currently is a very small pool – and why would such people want to move? Certainly, if they're any good, they're likely to be expensive.
- Category (iii) offers perhaps the best solution at present. The transition from client-side to an agency role is never easy, but at least there is a good chance that client-based managers will have had some experience of making decisions governing the allocation of marketing budgets between various candidate media, and will be able to take a dispassionate view in order to make choices between the various disciplines available. Of course, some individuals will be more broadly based than others, and in the jobs market for IADs, the 28–30-year-old who has worked at IBM, Procter and Gamble and Sainsbury's, including spells in market research, strategic planning, six months on the road as a sales representative, and marketing management roles including FMCG, business-to-business and retail, will be able to name his or her price (and may well be preparing for a second or third nervous breakdown). The next question is whether the integrated agency will be able to afford that price (that is, can such 'expensive' individuals pay their way in integrated agency structure C? I believe that they can).

As with all labour markets, supply and demand factors will operate, and as the pool of 'integrated account management' staff grows, the scarcity value of the individuals will fall and they will become more affordable. This will coincide with the passing of the old generation of 'die-hards' who will fight to preserve the old specialist status quo, with which they naturally feel comfortable. The IAD needs to be less of a jack of all trades and master of none, and more of an 'expert in everything'. The IAD needs to have all the traditional skills of the old specialist holders of the role: must be a natural salesperson, charming with people, an entertaining raconteur on any subject/able to hold an interesting conversation with anyone (or at least any client or agency person, which pretty well takes in the entire spectrum of mankind), organized and methodical, a capable administrator, patient and persuasive, an excellent communicator and builder of professional relationships. Moreover, s/he must combine these skills with an impressive array of specialist knowledge. To illustrate this point, s/he would ideally be capable of talking knowledgeably about:

- printing costs of 96-sheet posters;
- the practicalities of cropping transparencies for use in a brochure;
- buying a combination of regional radio stations to approximate to national coverage;
- designing layout grids for a 'lifestyle' magazine;

- costs of producing an animated TV commercial versus actors/film;
- the likelihood of getting a net names deal from a list broker of business lists;
- the ins and outs of putting together an advertorial feature;
- the comparative strengths of the various geodemographic segmentation systems currently available;
- the viability of using a client's stock footage (and library film) to make a video for use at the annual sales conference;
- and much, much more.

It may reasonably be pointed out that we appear to be looking for a superman/woman – the marketing equivalent of 'Renaissance man', perhaps Leonardo da Vinci in an Armani suit (or maybe Marks and Spencer in the more inwardly directed 1990s). Yes, ideally we are; moreover, since integrated agencies are still a relatively new phenomenon, few executives have joined them straight from university/college as integrated account executive and been promoted via integrated account manager to IAD. On the contrary, the vast majority of account directors in UK communications agencies have progressed either through advertising, direct marketing, sales promotion, PR, design, video, conferences or exhibitions, that is, they have *specialized*, because finding your specialist expertise and developing it has been the best method of 'getting on' in agency life.

This shortage of sufficiently broadly experienced staff is likely to apply across the whole integrated agency (including the 'generalist' heads of media, creative and production), but it will be most acute in the account management function, where there will be the greatest demand for multiskilled individuals. It will inevitably hold back the development of fully fledged multifunctional marketing communications organizations over the next few years. Professional training and education, as provided by organizations such as the Institute of Direct Marketing, the Chartered Institute of Marketing and the CAM Foundation, will be important in filling in the gaps in people's knowledge/skill sets. The good news is that, by the time that our 'integrated graduate trainees' have progressed up the agency ladder via integrated account manager and integrated account supervisor to IAD, a cadre of new, genuinely broadly based account directors will have been created. Until then, most integrated agencies will have to get by with a mix of account directors, each carrying their individual bias of experience and familiarity. It will be the task of the client services director (or 'head of account management' – a role for a *true* communications Renaissance man/woman!) to construct a sufficiently balanced team and then to develop the personnel through relevant cross-disciplinary training, all the while juggling people and roles to deliver a coherent, no-lead-discipline service tailored to each agency client according to their individual needs. (But who said it would be easy?)

Certainly, integration, like any change process, hurts. There are people with vested interests militating against it, and for an existing agency, attempting to 're-engineer' itself as a brave new integrated communications consultancy, the challenge is doubly difficult. Making the necessary changes will hurt. However, change is essential. Dinosaur agencies will be left to their fate; the cost of *not* embracing integration in the last years of the twentieth and early years of the twenty-first centuries will be higher than that of grasping the nettle.

So, *integration* is the future. In the next chapter, we examine how a client might select and work with an 'integrated' agency to deliver successful integrated direct marketing campaigns.

9 MAKING IT HAPPEN – INTEGRATION IN ACTION

> There are two words which are misused
> greatly by agencies talking to their clients.
> One of them is 'strategy' – usually applied
> to some minor subterfuge. The other is
> 'partnership' referring to a legendary state
> of affairs, a nirvana of equality between
> client and agency.
>
> Drayton Bird, 1993

Choosing an integrated agency

For the purposes of illustration, let us suppose you are the newly appointed marketing director of a company with a significant marketing budget. Your company has, historically, spent advertising and promotional moneys on TV, press, posters, point-of-sale, sponsorship and direct mail. You believe in integrated communications and you intend to appoint a single integrated agency to handle *all* of your company's marketing communications. Suppose in addition that you are unconvinced that your current agency is up to the task of handling *everything* from TV to shelf wobblers. So – where do you start?

Come to that, where does one ever start in the hunt for any type of communications agency? Ask any group of client-side marketers how they selected their agency (either integrated or not) and you'll get a variety of different answers, for example:

- A visit to a specialist 'search company' (such as the Advertising Agency Register). This company, and others like it, offers a service that is confidential and discreet: for a fee, clients can view showreels and portfolios provided by participating agencies and decide which to visit (without the unsuccessful agencies ever knowing who viewed their material). The process removes much of the pressure of the inevitable agency hard/soft sell.
- Someone you used to work with/or someone recommended by someone whose opinion you value, referrals, and so on.

- The result of a cold approach by the agency (direct mail with or without telephone follow-up – yes, it sometimes *does* work!).
- The agency was high profile, well regarded, well spoken of, regularly appeared in the marketing trade press, and/or was in some other way 'hot'(!). (In these respects, agencies are often guilty of not practising what they preach – indeed they often neglect to build their own brands in a situation where advertising, PR and direct marketing – and even, on occasion, a little sales promotion creativity – could pay off handsomely.)
- Your chairman liked the sound of the agency (and/or played golf with the agency boss).
- A combination of two or more of these.

Choosing an integrated agency is little different from the traditional search for an advertising agency, although the range of suitable 'shops' from which to make a selection is likely to be more limited. There is also the important extra consideration of whether you actually believe that a given agency is genuinely 'integrated', or, more to the point, whether it can actually deliver the various marketing communications solutions you believe you are likely to require, or whether it is merely a 'traditional' specialist agency in disguise (employing 'smoke and mirrors' to win and ideally retain 'integrated accounts').

The process typically comprises five stages which we shall examine individually with particular reference to the special requirements of you, the marketing director (let us assume) as you seek to select your ideal integrated agency:

1. The initial 'trawl'/drawing up a 'long list'
2. Viewing agency 'credentials' presentations and reduction to a shortlist
3. Briefing the shortlisted agencies
4. Viewing the agency pitches
5. Final selection/appointment.

THE INITIAL TRAWL

This can be daunting, especially considered as only the first stage of a potentially long-drawn-out process (and meanwhile you and your colleagues all have your jobs to do, which may involve working with the 'old' agency; whether they know your plans to review or not, the situation is unlikely to be a comfortable one).

Where to start? Visit the Advertising Agency Register – the AAR (now incorporating a number of genuine integrated agencies as well as traditional advertising, direct marketing and sales promotion agencies) or the Direct Marketing Agency Register or one of their competitor organizations. Read the brochures and view the showreels, and pick out those whose work you like. Does the creative (and the underlying strategy) make the work stand out? Do they show genuine creativity and imagination in below-the-line media as well as in advertising? Consider other factors. Do you like the 'feel' of the place? Do the people look like the kind you could work with? (Might you even *enjoy* working with them?) What about the agency philosophy (if any is discernible)? In short, does the agency, at first viewing, *feel* right?

You are beginning to note agencies you'd like a closer look at; you might wish to add to these AAR-selected shops others you have already worked with or had recommended to you, or where you or one of your colleagues (especially your MD or chairman) already has contacts, along with any you simply 'like the look of' from the press or by talking to colleagues in the industry. The 'grapevine' should, of course, be treated with scepticism, but it can suggest some agencies you'd like to visit at the next stage. Of course you should bear in mind that including more agencies at the outset means more time will be spent fixing and attending meetings, which is likely to delay the final selection.

Now look at this initial list and strike out all those which:

- your chairman/MD hates (like it or not, you'll be wasting everybody's time if you take things further);
- have a competitive account (unless you realistically believe they would resign it to handle your business, or unless they're about to lose it, which might well arouse your suspicions anyway!);
- have an ultimate parent/holding company which is for some reason unacceptable to you and/or your organization;
- are located somewhere so inaccessible that you just don't believe a relationship could work logistically (still a real issue, though less so with modern communications).

(An agency I worked for once failed to be shortlisted for an account I believed we were very well qualified to handle, after a 'credentials' presentation I was certain had gone very well. Believing I had nothing to lose, I took my courage in both hands and asked the client straight out where we had let ourselves down. She replied unhesitatingly that she had decided she needed an agency whose office was 'on the Piccadilly Line' of the London Underground.)

If you're still left with a list of more than ten, you must now go through it again, being more ruthless and eliminating your least favourites – maybe leaving in one 'dark horse' (or 'wild card') just to ensure the forthcoming pitch process isn't too boring! Seeing more than ten agencies will be a torture for you and your colleagues, as well as being unfair to the agencies, and is likely to be so confusing that it is far from certain to produce a better final decision, so be tough now and save a lot of grief later.

Now the fun really starts!

VIEWING THE AGENCY CREDENTIALS

Let us assume you are now down to eight or nine agencies, any one of whom, you could, at this stage, imagine yourself appointing and working with (if not, cut them out, *now*!). You must first decide which members of your organization should comprise the agency selection panel (ASP). This is an important decision, as the selected individuals should stay with the process right to the final selection (which could be anything up to three months down the line – but courage! the process can, and sometimes must, be 'telescoped'). The panel is likely to include you (remember we're assuming you're the marketing director and, as such, the driver of the whole pitch process) and (say) two members of your marketing team. You may well wish (or it may for a variety of reasons be expedient) to include managers from other parts of your organization (say, national accounts manager/sales director/financial controller/direct marketing director) and even in some situations an outside consultant (although the agencies will be deeply suspicious of such people), so that all relevant interests are represented. This panel should stay together consistently throughout the process. Now approach each of your longlisted agencies and invite yourself and your colleagues to visit them in their offices, to view a general agency credentials' presentation. Tell all the agencies the same; you will find it useful to give them some idea of who you are and what you are looking for, including which communications disciplines you require your integrated agency to be strong in. Thus if you only want creative advertising coupled with the ability to use the advertising images on the direct mail envelopes and the odd piece of point-of-sale, this is quite different from a requirement for in-depth expertise in database building and manipulation; also make clear to them the degree of confidentiality involved – do you wish them to sign any kind of 'Confidentiality Agreement' at this stage? Try not to lead them on too much; agencies are, generally speaking, enthusiastic enough at the best of times, without mistakenly thinking your planned annual budget is ten times the actual figure. If you're not reviewing your entire business, or if you're not sure you'll get the budget approved for this year, let the agencies know

CREDENTIALS PRESENTATION

AGENCY ....

DATE ....

PRESENTERS ....

YOUR NAME ....

SCORING: 5 = EXCELLENT, 1 = POOR. PLEASE CIRCLE THE APPROPRIATE NUMBER

1 IMPRESSION OF AGENCY PRIOR TO PRESENTATION	1	2	3	4	5
2 DID THE AGENCY DEMONSTRATE STRATEGIC THINKING?	1	2	3	4	5
3 WERE YOU IMPRESSED WITH THE CREATIVE WORK/CASE STUDIES?	1	2	3	4	5
4 IMMEDIATE REACTION TO AGENCY PERSONNEL	1	2	3	4	5
5 QUALITY OF PRESENTATION CONTENT FACTS/FIGURES	1	2	3	4	5
6 OVERALL IMPRESSION OF THE PRESENTATION	1	2	3	4	5

7 OTHER COMMENTS

Figure 9.1   Royal Mail Streamline agency assessment form

whatever you can – otherwise it will only lead to disappointment and/or embarrassment later.

At this point call the first meeting of the ASP. You must collectively agree in advance what you are looking for. 'We'll know the right agency when I see it' is really not good enough. This is also the time to draw up the 'ground rules': do you require a unanimous verdict to exclude, include or eventually appoint an agency? How *democratic* will the ASP be? Given the necessity of making a decision (the *right* decision), many marketing directors take care to equip themselves with (at least) the casting vote. The most professional 'pitchees' including, in the UK, Royal Mail and the

Central Office of Information (COI) have been known to draw up questionnaires/scoresheets in advance with all the key criteria listed with marks available from 1 to 10 in each category. (See Figure 9.1.)

This method has the virtue of quantifying people's otherwise subjective opinions, making it possible to score the agencies and compare overall ratings in a relatively objective, even 'scientific' manner; it can also be useful in limiting the potentially biasing effect of one particularly 'anti' or 'pro' individual on the panel who might dominate a group discussion and unduly affect the final outcome.

When you visit the agencies, arrive early. Sit in Reception. Pick up a newspaper by all means, but look around – and listen. Soak up what used to be called 'the vibes' of the place. How would you feel if you were waiting here to visit the agency to which you'd just agreed to entrust your entire integrated direct marketing budget for the next X years? If you don't like the thought at this stage, you may be in the wrong place.

In my opinion, the appraisal form scores should not be the sole determinant of who makes it to the final shortlist of three or four agencies. In addition to the 'hard' measurements, there will be a number of 'soft' impressions that the team carries away from a visit to any agency relating to the atmosphere, the people and the overall feel of the place.

It is also worth attempting to establish how important your account would be to the agency. (This is a crucial question, not always easy to get a definitive answer to, but certainly worth asking straight out at a first meeting. You might conclude that being, say, the second or third largest client of the agency is a comfortable place to be.)

Other questions, relating specifically to a future working relationship with this agency, might be:

- 'Would I be proud for my colleagues/peers to know I was working with this agency?'
- 'How convenient would it be for me to visit their offices regularly? – or for them to come to me?' As we have discussed above, despite the massive strides made by communications technology, client–agency relationships still stand and fall by personal relationships, which means a certain number of face-to-face meetings.
- 'Are they going to make my brand/s famous? and *sell*?'
- Can they really give me *integrated* communications?

All these questions are relevant at this point.

BRIEFING THE SHORTLISTED AGENCIES

After this, the selection of the final shortlist (three or four maximum) agencies is made and the pitch process enters its final phase. Now act – firmly, decisively and professionally. Give the unsuccessful agencies the bad news; invite the other agencies to pitch for your business, issuing the same brief to each, indicating the criteria on which you will base your final decision and telling all agencies which other agencies are involved. Thus everyone has a level playing field on which to operate. At this point some 'wobblers' might be thrown in: one or more agencies might decline to pitch; certain conflicts might come to light; worst of all, the chairman might even foist an 'eleventh-hour' 'dark-horse' candidate upon you. Be all this as it may, you now have your pitch lists. You must grit your teeth and steel yourself to sitting through perhaps four two-hour presentations. Think of the light at the end of the tunnel. This is not the end, but certainly the end of the beginning.

THE PITCH

> Life's a pitch. Then you die.
>
> Gerry Moira

Bill Bernbach, one of the all-time advertising greats, founder of Doyle Dane Bernbach (now DDB Needham – part of Omnicom) and reliable source of advertising sayings, once said:

> a principle isn't a principle until it costs
> you money.

The new business pitch is a time-honoured and much-debated ritual in the lives of virtually all agencies – advertising, direct marketing, sales promotion and, yes, integrated agencies too. It could be described, with varying degrees of truthfulness, as any or all of the following:

- an exciting, competitive, stimulating opportunity for the agency to impress the potential client with its ability to handle the account successfully;
- a relatively objective examination of several evenly matched professional organizations, so as impartially to compare their differing strengths;
- a frustrating, and ultimately pointless, 'beauty parade' or painting competition, in which allegedly professional companies effectively prostitute themselves (even more degrading, at their own expense) in a desperate and undignified attempt to seduce a client who probably doesn't know what they're looking for and quite possibly intends to reappoint the existing (incumbent) agency anyway and only instigated

the bogus 'review' in order (1) to satisfy his management that the advertising and promotions budget was indeed being wisely spent through the very 'best' supplier and/or (2) to keep the incumbent on their toes – in the belief that a bit of a scare will result in the 'phone calls being answered one ring earlier (and/or returned a bit sooner), in the artwork/production/print costs being pegged a bit lower and (perhaps secretly) a more up-market venue being selected for the next few lunches on the agency (!), that is, a monumental and obscene waste of everyone's time and money.

The general view among agencies (of all descriptions and degrees of integration) seems to be that pitches are unsatisfactory, often unfair, and frequently fail to deliver the 'best' agency for the potential client. The agencies who win the pitch are often expected to be so grateful that they will be happy to recover their (often substantial) pitch costs over the course of the first few jobs (but 'rest assured, we'll be keeping a close eye on your invoices, guys, as you would expect'), whereas losers frequently come out with nothing to show for enormous effort and much burning of midnight oil, which means that clients might have accumulated the best ideas of three (or more) different agencies about their business, without paying a penny! Is this any way for a so-called 'grown-up' profession to conduct itself?

At this point, one has to consider the alternatives to the agency pitch process (chairman's wife or husband's whim? golf club deals? AAR only?) and reluctantly conclude, with the majority of agencies and clients, that it is the best method among several which are unsatisfactory in different ways. There is certainly justification for the view that the client should commit (up-front) to a 'pitch fee' (of, say, £5000) to each of the agencies participating – this is no more than a fair recompense for the 'consultancy' proposals presented in the pitch and should be independent of the final result. Several (but not enough) clients offer such fees as part of the invitation to pitch. Several (but not enough) agencies ask for them. Few (and arguably nowhere near enough) agencies refuse to undertake speculative creative work (the real pitch money-eater). It is not uncommon for an agency to spend as much as £20 000 on a speculative creative pitch including *boards* (beautifully finished by an artwork studio), *slides* (expensively produced by a specialist presentations company) and *TV animatics* ('just to bring the storyboards to life' as the creative director explains). Even this takes no account of the costs of the time expended by agency people of all levels of seniority which could otherwise have been spent on existing clients' business.

However, the reality is that, for all its faults, the agency pitch process appears to be here to stay, and that if the agency wants new business (and which agency doesn't?), it had better resign itself to pitching and indeed, must positively *strive* to get itself on to pitch lists, and, having achieved that, expend every ounce of available effort to ensure (as far as is possible) the only acceptable result – VICTORY!

Meanwhile, as the client who has at last sat through the three or four pitches, the culmination of this frequently exhausting agency selection process, how does one make the final, all-important decision? It is after all vital that this admittedly unsatisfactory business at least ends with the selection of the best agency possible, a decision the client and his/her colleagues are likely to have to live with for at least a year, and probably two or three (and of course, the successful agency fondly hopes, for *much* longer).

Not surprisingly, the answer is – it all depends. It is hoped that your ASP or pitchee team has come through intact, if not unscathed, so that all three or four of you will have seen the entire process and been a party to all the decisions to include or eliminate the various agencies along the way. Refer to Fig 9.2 – the agency 'pitch evaluation form' (pages 192–193). Depending on your priorities in terms of what you are seeking from your integrated agency, you may include measures of:

- Creative/strategic planning resources
- Personnel: senior management and account team. Do you like them? Do they know their stuff? Can they deliver? Will you get enough input from the people you want on your business? Will there be someone around sufficiently senior for you to talk to when things go wrong? Remember this is your working life for the next X years. The chemistry will be as important as the accuracy of the typesetting or the IQ of the planners. 'Brains the size of planets' should be combined with loveable personalities, or life won't be much fun.
- Philosophy/attitude to your business. This is difficult to pin down, but you need to be able to strip out the agency 'hype' and establish:
  - Does this agency *believe* in integration?
  - Can it *deliver* integrated communications?
  - Do the functional specialists work together or do they compete as separate profit centres? (If the latter, how dispassionate can their recommendations actually be?)
  - Will all disciplines be considered equally seriously, be accorded equal importance and be executed to an equal standard of excellence by the agency?

PROMOTIONAL PITCH					
SCORE SHEET					
AGENCY:.................................	NAME:..................................				
Mark each element out of five 1 = Poor 5 = Excellent					
1 OVERALL IMPRESSION GIVEN BY ANY CONTACT PRIOR TO PRESENTATION	1	2	3	4	5
Notes or comments					
2 LEVEL OF RELEVENT BACKGROUND/ EXPERIENCE	1	2	3	4	5
Notes or comments					
3 UNDERSTANDING AND INTERPRETATION OF BRIEF	1	2	3	4	5
Notes or comments					
4 KNOWLEDGE OF ROYAL MAIL AND ITS WORKINGS	1	2	3	4	5
Notes or comments					

Figure 9.2 Agency pitch evaluation form

- Are the various specialists (advertising, direct marketing, sales promotion, and so on) genuinely masters of their trades (would they hold down jobs in major *specialist* agencies?)?

In short, ask yourself:

● Can this agency actually give me the integrated marketing communications I want *now*?

		1 = Poor	5 = Excellent		
5 PROPOSALS FOR: Key requirements of the brief	1	2	3	4	5
Notes or comments					
6 TIMING	1	2	3	4	5
Notes or comments					
7 VALUE FOR MONEY	1	2	3	4	5
Notes or comments					
8 TEAM POTENTIAL–COMPATIBILITY	1	2	3	4	5
Notes or comments					
9 ADDITIONAL WORK/INNOVATION	1	2	3	4	5
Notes or comments					
TOTAL SCORE					

- Does it appear likely that it will be able to *continue* to do so over time and
- Can I (and my team) *work* with them?

Then, having asked these questions about each of your shortlisted agencies, take a deep breath, advise your board/gain their concurrence and move on to the next stage.

FINAL SELECTION/APPOINTMENT

Make those 'phone calls!

Unless you are indeed a peculiar sort of person (which a few marketing directors admittedly are), you will have one pleasant 'phone call to make and several less pleasant ones. You may choose to agree terms with the winner before finally calling the losers, but make it as quick and painless as possible.

Agreeing the ground rules

> there are only three ways in which
> advertising agencies (and similar
> businesses) can charge for their services:
> i)   some type of commission system based
>   on turnover
> ii) some type of time or time–cost fee
>   package
> iii) some type of performance-related
>   arrangement
> . . . although each system is deeply flawed,
> each has great merits . . .
>
> Winston Fletcher, 1994

Congratulations! You've just got yourself a brand new integrated communications agency. When you 'get it home' and 'unwrap' it, you'll have the chance to examine it at leisure and find out exactly what you've really bought. To put it another way, there may well be an initial honeymoon period, but sooner or later the relationship must settle down.

How, then, should you, as a client, set about getting the most out of this new integrated agency?

Account must be taken of:

- the personalities of the client and agency (and of the key individuals from both organizations);
- the structures of the two organizations (who 'faces off' against whom?);
- the market conditions under which the communications are operating; what are the pressures? how busy is everyone?
- the importance of the relationship to each of the individuals involved (what are people's priorities?).

Clearly we are dealing with a complex matrix of complementary, overlapping and even conflicting agendas here. Individuals' personal goals may well not be entirely congruent with those of their organization, which in turn may not match those of the 'partner' organization. We are talking here about culture clashes, mutual suspicion, misunderstanding, even envy. These are some of the reasons that agency–client relationships are so volatile, so unpredictable, and so fascinating. They are one of the most enjoyable – and at times the most infuriating – aspects of working in marketing communications.

Let us now assume that you have appointed your integrated agency and that both parties have duly signed a contract including terms of the remuneration review procedure (*much* more about agency remuneration later). All this important and serious financial stuff having been sorted out, how do we make the day-to-day operational relationship as fruitful and productive as possible? We will look at the relationship under five headings:

1. Agree objectives
2. Formalize procedures
3. Adopt an *open* communications policy
4. Develop (and acknowledge) mutual respect
5. Agree the financial arrangements.

AGREE OBJECTIVES

In order to get the most out of your integrated agency, you should revisit the objectives you started with in the pre-pitch planning phase, which should now be openly discussed with the new agency to arrive at the joint marketing communications objectives of the new client–agency partnership. You may end up with something like the following:

Over calendar year X, achieve a consistent programme of communications, which delivers:

(a) W per cent increase in prompted awareness;
(b) X per cent increase in unprompted awareness;
(c) Y per cent reduction in the cost/response for specified direct mail campaigns with specified offers;
(d) £Z thousand worth of proven incremental sales from the 'database exploitation' programme.

The integrated direct marketing objectives for the year, like any marketing objectives, should be 'SMART', that is:

Specific
Measurable
Achievable
Realistic within budgets
Timed

Only with clearly defined and documented goals will it be possible to assess progress and achievements. Of course, there is also nowhere to hide in this situation – which, to good agencies and clients, is more of an opportunity than a threat.

FORMALIZE PROCEDURES

In order to achieve these objectives, it is likely that you will agree with the agency certain disciplines on the basis of 'how we do business', for example:

- Weekly status meeting (core agency/client teams to attend).
- Weekly status report (to act as agenda for above).
- All meetings to have typed agenda circulated in advance.
- All meetings to be contact reported with agreed actions clearly indicated and copies circulated within 24 hours to agreed list of personnel at client/agency.
- Each campaign to be the subject of a written brief from the client. Agency then to formulate a creative brief which client should agree and sign off before any work commences.
- All timings and costs to be agreed in advance before the start of the project and client to issue purchase order before the agency incurs any cost on the client's behalf.
- Any changes to the job to be notified by the agency and supplementary purchase orders issued as appropriate.
- Strict sign-off procedures for all creative work; signatories to take responsibility for what they are signing.
- Final agency invoice not to exceed sum of relevant purchase orders.
- Quarterly strategy meetings to review last three months' campaigns and ensure integration of all communications activity (that is, consistency).

The idea of the above is that surprises should be kept to a minimum: even if the brilliance of the agency's strategic insight and creative solutions should take the client's breath away, invoices and timings certainly should not!

ADOPT AN *OPEN* COMMUNICATIONS POLICY

As with any relationship (business or personal), the client–agency relationship must be nourished by interaction, by dialogue and by regular contact involving proactivity by both parties. So if you want to get the most out of your integrated agency, *talk* to them, *meet* them, confide in them. If things are going well, *tell* them. If not, *complain*. It may be that the agency is performing well in some departments/disciplines (say advertising) and less well in others (say sales promotion), or that their recommendations do not appear to be genuinely 'media-neutral'. All agencies worth their salt welcome feedback from their clients; in this respect (and perhaps only this) good agencies can be compared to good restaurants. Even bad news may enable them to take some action which avoids your having to give them even worse news at some time in the future. They may be able to convince you not to take your custom elsewhere, so that they can then return to their role of nourishing your brands! Encourage your new integrated agency to open up to you too: if they find your briefs woolly (so to speak), your juniors rude and unreasonable and are making a whacking loss on servicing your business, it's better that you know. If you're their biggest client and they'd do anything to keep you, you'd also better be in the picture. No relationship ever failed because of too much communication. (There may be exceptions to this one, but I can't recall any.)

DEVELOP (AND ACKNOWLEDGE) MUTUAL RESPECT

In theory (at least) the agency will never know as much about your business as you do (whether it be mail order clothing, cars or investment products). By the same token, your integrated agency would doubtless claim to be a source of considerable expertise in the field of integrated communications (at least you believed this when you appointed them). If this appears to both parties to be the case, then you're well on the way to that Holy Grail of 'mutual respect'. The agency–client partnership, like all relationships, can either deepen and grow towards 'mutual interdependency' or wither and die, grounded on the rocks of disillusionment and mutual incompatibility and almost certainly bound for the divorce court with all the attendant bitterness, grief, costs and damage to the progeny (the communications which were the innocent fruit of the ultimately doomed union). In short, respect is essential to a long and mutually beneficial agency–client partnership. Overall, agency–client relationships, like any other relationships, can be good, average or appalling.

Although it would be naïve to imagine that every client is solely committed to maximizing his/her company's profitability through successful and responsible commercial operations, just as it would to claim that every agency is a hard-pressed group of virtuous souls wholly bent on assisting the consumer to make informed purchase decisions, good agency–client relationships are certainly possible and there are many examples. Undoubtedly the existence of mutual understanding and respect is a necessary, if not sufficient condition for a successful and lasting client–agency relationship.

AGREE THE FINANCIAL ARRANGEMENTS

Agency remuneration is potentially the most sensitive issue of all – and no less so when we are talking about an integrated agency. There are a number of different bases on which clients can pay agencies. It is worth taking considerable care over sorting out this issue right at the start of the relationship, as it can be the cause of much tension and mutual suspicion later. Both partners must at least be *satisfied*, and preferably *happy*, with the arrangement. The agency is, of course, in business to make a profit, which enables it to afford to recruit the 'best' people to produce the most successful campaigns possible for the client. Moreover, a profitable agency is likely to be in business next year (and even the year after!) offering you, the client, the prospect of continuity and minimizing the threat of an unwelcome discontinuity in your marketing communications caused by the unexpected bankruptcy of your key strategic partner. Most importantly, if yours is a vital (big revenue-generating, that is, profitable) account for the agency, you'll get excellent service and the best people on your business, aware that they largely owe their livelihood to you – an enviable situation for any client to find themselves in.

The client must believe that the agency is delivering value for money; this evaluation is a complex process involving a number of interacting factors and is rarely entirely scientific. The only real basis of comparison (in weighing up the effort–reward/cost–benefit equation) is what might be available from another agency or even the client's own 'in-house' resource. By and large, though, clients know when they're being ripped off by excessive fees, say, and/or the agency is skimping on people resources in an attempt to make the account more profitable.

Hence the need to agree a firm and clear contract from the outset, to govern the relationship (and not only the financial aspects of it). It should stipulate exactly what will be the basis of charging. It should also incorporate a mechanism for reviewing the arrangement (say annually).

There are four main ways in which an agency (whether above-, below-the-line or integrated) can be paid: these are outlined below.

Mark-ups

Supplier costs are passed on with a standard 'margin' of 17.65 per cent on the net (equivalent to 15 per cent of the gross) cost. This is the historical basis adopted by advertising agencies of passing on production costs; in recent years, the introduction of something called the 'Pliatsky' form, along with the emergence of 'production cost auditors' has prevented some of the worst agency fiddles involving inflated TV production costs. These incidents have admittedly been few, and all reputable agencies take pleasure in seeing them stamped out for the good of all those attempting to earn an honest living in this business.

If you agree this type of arrangement with your agency, you should reserve the right to audit their supplier invoices (and exercise it at least once, to show you mean it) or alternatively demand to see all supplier invoices when the agency bills you. Even so, it has, regrettably, been known for agencies to conspire with their (that is, your) suppliers to produce inflated 'dummy invoices' which they duly mark up and pass on to you while pocketing a balancing 'early payment discount'; everyone gains except the client. The fact that some agencies have tried this in the past means clients would do well to do some cross-quoting from time to time, to ensure that the various supplier costs are 'within the ballpark'. This sort of mutual suspicion is of course extremely counterproductive to the building of a relationship based on mutual trust, and the greed and short-term focus of the few have to a large extent undermined the honesty of the many.

Another area of costs to be clarified is which, if any, agency expenses are to be reimbursed by the client. Again be specific (club class or economy flights? second-class rail travel? mileage rates? bikes/cabs/deliveries and so on) and devote some precious time to sorting these things out up front, as I have seen disagreements over these issues become the focus of bitter disputes (admittedly, in some cases serving as the flashpoint for more deep-seated underlying problems in the relationship). Clear them up early and remove possible areas of dispute which will detract from the attention directed to the task of 'getting the job done', which should be everyone's priority.

Media commission

Historically, the consultancy acted as a true 'advertising agent' and placed ads for the client, collecting a rebate (or commission) from the media owner (normally a newspaper or magazine) of 15 per cent (consumer press) or 10 per cent (business press); this discount was only available to 'recognized agents'. The advent of commercial TV and the spiralling cost of advertising time and space meant that agencies were in some cases receiving substantial 'windfall' revenues, in the shape of 'unearned' media commission, out of all proportion to the work they had done. In the late 1980s, the commission system began to break down. First, desperate agencies agreed to handle accounts on a reduced commission basis (11 per cent or even lower) and hard-pressed clients gratefully accepted. Second, we witnessed the rise of the 'media independent', doing no creative or production, merely planning and placing media at the lowest possible price; this separated the traditional 'full-service' ad agencies from the media owner and the commission-earning operation and encouraged a move to payment by fees.

Fees

Generally based on the time spent by the agency to plan and execute a particular project or campaign, this has long been favoured, especially by below-the-line agencies, as the 'fairest' of the available methods. The difficulty arises in arriving at a reasonable fee level – and indeed in monitoring accurately the exact agency resource which is being expended. Fees can be charged either 'one-off' or, ideally from the agency's viewpoint, as a monthly 'retainer' (for example, '£30 000 per month, to be reviewed in 12 months' time'). The great benefit of the retainer from the agency's point of view is that it enables them to plan staffing levels with a measure of certainty which is welcome in such a constantly changing, volatile environment. Indeed, an agency will often be prepared to settle for the security of, say, a 'guaranteed' £5000 per month rather than operate on project fees which could amount to £70 000 a year, or in a difficult year with a budget cut in September, to only £45 000.

The most unfair thing about time-based payment systems is that the arrangement does not incentivize the agency to do great (that is, successful) work; rather to fill in timesheets diligently and indeed to work as many 'billable hours' as possible on the client's business, regardless of how well spent such time might be, or of how talented those people who are putting in the time actually are; not, on the face of it, a recipe for cost-effective marketing communications.

Payment by results

I know of no instance of such an arrangement having worked to both parties' complete satisfaction. It sounds attractive, especially to clients; it also sounds eminently reasonable. The theory is that good work, which builds the client's brand and sells the product, is worth more than poor work, and consequently an agency creating and producing successful campaigns should be more highly remunerated. The difficulties come in agreeing the level of 'performance bonuses' and in devising a measurement system acceptable to both parties. Compared to advertising, direct marketing activity can, generally speaking, be measured relatively accurately (cost per response, cost per sale, percentage conversion of leads and so on) but, even so, disputes can occur about detail, and about the effect of outside factors (the state of the economy, the performance of the sales force, the retailers, the competitive advertising, price increases and the like), resulting in disagreements about remuneration which inevitably impinge on the all-important client–agency relationship. If you're arguing about money, it's very difficult to focus on producing effective marketing communications. As yet, it has proved difficult to devise a system of this sort that is agreed to be sufficiently robust to be generally 'fair'.

It is, of course, possible to combine one or more of the above four remuneration systems. It is becoming increasingly the norm for clients to pay agencies (especially below-the-line and integrated agencies) fees of some description; this is often combined with an agreement governing media commission (in some cases, the whole 15 per cent is rebated to the client) and specifying mark-up on production (often a blanket 17.65 per cent on all bought-in items/materials, although in other cases it is agreed that all supplier costs are to be passed on without mark-up).

Note on agency–client relationships

It is not difficult to understand why agency–client remuneration arrangements can be the focus of so many problems, particularly if not clearly laid down at the start of the relationship. Agencies naturally require as much security as possible before recruiting personnel with their attendant costs; clients need to be convinced that they are obtaining value for money. As with other aspects of the relationship, openness and honesty on both sides offer the best hope of a harmonious partnership.

The greatest advertising, sales promotion and direct marketing campaigns all have one thing in common – a successful agency/client partnership. It takes a great client to buy a great idea; sometimes this carries career risk for the client but when it results in a famous and successful campaign, it frequently makes them a star within their organization and hastens their progress into general management (or a better marketing job in another company!). Such relationships between two organizations work best when they operate at more than one level, and are invariably based on each party respecting the other's field of expertise. As has been suggested above, the agency is never going to know as much as the client about the client's brands and marketplace (if it believes it does, it certainly shouldn't let on!), and at the same time the client is never going to know as much as the agency about marketing communications (although sometimes the client may think differently!).

Each party should understand and respect the objectives of the other and there must be clearly defined working procedures and open and honest communications. Such relationships, based on:

- openness
- mutual respect
- confronting problems head-on
- regular reviews/appraisal meetings
- continuous improvement
- honesty
- integrity

are likely to be strong enough to withstand changing market conditions, changing brands and campaigns, and even changing personnel on both sides. Such long-term mutually beneficial relationships, where both parties, in addition to embracing the above principles, share a genuine commitment to making integrated communications work, with no discipline-specific prejudices, are likely to be the basis for the best integrated marketing campaigns. Achieving such a working partnership should be the objective of every client embarking on the (admittedly potentially daunting) agency selection process detailed in the first part of this chapter.

The process

We now arrive at the crucial part of this chapter – the process by which one works with one's integrated agency to plan and implement the aforementioned integrated marketing campaigns. Clearly no two clients and no two agencies (integrated or otherwise) are the same; we shall examine the various stages of the process as it might be followed by a typical client with a typical agency working on a real brand in the real world with limited budgets (as they all are) and under pressure to deliver on time. We shall tackle the process in stages:

- Planning the marketing communications mix
- The briefing process

- Creative development
- Presentation of creative work
- Media proposals
- Campaign implementation
- Post-campaign evaluation.

PLANNING THE MARKETING COMMUNICATIONS MIX

Since we are focusing on *integrated* marketing, we are likely to be looking for a response which includes executions in a number of media, for example, a fully integrated campaign including creative work for: TV commercials, press ads, direct mail, sales force presenters and in-store materials. I do not believe the *selection* of media is an issue to be left to the creative department; rather that decision should have been made by the agency and the client *before* the submission of the creative brief.

Indeed the agency's recommendation, which determines (in broad terms) what is required of the creative department, will to some extent be determined by what the agency claims to *offer*. If it positions itself as a purveyor of *advertising*, then it follows logically that a fair number of clients will walk into the agency looking for exactly that; if the shop is positioned as an 'integrated communications' vendor, then that is what clients are likely to be looking for, so that they will tend to be open to the agency proposing how budget should be split across a *range* of different marketing communications disciplines and media (indeed they may *demand* this service of their integrated agency). Then again, the mere fact that an agency claims to offer advertising, direct marketing and sales promotion doesn't necessarily mean that a given client will wish to purchase *all* these communications from the same agency. Thus an FMCG manufacturer (say) may require sales promotion and advertising from Integrated Agency X, whereas a financial services company may go to Agency X for advertising and direct marketing; then again, an automotive client may buy advertising, sales promotion and direct marketing from Agency X, while a retailer may buy just advertising from Agency X, but obtain sales promotion from Agency Y and direct marketing from Agency Z.

In other words, those clients who choose to control the integrated process by orchestrating the services of a range of specialist suppliers will inevitably work with their supplier agencies in a manner which will differ from that adopted by those clients who favour 'one-stop shopping'. The latter is the process on which we concentrate in this chapter, that of planning and executing a *complete range* of marketing communications activities sourced from a single agency. In reality, agencies will generally supply services in the manner that clients require (if only because failure to deliver what is demanded is, generally speaking, a short cut to economic ruin).

The selection of media (that is, the allocation of available budget between the various media options available above- and below-the-line) is an area where the integrated agency's planners can have a real input. The key here is to 'think outside the box'. For example, we might ask: 'Are we genuinely seeking to reach a mass audience with a common message?' (that is, a straightforward mass marketing brand proposition, for which the 'traditional' mix of broadcast TV, national press, radio and/or posters is likely still to be the best option) or are we in fact able to identify segments (niches) so that a mix including targeted direct mail, or telephone marketing, say, might be more appropriate? To borrow a phrase: 'When all you've got is a hammer, every problem looks like a nail'; specialist agencies are expected to deliver specialist solutions, but integrated agencies must do *better* or at least *more*.

Even though the major decisions about media type/selection will, generally speaking, already have been made by the time the creative brief enters the creative department, the creative people should still be encouraged to have an input – indeed their views, likely to be less influenced by what the client tells the account director *needs* to be done, often constitute a valuable contribution to the process.

THE BRIEFING PROCESS

This is a crucial stage in the development of integrated communications campaigns. Indeed, the old adage 'garbage in, garbage out' definitely applies in this case, so that great care and effort should be employed in formulating and expressing the brief, first by the client, and subsequently by the agency in distilling the client's brief into a document which is designed for the agency creative people to use in constructing the marketing communications. This process is generally performed by the agency planners/account management (keen to add value and thus justify their existence and possibly their remuneration packages).

Let us start with a typical creative brief document (see Figure 9.2) as used by an agency (this is very similar to the brief that was shown in Figure 6.1 on page 115). This document has also been used successfully by clients in briefing their agencies. It can accommodate various media choices. With certain variations, it is used by the majority of agencies working across the

---

INTEGRATED COMMUNICATIONS – CREATIVE BRIEF

Client:

Job name:

Job no:

Date issued:

Issued by:

Objective:

Positioning:

Proposition:

Substantiation:

Action required:

Tone of voice:

Mandatory inclusions:

Media/sizes/quantities:
  <stipulate mandatory and proposed communications disciplines/choices>

Budget:

Timing:

Approved by:

Planning Director   Date
Account Director   Date
Creative Director   Date

Figure 9.3 A typical creative brief

range of marketing communication disciplines. The various sections of the brief are largely self-explanatory; the flow of information is logical and by formalizing the brief writer's thinking, it forces him/her to get to the nub of the marketing task in question.

At this time the client should be asked to approve the agency's creative brief since this will highlight any misunderstandings/lack of agreement about what we are trying to communicate to whom; it is better that these issues are debated now rather than after the agency has expended a fair amount of its most precious resource – the time of its people. The client may also have certain fixed ideas about the communication, including which media/disciplines are appropriate, and if the client will never pay for a TV commercial, or if the client's chairman will never agree to running direct mail activity, then it's better to resolve such issues at this stage rather than down the line.

The most important section of the brief (which should, correspondingly, take the longest to write) is the proposition. It is the single most motivating and differentiating thing about the brand we can say to the audience; it is the core of the creative brief, against which the creative work should be checked at all stages of development and presentation, to ensure it is an appropriate response to the brief which everyone has signed off (and is therefore difficult for the client to reject, except by simply saying 'I just don't like it!' which is not, of course, unheard of).

Another approach to the creative brief is called the WHO? WHAT? WHAT? WHAT? format:

- WHO are we talking to? (our target audience)
- WHAT do they currently think and feel about our product or service?
- WHAT do we want them to think?
- WHAT do we want them to *do*?

This has very much the same effect in terms of controlling the thought process of the brief writer; it also gives the recipient creative much the same information in an easily digested format.

The brief is a crucial stage in the process; without a good brief, disaster is likely to ensue: at the very least, the creative work will be suboptimal; at worst, it will be a spectacularly imaginative and insightful response to the *wrong* marketing challenge and, as a result, entirely useless, a complete waste of everyone's time. Hence the importance at this stage of 'using the planners' heads to save the account managers' feet', that is, those involved must think now and avoid a lot of time and trouble (money) later. By and large, great work requires a great brief, which not only covers the basic requirements and imparts key facts about the product or service, but genuinely stimulates the fertile minds of the creative people, leading to the ideas which make great advertising (and direct marketing and promotions).

The creative brief is from time to time, of course, an occasion for some ritual creative versus suit 'cut and thrust'. Some creative directors seemingly take a delight in violently rejecting briefs timidly proffered by junior planners and account handlers (often, on these occasions, inadequately 'protected' by their senior managers). Indeed the only thing creative people resent more than a brief which is poorly thought through and generally 'woolly' (betraying lazy or inadequate thinking) is one that is unnecessarily tight and unduly influenced by the account handler's (or planner's) subjective opinions and allows them no room to contribute at the strategic level. This is an example of the creatives' frustration at being one step removed from the client's business (although they would in many cases find dealing with the client directly even more frustrating).

I would always recommend a formal face-to-face briefing of the agency by the client; by all means circulate the brief in advance, so that the session becomes a discussion and clarification meeting, but always mark the importance of this occasion by a physical meeting.

Attendees should normally be:

- Client:
  - Marketing director
  - Marketing manager
  - Brand manager
- Agency:
  - Group account director
  - Account director
  - Account manager/executive
  - optional – client market research manager and the agency planning director.

This stage is about 'taking a step back' to answer the questions:

- *Where* are we now?
- *Where* do we want to be?
- *How* do we get there?

The above process may appear unduly formal and structured, but it is my experience that imposing some discipline at this stage serves to concentrate the minds of all those involved and leads to better, more focused ideas from the creative department with the optimum end results – ideally cutting-edge marketing communications – which is what everyone is seeking.

On a practical note, the brief meeting should end with an agreement as to the date and content of the next meeting; this will normally be the response of the integrated agency to the client's brief. The agency is right to fight for as much time as possible here: in most cases, at least three to four weeks, while for a major integrated campaign, planned well in advance, two months might be an appropriate time to allow the agency to put together its best ideas. However, there will inevitably be times when the client needs something (almost anything!) back the following week, to put in front of the chief executive, say. Agencies don't generally let the client down on these occasions, but rightly stress that this is not the best way to get the best work and should not be taken as 'the norm' in future. Rushing the creative process may mean the agency presents its first ideas, which are unlikely to be its best.

Thus with, say, a three- to four-week response time, the integrated agency has the best chance of delivering the right solution. Now, having, as it were, lit the blue touch paper, the client must have the self-control to retire and let the agency earn its fees. Certainly make yourself available to answer questions and supply any information the agency people require, but don't stand over them – let the creative alchemy work its magic!

Meanwhile, back at the agency (aka the integrated dream factory), the planners will be translating the client's brief into something that the creatives can work from (this may require little work in some cases, much in others). As discussed above, a key part of this process will be planning working with account management, media, the client, and even on occasion creative, to decide on the media split; this may be as simple as 'We all agree it's TV, press, and some targeted direct mail' or more complex: 'How do we reconcile cutting the point-of-sale material budget in order to invest in building the database, with the fact that the client wants to up-weight the press media budget, despite the research telling us it's failing to build awareness?' (But who said it would be easy?) The planners are here adding real value to the agency's product by interpreting the client's requirements and, if necessary, challenging them (what they *say* they want may not necessarily be what they really *need*) and using their intellect and experience to encapsulate this in a single document. This will serve as a yardstick against which to judge all the creative solutions proposed by the assembled (and sometimes intimidating) ranks of art directors, copywriters, creative group heads and others.

The integrated agency must justify its role in the total communications process (and, in so doing, its fees) by adding value. This has to come from its unparalleled understanding of how consumers react to selling messages (howsoever delivered), and its creative ideas for marrying words and visual images in a powerful combination which lodges persuasive messages in the minds of the target end-user. To employ these skills to maximum effect, to the benefit of the client's brand and ultimately profitability, a crystal-clear understanding of exactly what is to be communicated to whom is essential; hence the pivotal role of the creative brief.

CREATIVE DEVELOPMENT

Inside our integrated communications agency, certain key players now come into their own:

- Planning director
- Senior planners
- Account director
- Creative director
- Creative group head

The above list of personnel is typical of traditional 'above-the-line' ad agencies. However, the situation may be more complex in integrated agencies where the account director and planning director may need to coordinate both creative and media solutions across the line (to coin a phrase), which may require a creative team (art director and copywriter) who are expert in TV commercials, to work with another team which specializes in direct mail and point-of-sale material. Meanwhile the TV media planner and database manager may be at work on various aspects of targeting the campaign via the various media/disciplines.

At this stage, the agency should focus on two things: (i) the creative brief and (ii) the deadline for presenting ideas to the client. Meanwhile, account management, as the level-headed, practical coordinators of the agency (and on occasion its conscience) should be compiling timing plans/critical paths/schedules and examining the cost implications of the various creative ideas (if any) coming out of the creative department.

This is often the most frustrating stage of the process for the account management people: they are divorced from the ideas process and often reduced to the role of onlookers, at exactly the time when their inbuilt paranoia and neurosis are in full flow. The deadline looms ever nearer – and the creatives don't seem to have done *anything* yet! Are they really discussing the *brief* over a beer? And what if their ideas are rubbish and presented as a *fait accompli* an hour before the pitch? How will we have time to get accurate costings? After all the work that went into getting the integrated brief exactly right! What's going on?

But the creative department is closed. Locked. No 'suits' are allowed in (this probably includes planners). 'Leave us alone to perform our black arts!' cry the unkempt and overpaid creative sorcerers.

Meanwhile, account management must fend off the client's enthusiastic enquiries, for example, as follows: 'Yes, in fact we're working on a couple of promising ideas at the moment, but no, I don't think it would necessarily speed things up if you came in for a "sleeves-rolled-up work-in-progress session to review where we are up to" . . . '

Within the creative department 'black hole' it is to be hoped that the process is genuinely integrated – much of this depends on the creative director and the group heads. The trick is to find the 'big idea' that can work 'through the line' and then adapt it to work optimally in each media specified on the creative brief. As part of the process, a good integrated creative department will often contribute media ideas of its own (such as 'This would also work as a cross-track poster!' or 'These poster ideas could also be used as a series of A5 teaser postcards!' and so on, which can add real value to the agency's ultimate product).

At last, the fateful hour arrives (perhaps a day or two later than originally suggested on the creative brief). The group account director and the senior planner are summoned to the creative director's office to find a room full of unsmiling creatives, standing around the walls with their arms folded. The best role in such meetings is often to be a fly on the wall rather than a participant. The creative director (with an air of 'welcome to my parlour') launches into a preamble which ideally involves acknowledging the creative brief (to sighs of relief from the account people). The creative director then presents the ideas, folds his arms and may or may not add, 'So now go and sell it!'

If the account director has reservations, these must be raised now, however difficult that may seem, for at the meeting with the client, the account director will have to support and indeed often *sell* the agency's recommendation (the creative product) 100 per cent. Often there are lively and heated debates at this stage, for example:

● Is this on strategy?
● Can we afford these executions?
● How does the ad translate into direct mail (or in-store)?
● Can we have it ready to run by 1 August?

Finally, peace breaks out, as it must, in the integrated agency. ('When a man knows he is to be hanged tomorrow, it concentrates his mind wonderfully.') All problems are resolved, all internecine disputes put aside, all wounds healed, all glass partitions reglazed and all minds turn to the client. Finished visuals/storyboards are produced and the account director and senior planner (ideally after a good night's sleep) prepare themselves to go and take the game to the client – an altogether different challenge.

PRESENTATION OF CREATIVE WORK

This is the closest to 'theatre' that the working relationship gets; there's slightly less acting (and nervousness) on the part of the agency (and generally speaking the client too) than at the pitch, but only slightly. The need to show an integrated campaign also raises certain questions, for example, whether to present the advertising first, or lead with the below-the-line work and so on.

It is normal, on such occasions, for the managing director or other senior account person to start with a preamble, effectively an overall regurgitation of the brief (as finally agreed before submission to the creative department); this serves to remind everyone of the marketing task in question, to which the creative work will (it is hoped) be a logical, strategically sound, and strikingly creative response.

During the meeting, at the back of the agency people's minds will be various concerns and paranoias; what will they tell the creative director when the work is rejected by the client? What will happen when the production people back at the agency learn that the campaign now has to start on 1 June? How should they explain to the client that the creative director *insists* on using this (expensive and unavailable) director for the new TV commercial? and so on. All these delays are threatening the schedule – and who'll have to take up the slack? These revisions will cost money – is the client good for the extra cost? Whose fault are the amends anyway? Such anxieties explain the high burn-out rate, and premature ageing, among account management staff (many would claim that junior hospital doctors and financial trading-floor dealers have a low-stress job by comparison).

The client, too, will often be uncomfortable. It is difficult to look into the ideas of the charming, enthusiastic, smiling agency people and say '*No* – I know you were up until 2 a.m. this morning working on this. I know you gave me everything I asked for (and more). I know the campaign will look wonderful and win stacks of creative awards, but – *no!*' Even worse, one could say 'Yes' and risk being overruled by one's boss (with the attendant embarrassment of crawling back a week later and explaining that you're so junior within your own organization that you can be completely overruled at a stroke).

The work is rarely 100 per cent right first time; thus the need for revamps, adjustments, amendments. The agency would normally present creative concepts (copy and visuals), budget costs, and an outline timing plan (timelines) at this meeting; any or all of these are likely to need amendment and they are all interlinked. The overall task of client and integrated agency is jointly to produce work which is on strategy, on budget and on time; this can often require a difficult juggling act. Indeed, changes to the creative work (depending on when in the process they occur) will invariably entail extra cost and possibly affect the timing – this complex system must be optimized to achieve the necessary end result.

In terms of creative work, the agency may present the main ideas as 'adcepts', that is, rough visuals sketched (or, more likely these days, originated by Apple Mac) on a concept board, before translation into the various media executions (press, direct mail, in-store and so on). The client may be happy to look at rough scribbles and be perfectly capable of visualizing what the finished version of such communications would look like, but the agency may not believe this; thus considerable expense may be incurred on highly finished visuals (this is normally fuelled by paranoia and may well not be recoverable, that is, it's bad business – see the earlier section on pitches, page 189).

MEDIA PROPOSALS

Advertising agencies used to allow the media director a few minutes at the end of a long discussion of the creative work. Things have changed, even in pure ad agencies, as media have become more complex and targeting increasingly important.

In the integrated agency, media becomes a complex art/science which addresses the question of how best to spread an overall budget not just across (say) TV and press, but also across the various 'below-the-line' disciplines. The agency may present its recommendations at the same meeting as the creative work is presented, or there may be a separate targeting meeting. In any case, we shall need a senior media planner who will present a costed media schedule (split across any or all of TV, press, radio, cinema, posters and the like), but we may also need a direct marketing targeting expert to present the direct mail proposal (lists, offers, creative test matrix and so on). Thus we see how important is the account director's role; s/he must be present at all these client meetings to take an overview of the work of the specialists and to preserve strategic and creative integrity.

The agency should therefore present an integrated media plan – this is not a common event even in some agencies which claim to be integrated; it may include any media but the key factor is that the total cost adds up to the available budget and that it represents the agency's wholehearted and *media-neutral* recommendation.

It is also necessary at this point for the agency to formulate and present a production schedule/critical path which keeps everything on track and serves as a checklist as the project progresses. Key 'milestones' might be:

- Retailer head office sell-in
- Sales presentations to key accounts
- Teaser direct mail
- Response handling/fulfilment
- Stock delivered to retailers
- POS arrives in store
- TV commercial breaks
- Press ads break
- Door-to door coupon plus sample drop
- Targeted direct mail
- Evaluation and review meeting.

Each of the above items will have its own production schedule which will need to be dovetailed if the 'integrated' campaign is to look integrated and achieve economies of scale in the production process (for example, just one photographic shoot, consistent design images, typefaces and so on).

Indeed, one successful integrated creative director has said he can achieve 'a fair approximation to integration' if he gets agreement on:

- key colours;
- key phrases/straplines; and
- typefaces.

Even achieving the above can be problematical, given the different lead-times of the various elements. For example, if the direct mail and catalogues/publications are to take their lead from the advertising, there is a 'drop-dead date' by which the layouts of the ads must be firmly agreed if the direct mail is to be ready on schedule – this often depends on which creatives are responsible for the ads and how much they and the creative director care about the direct mail. Thus the date for the presentation of creative work to the client must be set to accommodate the slowest process (generally speaking, the below-the-line elements). This all requires that the process be overseen by senior agency people who think and act in a genuinely media-neutral manner. Their main concern is to meet the client's needs, that is, deliver the best possible integrated campaign, on strategy, on budget, and on time. As we have seen, one of the biggest challenges will be the shortage of such people – people who are not emotionally committed either to the 30-second TV commercial or to targeted direct mail (say) as the 'best' marketing technique.

CAMPAIGN IMPLEMENTATION

The client reacts to the agency presentation, normally along the lines of 'We all really like it – but . . .'. And as the final media deadlines loom, the necessary amends are completed and the agency moves into 'execution mode' at last. The agency production people brief photographers, illustrators, Apple Mac studios, TV commercials directors (and production companies). Agency traffic people rush about attempting to liaise between the account management people (who at last have something to do) and the creative team(s) who now must actually deliver the campaign that the client fell in love with when it was presented as finished visuals.

The traffic people act as an invaluable 'buffer zone' during the production process. Their crucial role is to 'make the trains run on time' in a situation where the account director will say: 'We're not creating fine art here – it's useless if it's a day late', while the creative director might retort: 'In six months' time, no one will remember how fast we had to do it – they'll only see that the work is sub-standard, so we must refuse to rush it.'

Both, of course, have a point. No job can be 100 per cent right; rather one must employ 'the art of the possible' and be prepared, on occasion, to accept a 99 per cent job in order that the activity appears as scheduled. It also means that someone should be thinking about the sales leaflet (accounting for maybe 5 per cent of the total budget) while someone else is (quite rightly) watching the TV production costs which are threatening to spiral and already account for 30 per cent of the total campaign cost (say).

Account management must restrain the creatives, whose personal agenda may well be to produce the longest, biggest, most lavish campaign (that is, the most expensive, with the longest lead-time); in the real world, this objective may be unrealistic and incompatible with producing the campaign on time, which means there is a real risk of the whole idea failing to see the light of day. Thus deep strategic insight and inspired creative thinking must go hand in hand with tight project management if the campaign is actually to happen, and so benefit the client's brand.

To achieve great integrated marketing communications, one needs great creative ideas that will work across media and great execution. The latter requires the best production people, the best suppliers and overall the best attention to detail – this part of the process is in many ways still a 'craft' and needs people who take a pride in their work (both agency and client) and who are committed to 'going the extra mile' to get it right. This same diligence and scrutiny should be applied to every detail of the integrated campaign – not just the TV commercial but also the dealer mailings, the shelf talkers and the sales force give-aways. Integrated thinking must be accompanied by integrated execution across the full range of media. This means the agency creative director and the client marketing director must care about every manifestation of the campaign so that no detail is overlooked and no executions are considered to be of secondary importance. This is asking a lot, and the difficulty of achieving it should not be underestimated. The need here is for high-quality discipline-specific implementation skills and broad-visioned coordination and scheduling. Two pertinent analogies are the musical conductor coordinating the various elements of the orchestra into an integrated symphony of sound, and the master chef preparing all the elements of a dish to be ready simultaneously and each exactly right.

It is also important to give thought to what happens after the consumer sees/hears/reads notices the campaign, that is, response management – the charmingly termed 'back-end'. Is the handling house briefed? Do the telemarketing operators have their scripts ready? Are there enough people to handle the calls? Is the fulfilment literature ready to send out? Are the sales force and dealers briefed? What about customer service? Such details can, if neglected, negate all the effort put into the campaign in the first place.

The implementation process of integrated campaigns is of critical importance. Any agency claiming to offer such resources and any client looking to achieve such campaigns must be appropriately organized and possess the necessary determination, if the great integrated ideas presented and bought by the senior people are not to fall foul of real-world obstacles.

POST-CAMPAIGN EVALUATION

At the end of every campaign, the easiest thing to do is to rush on the next one – both client and agency want to get ahead with the planning process so that it won't be such a mad scramble as it was last time. But no – we should take a little time to take a step back and review what we were trying to achieve (our objectives) and what we did indeed achieve (the results). The client and the agency should have an honest discussion about the planning and implementation process so as to improve the way it works next time.

Thus the review meeting should encompass, first, the *process*. We should ask: What went right? What went wrong? What could we do better next time? (assuming there is a next time). This is an important part of the development of the client–agency relationship – an honest appraisal of the experience by both sides. It can easily be overlooked under day-to-day pressures. It needs to be planned for, with diaries coordinated, and it is best conducted off-site, say in a hotel, away from the 'phones, faxes and other distractions. In my experience, such sessions usually work extremely well. Both parties do see the other's point of view and a greater mutual understanding generally results – which is of course good for the overall relationship. (Indeed, even calling such a meeting is a gesture of commitment to building the relationship on the client's part.) This exercise can also be surprisingly revealing, throwing up insights into frustrations and problems hitherto unknown to the other party. (But beware – soul baring can be addictive!)

Second, the review meeting should deal with the *communications*. An analysis of a typical direct marketing campaign might take the form of Figure 9.3.

This chart (Figure 9.3) would be appropriate for a direct response campaign, where cost per sale is the ultimate measure of success. However, as we have seen, advertising generally has other objectives including awareness and attitude change, so that the effectiveness of an integrated communications campaign must be measured by the full range of available techniques:

- Research (pre- and post-awareness monitors, tracking studies and so on) as practised by ad agencies for years
- Enquiries/responses (to DRTV, press coupons, 0800 'phone calls, reply cards/coupons and the like)
- Redemptions

Medium	Quantity	Cost (£)	Projected response (%)	No. of enquiries	Cost/enquiry (£)	Conversion (%)	Sales	Cost/sale (£)
TV								
Press space								
Loose inserts, door-to-door								
Direct mail								
(i) Brochure (ii) Two-stage								
Total								

Figure 9.4 Campaign response projections

- Sales/market share (for example as measured by Nielsen data) in cases where it is possible to create control cells to isolate the effect of the communication on sales.

Agency and client should, of course, work together to evaluate the effectiveness of the marketing communications activity; indeed, this would normally be a key offering of the integrated agency via its planning department. Moreover, our integrated agency should be in a position to take an overview of the effectiveness of all the activity without fear that it will result in a budget cut – this represents a significant advantage over the situation where the client is orchestrating a range of specialist suppliers, all trying to justify their own contribution and to secure their future share of the budget.

The process of creating and implementing integrated marketing communications is central to this book; it is never easy but the prizes for those who do it successfully can be substantial. The outline above is somewhat idealized and inevitably conceals a myriad of operational challenges and difficulties, for example:

- Everyone loves the 'big creative idea', but it becomes clear that the TV commercial cannot possibly be realized within the available production budget.
- The client marketing director approves everything. Everyone at the agency believes the work is on strategy and that this will become a

famous campaign, and everyone joins in a celebratory drink. Two days later, the client managing director overrules him/her without explanation (politics is suspected), thereby blowing the budget and the timing plan. Then the decision is taken to postpone the entire campaign until next year (with impact on agency revenue).

- The agency creative team takes so long to 'crack' the press ad brief that the direct mail and the product brochure have to go to press using a different creative idea; the planned origination cost savings are not achieved and 'integration' is a casualty yet again.

This process of strategy and implementation is often painful, but of course necessary, and it is no coincidence that we see so few truly integrated campaigns; to achieve them needs persistence, planning and an overall political will to 'get it right' in all disciplines/media, which is rarely found. However, when a client and its integrated agency succeed in working together, the resultant rewards are of course correspondingly great.

The following case histories illustrate how companies and their agencies have made the relationship work to produce successful integrated marketing campaigns.

Case history

Company	Whitbread (Boddingtons)
Background	Whitbread bought the Boddingtons brewery at the end of 1989 as a strategic move; Boddingtons Bitter was a declining regional brand from Manchester, in the north of England, but Whitbread had identified it as an opportunity; consumer tastes in beer were moving towards unpasteurized, cask-conditioned bitters like Boddingtons, and away from 'keg' bitters such as Whitbread's own fading former stars, Trophy and Whitbread Best.
	The bitter drinker in particular is discriminating, cynical and resistant to 'marketing hype' as well as being slow to accept anything new. The influence of organizations such as CAMRA (The Campaign For Real Ale) in resisting the perceived manipulation of the market by the major brewers is also a major factor in this case history.
Marketing objectives	The plan was to roll out Boddingtons draught (the variety available as a 'pub pint') nationally, at the same time as launching a canned version, with new technology – a 'widget' that delivers a creamy head previously only used in stout – both without

alienating the loyal Boddingtons drinkers in the Manchester heartland (where it was the market leader). The process couldn't be rushed, as research had shown that word of mouth, and a process of gradual acceptance and progressive market penetration, was the most effective means of building a sustainable brand franchise based on long-term consumer loyalty.

Solution

Most beer advertising in the UK, constrained as it is by codes of conduct and voluntary agreements, has tended to major either on humour (especially lager) or sociability/user imagery (especially bitters).

Whitbread took the unusual (and in many ways brave) route of focusing on *product attribute*. The main feature that led the advertising was *smoothness*, as evidenced by a creamy head and golden colour. The advertising was single-minded and consistent: 'Whoever you are, whatever you drink, the product truth remains the same.' The campaign positioned Boddingtons as the ultimate, smooth-drinking pint, and to do it in an accessible, humorous way, adopting the tag line 'The Cream of Manchester'.

Unusually, Boddingtons led on press advertising, rather than TV. This not only made the budget go further, but by clever media planning and buying (featuring the outside back cover of key magazines), Boddingtons achieved extremely high awareness despite being considerably outspent by competitors. TV was gradually introduced into the media schedule over a period of two years. The press work featured visual puns based on 'cream' whereas the TV work, when it arrived later in the campaign, retained the cream/smoothness references, but introduced a series of spoofs on 'luxury' goods advertising featuring the Northern dialect expression 'By 'eck'.

The success of the campaign is undeniable. Boddingtons has strengthened its position as the market leader in its north-west heartland, and overall is now the UK's fourth largest bitter brand. The canned variant is market leader, with 48 per cent of bitter drinkers claiming they drink it 'nowadays'. And the success has continued as the brand goes from strength to strength. Outside the North-West, Boddingtons share of cask ale sales rose from 51 per cent to 66 per cent and in the North-West from 87 per cent to 91 per cent over a three-year period.

Below-the-line extensions of the campaign include retailer promotions, point-of-sale material and Boddingtons merchandise. All reinforce the essential Boddingtons branding, which has been powerful and consistent throughout the period of this 'slow-build' strategy.

Case history

Company	Digital Equipment Corporation (DEC)

Background Digital is the world leader in open client/server computer solutions – from personal computing to integrated information systems. Their Alpha AXP platforms, storage networking, software and services are designed to help clients manage their information more effectively and thus compete better in their respective markets.

Marketing objectives Digital was in the process of launching 64-bit workstations and servers whilst its competition had only 32-bit offerings. It was important to promote the customer benefits of 64-bit technology over 32-bit so as to gain customer acceptance and desire to purchase Digital products, enhanced by the exceptionally fast and powerful Alpha microprocessor (known at the time of the campaign as Alpha AXP).

For this campaign, the primary target audience was 'IT functional heads', that is, IT directors, managers and senior professionals in major organizations. The goal, in the first instance, was for the audience to 'put Alpha AXP on the shopping list'. Secondary and tertiary audiences included business associates, press, analysts and employees.

Solution The creative approach selected to convey the message for this integrated campaign involved the use of the tagline:

'Imagine being the one without Alpha AXP'.

The advertising featured a number of powerful executions, with strong visuals (horses, bikes, trains and so on) using predominantly non-technical copy with a strong suggestion that the individual could find their company left behind (and, by implication, be failing in his/her job) if they did not consider purchasing Digital products, based on 64-bit technology. This was, however, communicated in a non-threatening manner using humour, so as not to alienate the target audience.

The advertising campaign ran in the following categories of media:

● Print:
  – national press (*Financial Times, The Daily Telegraph, The Times* and so on);
  – computer and business press

Plate 9.1   Digital – the Alpha AXP campaign
Source: Digital

- lifestyle/interest titles (*Golf Monthly*, *Yachting Monthly*, *Car magazine*, *InterCity*, and the like)
- Poster: poster sites throughout the UK.

The fully integrated campaign also included direct mail, seminars, an extensive PR campaign, research and merchandising items.

A full programme of internal communications was also implemented, with copies of the ads circulated to employees and business associates of Digital. The campaign strapline, 'Imagine being the one without Alpha AXP', also appeared on the company franking stamp, on umbrellas, calendars, pens, Post-it notes, car stickers, Christmas cards and even the company trucks – a truly *integrated* communications campaign.

Throughout the implementation of this high-profile campaign, the goal was to exert (subtle) pressure on the IT manager both from above (senior management) and below (influential computing professionals) by giving the message that to leave Alpha servers off the shopping list was to risk missing out.

Campaign feedback from business associates, customers and employees was extremely positive, whilst benchmark research undertaken pre- and post-campaign demonstrated considerable improvement in the awareness of Digital and the availability and benefits of 64-bit technology.

Susan Goldsworthy, Digital's Director of Marketing Services – Europe, makes the following observations concerning successful implementation of integrated communications campaigns, based on her experience:

> Remember three of the critical elements of a successful campaign –
>
> - Targeting – detailed audience segmentation, then 'think beyond the box' on how to reach them
> - Impact – stand out from your competitors and ensure your campaign is noticed
> - Consistency – constant change to your image and approach will only serve to confuse your audience

Engage all your employees prior to the launch of your campaign. Address any opposition positively and enthusiastically. Encourage each individual to be a 'campaign ambassador'.

Brief all your communications agencies at the same time, making them members of the team, and encourage open communication between all parties throughout the planning and implementation of the campaign.

10 AN INTEGRATED FUTURE?

Experience has convinced me that the factors that work in mail order advertising work equally well in ALL advertising. But the vast majority of people who work in agencies, and almost all their clients, have never heard of these factors. That is why they skid helplessly about on the greasy surface of irrelevant brilliance . . .
David Ogilvy, from the foreword to *Tested Advertising Methods* by John Caples, 1975

A measure of the interest in any new discipline is, of course, how much discussion, writing and teaching there is on the subject. On that basis, direct marketing looks as though it's going to take over the world . . . I *do not* believe direct marketing is going to conquer the world . . . I am not at all sure that the advertising and marketing business will be organised as it is now in the year 2000. I certainly hope not.
Drayton Bird, 1993

What I do see is a change that I have wished for during my whole career. Direct marketing is now accepted as a serious marketing tool in every size and kind of business. Sophisticated marketing executives . . . now respect the fact that direct marketing is different, that it is professional . . . Today and tomorrow, we in direct marketing are experiencing what we have earned and most desired . . .
RESPECT!
Ed Nash, 1994

> The days of traditional mass marketing are over. Technology ended them. They will not return . . . the environment in which modern marketing developed – one that was subject to the laws of mass production, economies of scale, homogeneous consumer and customer markets, national brand domination of a limited number of channels – is unrecognisable today . . . Successful marketing in the 1990s and beyond requires *real* customer orientation. It means communicating with individuals, not shotgunning markets. It is based on long-term relationships . . . it is based on customer satisfaction not just volume and share . . . the 1990s call for integrated, coordinated, cohesive marketing communications which inform, assist, involve and, yes, persuade customers and prospects.
>
> Schultz *et al.* 1993

Direct marketing in the integrated mix

This book has explored what has become *the* issue within marketing, and specifically direct marketing, at the end of the twentieth century, namely that of integration of the various marketing communications disciplines. It calls into question the very existence of direct marketing (as well as advertising and sales promotion) as a distinct discipline. It challenges the existence of such job titles as 'Direct Marketing Manager' and 'Sales Promotion Manager'. It places question marks over the future of self-declared specialist 'direct marketing agencies' and 'sales promotion consultancies', not to mention the separate existence of such specialist trade organizations as the Direct Marketing Association and the Institute of Sales Promotion (to name but two).

However, the day when there is no visible separation between direct marketing, sales promotion and advertising is certainly not yet with us. It is interesting to reflect that, should such a day arrive, the following expressions would become meaningless:

- 'a typical adman' (except when used to refer to *any* marketing communications professional)
- 'a below-the-line agency'
- 'the sales promotion department'.

The same would apply to many other currently commonplace pieces of marketing terminology. If understood at all, they would be recognized solely as largely irrelevant relics of a bygone age.

So *will* such a day come? As already established, I believe there are certain very real limits to this process. I do not believe that integration will ever take hold to the extent that TV advertising (say) is considered, either by clients or agencies, in the same breath as shelf wobblers; some media are just inherently sexier! I don't believe that certain 'image advertising' specialists will ever cease to regard practitioners of direct mail or telephone selling (say) as second-class marketers. And I don't believe that senior marketing decision makers in client companies will ever choose to involve themselves as closely with, say, a direct mail letter or the selection of a premium item for an on-pack self-liquidating promotion, as with the creative treatment featured in the blockbuster TV launch campaign for a new product, even when the TV commercial has to be aired on over 50 separate cable channels in order to cobble together the required aggregate audience! In the intellectual and artistic 'pecking orders' of the world of marketing communications, what has come to be known as 'above-the-line' will retain something of its present aura of being 'above reproach' while other disciplines (today termed 'below-the-line') will continue to be regarded by an (admittedly diminishing) number as 'beneath contempt'. To pretend otherwise is unrealistic.

Despite all this, major and fundamental changes have undoubtedly already occurred in the planning and implementation of marketing communications, and this trend can only accelerate as we move into the next millennium. The attitudes reflected above will change as some of the 'old-timers' currently managing marketing departments and agencies leave the industry, to be replaced by integration-minded managers with no intellectual baggage about 'above' and 'below'-the-line and no ideological axe to grind about the 'best' solution to marketing communications problems. There will be no favourites, with each discipline considered solely on its merits. There is already some evidence of this, although there is also the counter-phenomenon of the advertising snob 'young fogeys' in above-the-line agencies, misguidedly allowing themselves to be led astray by their dinosaur bosses, and short-sightedly looking down their noses, dismissing below-the-line disciplines, even in the late 1990s, as somehow inferior to what they do and irrelevant to their career development – more fool them!

Despite the attitudes of some die-hard separatists, integration of marketing communications is here to stay; the logic of harmonizing and synchronizing one's marketing communications activities for maximum cost-effectiveness is inescapable. Indeed, there can no longer be any excuse for a company organizing its marketing department structure and its marketing suppliers in any manner that does not positively assist the process of making all customer-facing communications work together in a coordinated and mutually reinforcing way (if there ever were any excuse!). Certain agencies now offer a genuinely integrated resource, fielding capable practitioners in direct marketing, sales promotion and advertising, although, as we have seen, some clients can and do choose to 'cherry-pick' and supply the integrating glue themselves, achieving integrated multidisciplinary campaigns by coordinating the specialists themselves.

The 1980s and 1990s have certainly been watershed decades for UK (and indeed international) marketing communications; a combination of boom followed by recession, then gradual recovery, and the application of some basic commonsense has started a process of convergence and redefinition which cannot be reversed. Direct marketing, in particular, has not only at last risen to take its place alongside advertising as an integral part of 'the marketing mix', but also achieved recognition by most marketers as a necessary part of any long-term integrated customer acquisition and retention strategy. This development is fundamental and is already changing marketers' use both of traditional media such as TV and direct mail and of new media, including the World Wide Web. It will inevitably in due course also underpin strategies for communicating via other as yet unimagined media. Whatever changes the future holds for marketing communications, integrated *direct* marketing is certain to play a significant role.

Making it work

So much for the brave new world of integrated direct marketing. But how to do it? Leaving aside any hang-ups, entrenched prejudices and natural cynicisms, let us bring this book towards its conclusion by indulging in something of an exercise of the imagination; idealized perhaps, but certainly not a wild flight of fancy. Suppose we transport ourselves to the integrated marketing department of Brandex. The time is the (near) future. The task in hand is the planning and execution of a year's marketing communications activity.

PLANNING INTEGRATED DIRECT MARKETING

Let us suppose our integrated marketing director has elected to appoint an integrated communications agency to plan and execute his/her campaign (although, as we have seen, this choice is by no means forced; I believe specialist agencies will survive for the foreseeable future because there will be a client demand for them).

Our integrated marketing campaign for Brandex will be planned in much the same way as the old marketing communications, so let us first consider how marketing communications are generally put together:

- set objectives;
- devise a strategy for achieving them;
- come up with a creatively arresting and persuasive execution, in the right media, to implement the strategy with maximum cost-effectiveness.

So far, nothing new. The difference is, of course, a matter of how broadly one thinks. It is of course important to leave one's mind open to all possible media (point-of-sale may be just as relevant to the task as TV advertising), but true integration goes far beyond this. The people formulating the strategy need to apply a *fully integrated mental approach* to the strategic marketing communications task. This is more easily said than done: all the individuals involved will have cut their teeth in other organizations and their experience is likely to be discipline-specific; a traditional account planner from an advertising agency is unlikely to be particularly comfortable discussing the intricacies of database or shelf wobblers, for instance. However, this concern, to an extent, misses the point: *execution* is not the most important thing at this stage; rather, the strategists need to understand the *potential* and the *limitations* of each of the candidate media, in order to make informed (and dispassionate) choices between them; they do not need to be experts at implementation. (And in any case, in time, prejudices, hang-ups and simple ignorance of the type currently exhibited by many of the key players in today's agencies will not be a factor.)

Certainly the new agencies will require people experienced in direct mail list selection, scratchcard technology and TV production costs, but there will be no need for such specialist knowledge in the planning department. Indeed, having the right individuals in key positions, both in agencies and in client companies, will be a prerequisite of the new integrated marketing.

From the viewpoint of an integrated agency, the requirement is thus for a planning department staffed by *broadly based* (that is, *integrated*) marketing thinkers, free from the petty hang-ups and biases found in many of the old non-integrated agencies. From the client point of view, the need is similar: to spend time, at marketing director level, probably in conjunction with the agency, formulating marketing communications strategies which potentially embrace any marketing communications discipline and in which direct marketing is as important as TV advertising, and shelf wobblers stand alongside double-page spreads. Indeed, the best marketing directors already operate in a manner similar to this. In this scenario, integrated direct marketing is planned as part of the overall marketing communications strategy by people who may not be specialists in its *execution*, but are experts in its *role within the marketing mix*. In specific terms, it comes down to hiring the right mix of thinkers, getting them round a table in the integrated agency with the agency planners, account handlers and (at least by the second meeting) media specialists and senior creatives, and thrashing out the strategy in an 'open communications' environment.

Once the objectives and strategy are agreed, the next task of our integrated agency is the media plan (supposing, say, that we are looking at a calendar year). These 'new age' media planners are part of an *integrated* department, and between them are equally at home in all media, including direct mail, press space and inserts, TV, radio, posters and the World Wide Web. They know their lists and door-to-door targeting as well as their television ratings (TVRs), a measure of the 'weight' of a TV campaign, and opportunities to see (OTS) figures, a measure frequency of viewing of the commercial by the target audience. Of course, if the strategy arrived at includes direct response (that is, gathering enquiries/leads/data generation) this will fundamentally affect the media solution (early bottom right-hand pages facing relevant editorial matter pull well in the press; display the 0800 phone number for at least 15 seconds on TV and so on). Thus successful integrated direct marketing will depend as much on the media department as on any other agency department and such a department must include specialists in planning and buying direct response media as well as traditional 'awareness' media.

IMPLEMENTING INTEGRATED DIRECT MARKETING

Concurrently, the creative department will be getting to grips with their key document – the creative brief. This will have been written by the planning department as the encapsulation of the communications strategy; each campaign needs its own creative brief (see Figure 6.1; page 115). For a campaign involving direct marketing, the brief will state what materials are required: DRTV, press inserts, direct mail and so on, which could well be launched into the marketplace alongside other communications (advertising, sales promotions) but *crucially*, these materials will flow from the same creative idea(s) which were a response to the same creative brief. It is inevitable that the integrated agency creative departments will need specialists in, say, direct mail, just as traditional ad agencies did in press or TV. The important thing is that the thinking will be integrated across all relevant media: integrated direct marketing will work seamlessly with the other communications coming from the same client company. This is extremely difficult, although not impossible, to achieve when the client is coordinating a range of separate specialist agencies.

Thus integrated direct marketing, properly planned in the agency of the future, will build on all the expertise of, and lessons learned by, the traditional agencies of the past. The 'direct marketing experts' currently huddling together for warmth within specialist direct marketing agencies will confidently take up their positions alongside advertising and sales promotion experts, each respecting the other's specialist skills and experience (and even perhaps learning from each other!). Achieving 'integrated direct marketing' should always have been part of the responsibility of marketing management; the closing years of the twentieth century have not only ensured that this is widely recognized, but have also witnessed the genesis of a new wave of integrated agencies equipped to deliver it 'under one roof'. We may not be there yet, but we're certainly on our way.

Direct marketing – super discipline(!)

To recap, direct marketing is:

- 'an interactive system of marketing, employing one or more advertising media to generate a measurable response/transaction at any location'
- 'a range of marketing communications which create and exploit a profitable relationship between a company and its customers and prospects over time'
- 'accountable advertising'

(Select any or all of these definitions!)

This book has examined, in some detail, the whole spectrum of marketing communications – from 90-second pure image commercials on broadcast

TV, to a 10p money-off coupon on a box of soap powder and passing through all points in between – with particular reference to the role of direct marketing.

I have sought to dispel various myths, for example:

- 'Advertising is more creative (or sexy or respectable) than direct mail or promotions.'
- 'Direct mail is more cost-effective than other media.'
- 'Below-the-line people are either spivs or failed admen.'

But why is this book called 'The New Integrated *Direct* Marketing?' Why not call it something safe and bland like 'Integrated Marketing Communications'? Well, because we have saved perhaps the most controversial claim until (almost) the very end:

ALL MARKETING COMMUNICATIONS SHOULD OPERATE AS PART OF A DIRECT MARKETING APPROACH.

In other words, *direct* marketing is the *broader* concept – it should, and increasingly will, contain all other marketing communications! This is not to say that every communication should have, as its *main* objective, volume response. Image building, creating awareness and shifting attitudes will always be necessary; it is important that people are not merely persuaded to buy the product once, but that they feel good about buying it so that they come back for more. Indeed, for some brands, (such as fine fragrances or designer fashion labels) creation and maintenance of *image* will continue to be the key role for marketing communications. However, communications that offer the consumer a response channel (and in so doing allow the advertiser to gather data) will rapidly become the norm – evidence of this is already all around us. Every advertiser, regardless of their preferred media mix, will have a marketing database. In effect, all marketing will be *direct* marketing. This is for some, no doubt, difficult to accept at the time of writing, but in retrospect (and I hope during the lifetime of this book) obvious and entirely logical. The best advertising account managers, planners and creatives will by this time be working with their ablest colleagues from the old direct marketing and sales promotion agencies in the most successful of the new integrated agencies, and all the fuss made in the early 1990s (which filled a lot of columns of the marketing press and sold a fair few books!) about whether or not to integrate one's communications will appear to have been, at best, interesting and amusing, and, at worst, a monumental waste of many people's time and energy (I naturally hope the present book can escape such opprobrium).

Underlying the controversial proposition above is, of course, a fundamental belief that direct marketing is *not* a communications medium (unlike direct mail). Nor is it a range of techniques, nor yet an esoteric sub-branch of marketing. Rather it is a *fundamental approach to marketing*. It is more than direct mail and direct response advertising and more than mail order. It is a robust commercial discipline. It represents a view of marketing that sees consumers as individual customers and prospects with differing wants and needs.

Of course, not every communication can (or indeed should) be personalized, one-to-one. But the vast, sprawling mass of consumers, previously considered as a homogeneous whole, can and must be segmented so that distinct prospects receive targeted messages. Call this direct marketing or call it enlightened integrated media planning; the point is that good marketing communications must, in addition to being creative, also be *relevant* to the recipients, and this requires *targeting*. Individuals can raise their hands to supply information about themselves, which assists the advertiser in his/her efforts to direct ever more relevant messages and offers towards such people. Wasteful and inappropriate communications are eliminated. Communication budgets are deployed most effectively. Everybody wins.

This is the direct marketer's view of marketing. It is the only view appropriate as the twentieth century gives way to the twenty-first. Data will drive this new marketing. Names and addresses will just be the start; demographic, transaction and lifestyle data will be acquired from an increasing range of sources and accessed, with increasing skill, for a widening range of marketing purposes. The individual will receive appropriate protection from an ever-more rigorous data protection regime from which responsible direct marketers have little to fear. *Intelligent* collection, storage and manipulation of data will take on even greater importance, even as the associated costs fall still further. The majority of advertising communications will offer some kind of response facility, thus keeping the channels of communication with the individual consumer open, as part of the overall objective of building a *relationship*. Direct mail and telephone marketing will take an increasing share of advertising and promotions budgets, but so too will interactive electronic media – fortunes will certainly be made via cable/satellite/home shopping /the Internet, the World Wide Web and other interactive media, and via advertising/sales media not yet invented. Already Website construction and Web advertising sales have spawned specialist agencies, while the multinational agency networks, spotting (arguably somewhat belatedly) a direction in which some of their clients' budgets were likely to be diverted, have moved to grab their share of these developing new branches of marketing communications spend. As always, the agency–client relationship is evolving, transmuting and reinventing itself; marketing communications are as exciting and as fast-changing a business as ever in which to operate. These are already, or will be in the future, some of the varied advertising media employed by the new integrated direct marketing. Moreover, the integrated agency which is the focus of Chapter 8 will in fact (if not in name) be an integrated *direct marketing* agency.

Having boldly stated that integrated direct marketing is the only viable way forward for marketing communications, I should make it clear that this does not for one moment imply that the current direct marketing specialists in direct marketing agencies (nor even direct marketing managers in client companies) will shortly take over the world. On the contrary, the best marketing brains, whether marketing directors, MDs of advertising agencies or direct marketing agency account managers are already thinking like integrated direct marketers, regardless of the labels pinned on them as job titles; by way of a comparison, remember that (except for a few US expats) the UK had no experts in TV advertising before 1956! I am certain that the best of today's TV admen will adapt to become leading practitioners of the new marketing communications, working alongside equally talented individuals from backgrounds including direct marketing, sales promotion, design and PR in the new integrated agencies. The best specialist craft skills of the old agencies will be transported into these new agencies and applied to clients' problems in a properly coordinated manner.

Client marketing departments will orchestrate integrated communications solutions as they always have: in some cases sourced from a single agency; in others 'cherry-picked' from a number of specialist sources, as many are currently. However, there will be a fundamental difference from the UK marketing scene of the 1970s, 1980s and early 1990s: the disappearance of the old value-laden categories and the accompanying snobbery and prejudice – increasingly so as 'traditionalists' move out of the industry and more open-minded, younger practitioners take their places. In time, direct mail will cease to be regarded as inherently 'inferior' to TV commercials (except in the minds of an irrelevant few). 'Traditional' sales promotion will survive primarily as a set of techniques for influencing consumer behaviour at the point of sale. Partner promotions offering, as they do, opportunities for data generation and collection, will be pursued in a more thorough, systematic manner. Sales promotion will be planned more strategically as part of the integrated communications mix. The World Wide Web will take its place alongside more traditional disciplines, finding its most powerful role as a 'fulfilment medium *par excellence*'.

Marketing communications will at last be viewed holistically, as a planned system of activities, establishing, developing and controlling a set of relationships with consumers on as personal a one-to-one basis as can be proven to be cost-effective (after all it is indefensible to advocate a precise 'rifle' targeting approach in those – few – cases where a 'blunderbuss' is manifestly more appropriate!). All this is to say, as indicated previously, that:

ALL MARKETING WILL BE *DIRECT MARKETING.*

In other words, of course marketing communications will be integrated; the point is that they will also be 'direct'.

We must never lose sight of the fact that marketing involves much more than marketing *communications* (including, as it does, product development, packaging, pricing strategy, and aspects of production and distribution). However, marketing communications are an essential part of building profitable customer relationships; the key point is that the fundamental attitude exhibited by the successful new marketer will be one of *consumer focus* rather than *mass marketing* (what has been called mass customization or one-to-one marketing). Of course, such marketing won't be called 'direct' anymore; the term will have outlived its usefulness, along with 'above-' and 'below-the-line' and other soon-to-be quaint anachronisms – and we're not talking far into the future here. In a sense, then, direct marketing will have 'won' the integration battle of late twentieth-century marketing. But only in a sense. In reality, marketing will be the winner. Artificial labels and internecine disputes within the marketing community have not served marketing well, and have distracted many highly capable marketers from the real task of improving the effectiveness of their activities and thus raising the regard in which marketing, as a discipline, is held within the senior managements of major corporations. The new integrated direct marketing will be stronger. Its effectiveness will be increased. Consequently its stature, within organizations which sell products and services to people, and within the international business community, will be enhanced. This will be good for those who understand what is currently called 'direct' marketing. It will be good for those marketers who have taken the trouble to understand their customers – who they are, what they want, both now and in the future. Above all, it will be good for business.

BIBLIOGRAPHY AND FURTHER READING

Bird, Drayton (1993), *Common Sense Direct Marketing*, London: Kogan Page

Caples, John (1975), *Tested Advertising Methods*, Englewood Cliffs, NJ: Prentice Hall

Cummins, Julian (1989), *Sales Promotion*, London: Kogan Page

Evans, Ivor H. (1913), *Brewer's Dictionary of Phrase and Fable*, London: Cassell

Fletcher, Winston (1994), *How to Capture the Advertising High Ground*, London: Century

Foster, Nigel (1988), *Bluff and Pace Your Way in Advertising*, Horsham, Sussex: Ravette

Fraser-Robinson, John (1989), *The Secrets of Effective Direct Mail*, Maidenhead, Berks: McGraw-Hill

Harris, Thomas L. (1991), *The Marketer's Guide to Public Relations*, New York: Wiley

Hopkins, Claude (1923), *Scientific Advertising*, New York: Bell Publishing

Institute of Direct Marketing (1992), *The Practitioner's Guide to Direct Marketing*, Teddington: Institute of Direct Marketing

Kobs, Jim (1992), *Profitable Direct Marketing*, Lincolnwood, ILL: NTC Business Books

Kotler, Philip (1994), *Marketing Management*, 8th Edition, Englewood Cliffs, NJ: Prentice Hall

Levitt, Ted (1983), *The Marketing Imagination*, New York: Free Press

McCorkell, Graeme (1990), *Advertising That Pulls Response*, Maidenhead, Berkshire: McGraw-Hill

McCorkell, Graeme (1997), *Direct and Database Marketing*, London: Kogan Page (in association with the Institute of Direct Marketing)

Nash, Edward (1994), *Direct Marketing – Strategy, Planning, Execution*, 3rd Edn, New York: McGraw-Hill

Ogilvy, David (1962), *Confessions of an Advertising Man*, New York: Atheneum

Ogilvy, David (1983), *Ogilvy on Advertising*, London: Pan Books

Packard, Vance (1981), *The Hidden Persuaders*, Harmondsworth: Penguin

Pearson, Stewart (1996), *Building Brands Directly*, Basingstoke: Macmillan

Peppers, Don and Rogers, Martha (1993), *The One to One Future*, London: Piatkus

Peterson, Christian (1979), *Sales Promotion in Action*, London: Associated Business Press

Rapp, Stan and Collins, Thomas L. (1987), *Maximarketing*, New York: McGraw-Hill

Rapp, Stan and Collins, Thomas L. (1996), *The New Maximarketing*, New York: McGraw-Hill

Schultz, Don E., Tannenbaum, Stanley I., Lauterborn, Robert F. (1993), *Integrated Marketing Communications*, Lincolnwood, ILL: NTC Business Books

Stone, Bob (1994), *Successful Direct Marketing Methods*, Lincolnwood (Chicago), ILL: NTC Business Books

Watson, John (1993), *Successful Creativity in Direct Marketing*, Teddington: Institute of Direct Marketing

Toop, Alan (1994), *Crackingjack! Sales Promotion Techniques and How to Use Them*, Aldershot: Gower

Toop, Alan and Petersen, Christian (1994), *Sales Promotion in Postmodern Marketing*, Aldershot: Gower

Williams, John (1996), *The Manual of Sales Promotion*, London: Innovation Licensing

INDEX